Memories of World War I

North Carolina Doughboys
on the Western Front

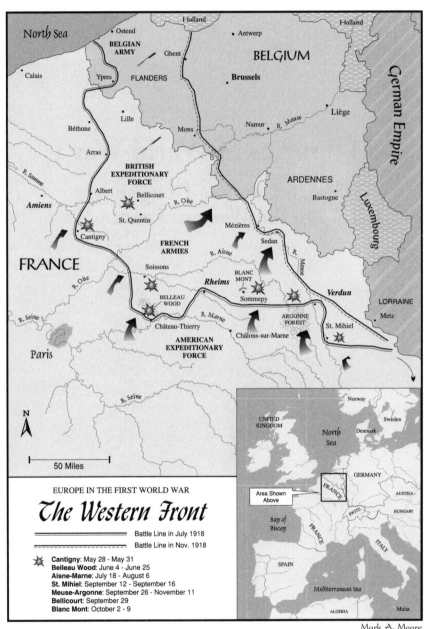

North Sea

Holland

Ostend
BELGIAN
ARMY   Ghent

Calais

Ypres   FLANDERS

Béthune   Lille

Arras

BRITISH
EXPEDITIONARY
FORCE
Albert   Bellicourt
Amiens

St. Quentin

Cantigny

FRANCE

R. Oise

R. Seine

Paris

R. Seine

N

50 Miles

Antwerp

BELGIUM

Brussels

Mons   Namur   R. Meuse   Liège

ARDENNES

Bastogne

Mézières

FRENCH
ARMIES   R. Aisne   Sedan

Soissons   BLANC
                        MONT
             Rheims
BELLEAU   Sommepy
WOOD
R. Marne

Château-Thierry   ARGONNE
                            FOREST
                 Châlons-sur-Marne
AMERICAN
EXPEDITIONARY
FORCE

Holland

German Empire

Luxembourg

R. Meuse

Verdun

LORRAINE
Metz

St. Mihiel

EUROPE IN THE FIRST WORLD WAR

The Western Front

Battle Line in July 1918
Battle Line in Nov. 1918

Cantigny: May 28 - May 31
Belleau Wood: June 4 - June 25
Aisne-Marne: July 18 - August 6
St. Mihiel: September 12 - September 16
Meuse-Argonne: September 26 - November 11
Bellicourt: September 29
Blanc Mont: October 2 - 9

Norway

UNITED
KINGDOM   North   Sweden
               Sea   Denmark

Area Shown
Above   GERMANY

FRANCE   AUSTRIA -

Bay of   SWITZ.   HUNGARY
Biscay   FRANCE

SPAIN   ITALY

Mediterranean Sea

ALGERIA   Malta

Mark A. Moore

Memories of World War I

North Carolina Doughboys on the Western Front

R. Jackson Marshall III

Division of Archives and History
North Carolina Department of Cultural Resources
Raleigh

1998

For Dalton and Stuart

Contents

Illustrations

Foreword

As the twentieth century draws toward its conclusion, North Carolinians who reflect on the tremendous events that have shaped the century must consider the historical significance of World War I. That war—the Great War, the war supposedly to end all wars and preserve democracy for the world forever—will have to be remembered as one of the most brutal, costly, disastrous, and disillusioning conflicts in history. It was the world's first "modern" war, which introduced weapons like the machine gun, poison gas, the airplane, and the armored tank. Despite the deadliness of such weapons of destruction and the horror of massive artillery bombardments, generals on both sides persisted in a primitive, outdated concept of waging war. The result was an awful trench warfare that inflicted a staggering loss of life among the soldiers who fought on the western front.

Jackson Marshall has thoroughly recorded and skillfully described the experiences of the North Carolina doughboys who endured the fright and hardships of fighting on the battlefields of Belgium and France. Through the graphic testimonies of thirty-six now-deceased North Carolinians from sixteen counties, Marshall has captured the pain, sacrifice, and courage of a generation of North Carolina's sons. Because of his diligence and the veterans' patience and cooperation, this aspect of the state's history has been preserved for future generations in *Memories of World War I: North Carolina Doughboys on the Western Front.*

Marshall is a historian and former administrator with the North Carolina Museum of History. A native of Winston-Salem, North Carolina, he earned his B.A. and M.A. degrees at Wake Forest University. He is the author of a number of articles, essays, reviews, guides, and reports related to North Carolina history. He also served as historical consultant on the award-winning film *Goodnight Alden*, based on a story of the Civil War. *Memories of World War I* is his first book. Marshall was assisted in the production of this title by Lang Baradell of the Historical Publications Section, who edited, indexed, and saw the work through press. Section editor Lisa D. Bailey applied her proofreading skills to the project. Mark A. Moore provided the map of the western front used as the frontispiece.

Joe A. Mobley, *Administrator*
Historical Publications Section

July 1998

Preface

In 1917 the United States went to war against the Imperial Government of Germany. Thousands of young Americans volunteered or were drafted into service, including many North Carolinians. These troops were trained and sent to the western front in Belgium and France to join the weary Allies in the struggle against the kaiser's forces. Through the hard months of 1918, many battles were fought, and North Carolinians participated in most of them, sometimes at great cost.

In this study the history of the war is documented as experienced by common soldiers from North Carolina. Here they describe the horrific battles in which they fought, including Château-Thierry, Soissons, St. Mihiel, Blanc Mont, Ypres, Bellicourt, Montbrehain, and the battles during the Meuse-Argonne offensive. They also tell of the discomforts of war: insufficient food, tattered clothing, ubiquitous rain and mud, and the irksome lice. This is not a history of World War I, nor is it the total story of North Carolina's role in the war. This is the story of individual soldiers and their struggle to survive war on the western front.

This volume is based primarily on a collection of tape-recorded interviews I made with North Carolina veterans of World War I between 1976 and 1985, and their diaries and letters. Originally much of this volume was presented as a master's thesis written at Wake Forest University under the direction of Dr. Richard L. Zuber. I consulted numerous military and political histories in preparing this study, but the veterans remained the main source of information and the focus of this history. I have found through this experience that oral history, when combined with previously written records, is a valuable source of information that can increase the overall understanding of history.

This volume could not have been completed without the assistance of many people. I thank all of the families of the veterans interviewed for their willingness to help me complete this study, for their time, for additional information, and for access to family photographs. I also thank Dr. Richard Zuber for his invaluable guidance and advice. And to Torrey McLean, World War I scholar and friend, I offer my sincere appreciation for his support and encouragement.

I thank Joe A. Mobley for the opportunity to work with him and his Historical Publications staff, and Lang Baradell, who as editor of this volume offered great expertise and advice in the preparation of this manuscript.

To Sion Harrington of the State Archives and to many others in the North Carolina Division of Archives and History, thank you for your assistance and interest in this project.

I offer my greatest appreciation to family members and friends; to the late Lucy Gray Drake, who redirected my career at a critical moment; to my wife, Patricia Marshall, for her constant love and unfailing support; and to my parents, Mr. and Mrs. R. Jack Marshall Jr., for their continued self-sacrifice and confidence in me.

Lastly, I dedicate the following pages to the memory of my grandfather, R. Jack Marshall Sr., a 1917 volunteer and veteran of World War I. It was through his inspiration that this study was initiated and continued. To him, and all of the veterans who gave me their time and were patient with my unending questions, I owe the greatest tribute.

Prologue
"They Call It World War I"

In 1917 and 1918, the United States fought in World War I, or the Great War as it was then called, a conflict that to most Americans is now merely an old, almost forgotten memory. Images of trenches, "old-timey" biplanes, horse-drawn artillery, and rattletrap tanks stick in our minds. It was an ancient war of sorts, of black-and-white photographs and silent, dreamlike moving-picture shows. But it was also a deadly war of terrible waste and sacrifice, and for the men who fought on its battlefields, a very real, terrifying experience. This volume describes the Great War as seen through the eyes of North Carolina doughboys who fought on the western front in Belgium and France. From their recollections color is added to the photographs, sound is affixed to the films, and some feelings are rendered for the men who fought and died.

Written records reveal little about the experiences of the common soldier in World War I. The military histories relate only the dry statistics and battle movements, but as one marine officer of this war pointed out, "It is only from the individual soldier that we can learn how the war appears to the man who is doing the fighting."[1] To better understand their history of the Great War it was necessary to go beyond the published accounts and talk to the veterans themselves. To this end about four hundred veterans were located, and of this number, eighty were contacted. Some of the men who were sought after were dead, many did not go overseas, and many were too ill to be disturbed for an interview. Others, however, were more than willing to discuss their experiences, and interviews with forty veterans were recorded. Of these, the recollections of thirty-three were chosen to be the basis of this book. The diaries and letters of three others have also been included.

What follows is a description of the experiences of thirty-six North Carolinians from sixteen counties, all of whom went through training, served in France, and returned home wishing that they could forget much of what they had seen. Fifteen volunteered into service, and twenty-one were drafted. According to rank when discharged in 1919, the group consisted of six sergeants, nine corporals, seven privates first-class, and fourteen privates. These men were not unique in any way; their interviews simply provided a better quality of material, and their characters were such as to prove them sincere. For some it was the first time they had discussed their experiences with anyone, and they were cautious about sharing some of their recollections. They were even less inclined to embellish their stories. It became apparent that the men of this generation wasted few words, answering questions directly and sometimes bluntly.

What can these men tell us about this seemingly ancient war? What can they tell us that we do not already know? Their history is not of great battles, grand strategies, or political upheavals. Those accounts have already been written. Their history is about the individual, the average man, who was caught up in a conflict he little understood and felt lucky to have survived. One veteran, speaking for all of the soldiers of his war, questioned our appreciation of what his generation had endured: "Do you know we didn't have any anesthetic or any kind of medication to give [the wounded] other than iodine or aspirin? Isn't that something? I hope that isn't the way war is today. Just think of having to wear your clothes until you wore them to shreds before you could get a decent uniform. Think of having to wait a year to get across. It took us a year after we declared war to even get over there and get to war. Think of that."[2]

These old doughboys, all of whom are now dead, hoped that readers would gain a greater understanding of why they fought and of the sacrifices they and many others of their generation made for our future. They did what they thought was best for this country—they went to war. "World War I, I think that's what they call it," recalled one veteran.[3] Another veteran reminded us that "it was the only war that any soldiers in the world have ever fought specifically to end all wars."[4] World War I, it was to be "the war to end all wars," so these men thought at the time. This nineteenth-century war fought in the early twentieth century destroyed the idealism of a young generation of Americans. World War I actually was not so long ago, the veterans pointed out, but they feared that their sacrifices were already forgotten. These North Carolinians wished to leave behind this, their testament of a sacrificed generation, so that they are not completely forgotten by a hurried future.

Notes

1. A. W. Catlin, *"With the Help of God and a Few Marines"* (Garden City, N.Y.: Doubleday, Page and Company, 1919), 171.
2. Felix Elbridge Brockman, interview with author, Greensboro, N.C., January 5, 1984.
3. Lamar Gladney Clarke, interview with author, Greensboro, N.C., January 4, 1984.
4. Harvey Clinton Maness, interview with author, Raleigh, N.C., December 19, 1985.

Chapter One
"To Keep the Kaiser Away":
Army Organization and Training

"I voted for President Wilson. Before the election many a car would pass on the railroad that had the sign: 'He Kept Us Out of War.' People really believed we wouldn't get in the war because Wilson said we wouldn't."[1] Otho F. Offman of Randolph County was only twenty-two years old in 1916. He and the majority of North Carolinians who voted that year helped to reelect Woodrow Wilson to a second term in the White House. Many of those who voted for Wilson did so because he had kept the United States out of the war that had been raging in Europe since 1914. Guy E. Wise from Stanly County also remembered the Wilson campaign slogan, "but that was in the fall of the year when the election was, and then in April he declared war."[2] Wise did not blame Wilson for breaking his campaign promise. The president had no choice, as Wise saw it. "The Germans were going to take over the whole country," he said, and we had to fight because "they started sinking our ships, and we couldn't stand for that."[3]

Wilson went before Congress on April 2, 1917, and asked for a declaration of war against Germany. On April 4, the Senate passed a war resolution with only six dissenting votes, and on April 6, the House approved the measure by a vote of 373 to 50.[4] Among the dissenters in the House was North Carolina's Claude Kitchin, the House majority leader. In his speech to Congress, Kitchin stated that he could not vote for war because the United States was under no threat and should not become involved in the slaughter in Europe. He added, however, that he would support the war effort "with all of his soul" once war was declared. As a result of his vote, Kitchin received many angry telegrams from his home state and some thanking him.[5] With the passage of the war resolution, North Carolinians, like other Americans, found themselves locked into an uncertain future, fighting an enemy they little understood in a European war for which they were unprepared.

Despite warnings from some political figures, including Theodore Roosevelt, and the hostile actions of the German navy since 1915, the Wilson

President Woodrow Wilson (left) asked Congress for a declaration of war against Germany on April 2, 1917. North Carolina's Claude Kitchin was one of fifty members of the U.S. House of Representatives to vote against the measure. Kitchin, a Democrat, was House majority leader. Despite his vote against the war, Kitchin promised to support the war effort fully once the measure passed. Photographs from the files of the Division of Archives and History.

administration had made little progress in preparing the American military for war. General John J. Pershing, who would lead the American Expeditionary Force (AEF) in Europe, wrote years later that Wilson did not understand what was necessary to prepare for war.[6] This lack of readiness became obvious in government and military circles as soon as war was declared, and to each man called into service during the following year. Otho Offman summed up the American dilemma: "We were caught napping. That's all there was to it. We were not prepared for it. We were misinformed—or just bullheaded."[7] Whatever the reason, the United States in April 1917 soon began scrambling to mobilize the existing armed forces, however small, and to organize the country for the war effort.

Once Congress adopted the war resolution, the nation's political leaders had to solidify support for the decision to fight. Wilson, in his declaration of war, stated that America was to fight "for democracy" and the "rights and liberties" of the people of the world.[8] Governor Thomas Walter Bickett of North Carolina said, "This is no ordinary war. It is a war of ideals."[9] He traveled across the state, speaking to women's clubs, at church functions, and

4

at civic meetings to explain why the United States needed to fight this war. In an address at the University of North Carolina Founders' Day, Bickett explained that our involvement was a sign of gratitude to France and was necessary to secure peace and to ultimately "send militarism to the scrapheap of civilization."[10] The speeches supporting the war were well received, as indicated by various newspapers around the state. Even the *Greensboro Daily News*, which before the declaration of war had stated that its readership had "little desire to take a hand in Europe's slaughter and confusion," fell in behind the *Fayetteville Observer* and *Charlotte Observer*, newspapers that had favored involvement before Wilson's call for war.[11] Despite hesitation by some in the state, there was support for the war effort based on a strong sense of patriotism—the essential ingredient in this time of crisis.

At the outbreak of war, the United States had only a small regular army, well understrength for a war in France, and a poorly prepared National Guard, or militia organization. Reports of the strength of the regular army and National Guard in April 1917 vary, but most agree that the total was about 200,000 men.[12] Congress quickly authorized the president to increase the size of the armed forces. This was to be accomplished by voluntary enlistment, if possible, with a goal of 287,000 in the regular army and 450,000 in the National Guard.[13] Recruiting stations were established across the nation, and young men everywhere were encouraged to do their patriotic duty and enlist. Felix E. Brockman of Greensboro had been preparing

Thomas Walter Bickett had been governor of North Carolina less than three months when the United States entered World War I. Calling the conflict a "war of ideals," Bickett traveled the state building support for the war effort. Photograph from the files of the Division of Archives and History.

physically for enlistment for several months by working on a construction job in Mecklenburg County. On June 27, 1917, he returned to Greensboro and volunteered in a local ambulance company. He did so, he said, "because the Germans had sunk the *Lusitania*, and I didn't see why we should stand for anything such as that."[14] William C. Grubb, also of Guilford County, left his job at the National Biscuit Company and joined the same outfit. "I just felt it was my duty," he said, "and of course, when you are young like that you don't know everything, . . . so I enlisted, all of us enlisted."[15] Marion A. Andrews of Forsyth County joined up because he "got tired of all the boys going off and leaving me, and all the girls bragging about them going."[16]

North Carolina responded strongly to the call for volunteers. In addition to exceeding its national quota in the regular army, navy, and marines, the state also organized six companies of coastal artillery, a cavalry squadron, a field hospital, an ambulance company, and several National Guard units. These volunteers had a deep sense of patriotism and a great deal of pride. They saw themselves as being different from the hard-luck regulars, the "tin-soldiers" of the militia, and the draftees.[17] In fact, many of the volunteers viewed draftees with great disdain. One Forsyth County volunteer expressed an opinion held by many when he said that "the ones who were drafted, . . . they never were worth a durn."[18]

The volunteer system was inadequate, however, and the Wilson administration had to use conscription. The first selective service bill stipulated that all males between the ages of twenty-one and thirty-one were to register on June 5, 1917. This registration totaled nearly ten million men.[19] From this number an initial half million men were inducted to create a national army, with an additional 187,000 called to serve in the National Guard.[20] The following year, on June 5 and August 24, those who had reached the age of twenty-one since 1917 were registered, adding an additional one million men to the rolls. The total for all three dates was 10,679,814 men, of which 2,666,867 (25 percent) were drafted. Still more soldiers were needed. In August 1918, Congress amended the selective service law to require that all men from eighteen to forty-five register on September 12. This registration brought an additional 13,228,762 men to the conscription lists, of which 120,157 were inducted. All told, just over twenty-four million men were registered, of whom nearly three million were called into active service.[21]

The conscription issue, at first, divided Congress. Representative Kitchin and many others had reservations about the draft but reluctantly allowed the measure to pass under pressure from President Wilson.[22] Reaction to the selective service laws was favorable in North Carolina, though there was some debate over the exemption of college students. Governor Bickett and Chief Justice Walter Clark of the state supreme court disapproved of the exemption.

Immediately after the United States entered the war, a recruitment campaign was launched to increase the size of the then understrength armed forces. Posters, such as this one, appeared across North Carolina to encourage young men to volunteer. Photograph of poster from the files of the Division of Archives and History.

When voluntary enlistments failed to provide enough soldiers, conscription was started. This is a group of draftees in Lexington on March 5, 1918. Wearing identification tags on their coats, they were put on board a train and sent to Camp Sevier, South Carolina. Carl William Clodfelter, one of the veterans interviewed for this volume, is shown standing, second from right. Photograph courtesy of the Carl William Clodfelter family.

Clark found no reasoning in drafting workers off productive farms while leaving wealthier boys to their studies in the safety of the universities.[23]

Responding to a sense of patriotism, North Carolinians had a 106 percent registration rate, suggesting that some had lied about their age in order to be included.[24] In North Carolina the registration dates for 1917 and 1918 brought a total of 480,491 men, of which 60,822 were drafted.[25] Some of those called avoided service. About 1,612 North Carolinians, or 2.65 percent of those drafted, evaded the draft during the war.[26] Most of the men, however, were willing to serve if called.

The selective service system, at times, interfered with volunteer enlistments and created confusion.[27] One recruit, Gladney Clarke, volunteered and was in training when he was called home to be drafted. He had to turn in his uniform and leave Camp Sevier, South Carolina, after three months of service. "That sounds crazy to me but that's what happened," Clarke recalled. "They had to send me home so they could draft me."[28]

On July 25, 1917, President Wilson called the National Guard into federal service, which in North Carolina numbered 7,454 men.[29] Many of these guardsmen had only recently returned from duty on the Mexican border. The North Carolina troops were sent to Camp Sevier to become part of the Thirtieth Division. Within the division, most of the First North Carolina Infantry Regiment became the 105th Engineer Regiment, while the Second and Third Infantry Regiments became the 119th and 120th Infantry Regiments, respectively.[30] Though these two infantry regiments were made up mostly of North Carolinians, they also included soldiers from Tennessee. These two regiments were part of the Sixtieth Infantry Brigade, which was the largest single unit made up primarily of men from the Old North State.[31] The Thirtieth Division also included two other infantry regiments, the 117th, which had been the Third Tennessee, and the 118th, which had been the old First South Carolina.[32]

When these various National Guard units were organized at Camp Sevier, they lacked a sufficient number of men to bring the division up to war strength. As a result, drafted men were sent to fill the ranks. Although some of the draftees came from other parts of the country, most were from North Carolina, South Carolina, and Tennessee, thus making the division's nickname, the "Old Hickory Division" for Andrew Jackson, all the more appropriate. Among the thirty-six veterans included in this study, eleven belonged to this division, six of whom were volunteers. It is also worthy of mention that the Thirtieth Division differed from many of the other new American divisions in that 95 percent of the men were of American-born parents.[33]

The only other division containing a large number of North Carolinians was the Eighty-first Division, organized at Camp Jackson, near Columbia,

National Guard units were federalized in July 1917. Many North Carolina guardsmen had just returned in March 1917 from service on the Mexican border, only to be called back into service for the World War. The Third North Carolina Infantry became the 120th Infantry, Thirtieth Division. Members of that unit are shown on Capitol Square, Raleigh, in May 1918, shortly before being sent to France. Photograph from the files of the Division of Archives and History.

South Carolina, in August and September 1917. Twelve of the veterans included in this study were members of the Eighty-first Division. This division, known as the "Wildcat Division," was made up of men drafted in the fall of 1917 and spring of 1918 from North Carolina, South Carolina, and Florida, in particular, and other southern states, in general. This was one of the first national divisions organized, but the unit's assignment overseas was delayed when 50 percent of the men were transferred to other units in October 1917.[34] Most of them went to the Thirtieth Division. One soldier who happily remained with the Eighty-first recalled that "they picked the sorriest men out of our outfit and sent them."[35] These men were replaced by additional conscripts from the same states as before, with a mix of northern draftees. Even with the transfers, North Carolina still had a high percentage of men in the Eighty-first. Three units in the division in particular, the 321st Infantry, the 316th Field Artillery, and the 321st Ambulance Company, included large numbers of North Carolinians.[36]

For every man, volunteer or draftee, the call to arms meant leaving home for an uncertain future. They were off to war, whether or not they understood the reason for fighting. The journey to the western front began when each recruit boarded the train to camp. Felix Brockman, who volunteered for an ambulance company, described a typical departure: "There was a large crowd at the station and there was some crying. This was not a familiar sight at this time, as we were the first soldiers to leave the State since the Spanish-American War in 1898. Our train pulled out at about 7:30 P.M. [June 26, 1917], and there are not many of the fellows who do not recollect the doleful sound of the whistle on our engine as it pulled us away from our homes. People in Greensboro later wrote us of how mournful it sounded to them and thought that the engineer did it on purpose."[37] Robert Gaither remembered his departure from home in Davie County on the morning of May 31, 1918: "The train came through Mocksville at ten or eleven o'clock, and of course, my family came with me. I was told later that my daddy just sat down and cried when I left. And then my mother scolded him for doing it in public. But when she got home she cried. . . . I felt different after I got on the train. It wasn't what I thought it would be. And I never came back home until the next year, it was over a year later, after I went to France."[38]

In many cases the trains arrived in camp in the middle of the night, which made getting up the following day all the more difficult for the new soldiers. William Morris was a member of the 365th Infantry Regiment, Ninety-second Division, which was made up of African Americans but commanded by white officers. He recalled the night he arrived at Camp Grant in Illinois: "You are on your own then, you understand. You go out to the straw ricks and pick up your own straw, come back to the barracks and make your own bed. That was about one at night when we got there; it was cold, with snow piled as big as a box car. . . . We came back in and got settled down on the cots in the barracks at about two that night and made reveille at five the next morning."[39]

John F. Adams of the 321st Infantry Regiment, Eighty-first Division, arrived at Camp Jackson, South Carolina, in the middle of the night and, like Morris, got very little sleep. Adams always remembered his first morning reveille: "About the time we got to sleep the sergeant came in and hollered, 'Everybody up!' It seemed like we just had gotten in bed. He turned the lights on right bright, and he called us out. He called the roll alphabetically, and some said present and some could hardly speak."[40]

New recruits soon learned that it was better to stand in line for roll call half asleep than to miss it entirely. David N. Edwards of the 306th Ammunition Train, Eighty-first Division, also spent his first night at Camp Jackson, and to his surprise, "when they sounded reveille the next morning I slept right through it, and they had to yank me out of the bed."[41] Having to get up with little sleep soon became routine, however, and like William Grubb of Guilford County, a volunteer in training at Fort Oglethorpe, Georgia, the new soldiers learned to "fall in" in a hurry. "We had a colonel who would call us out at three in the morning for inspection," Grubb remembered. "I've stood out many a morning with my shoes and overcoat on and not have another durn thing on except my drawers; I had them on."[42]

Several men remembered that no matter what hour of the day or night they arrived in camp, their first task after stepping off the train was to fill bed sacks. Horton B. Hall of the 323rd Infantry Regiment, Eighty-first Division, recalled: "The sergeant who was in charge lined us all up and had us to march to the supply room where we were given our bed sacks. . . . He marched us out to the countryside about half a mile to big straw ricks . . . and every man was told to fill his bed sack with straw as full as he could pack it. We carried our bed sacks back to our bunks, and we were given a sewing kit and were told to sew that hole up in the bags."[43]

The men had to pass two physical examinations, with the first one being given by a local board. Within a few days of their arrival at camp, they were subjected to a second examination. Between 65 and 69 percent of North Carolina inductees passed both tests.[44] Following the examination, the men went to the supply room where they were fitted for clothing. Typically, each soldier was issued one uniform coat and pants, two suits of underwear, two shirts, two pairs of socks, a hat, a pair of shoes, and a pair of canvas or cloth leggings. There was, however, an extreme shortage of supplies when war was declared, and many of the veterans interviewed did not receive all of their clothing. Several of the men also remembered having to wear wool uniforms in the summer or cotton in the winter. Felix Brockman, who was training at Fort Oglethorpe, Georgia, recalled: "We did not get a piece of uniform for the first five weeks we were in the service. You can well imagine what a set of tramps we looked like after so long a time in one suit of clothes. We were told not to bring any clothes except that which we wore and we wore our oldest having faith that they would give us more when we arrived at camp, but for some reason they didn't."[45] Finally, Brockman's company showed up at roll call in their bathrobes and torn clothes to impress upon their officers the need for uniforms, which they received that very evening.

Not all soldiers were fortunate enough to train in camps such as Jackson, "a big city of sprawling barracks," with its relatively comfortable quarters.[46] Insufficient funds prevented the construction of permanent barracks in some camps. As a result, sixteen National Guard units were forced to live in tents in camps in the South.[47] One of these canvas camps was Camp Sevier, near Greenville, South Carolina, and the first troops trained there were members of the Thirtieth Division. Archie C. Ingram, a Buncombe County native, was one of the first men to arrive in camp and remembered that they "had to pull up the corn to clear the drill field."[48] William F. Crouse of Forsyth County recalled that the camp "wasn't anything but an old pine field" and that they had to put up the tents when they got there.[49] Clarence C. Moore, also of Forsyth County, remembered digging up pine stumps to clear enough land for the tents and never forgot having to stay in the tents during the winter of 1917-1918. "It was one of the worst winters you ever saw," he said, "snow and ice half waist deep, and limbs and tops breaking out of those trees all night long."[50] John H. Collins of Surry County was also at Camp Sevier during that winter and recalled one night when conditions were particularly severe: "There came up a storm one night, and it blew all the tents down. They all fell in on us, but we just laid there until the next day and got up and put the tents back up. It was rough, but I enjoyed it."[51]

When some of the draftees were sent to camp they were placed in depot brigades until sorted out and transferred to the various divisions that needed men. Clarence Moore was drafted and, along with other men from Winston-Salem, placed in such a brigade for several weeks, until they were separated and "spread out like a covey of quails."[52] Moore, who had been a barber in civilian life, was sent to the Thirtieth Division, and as in the depot brigade, he was pulled from the ranks and made company barber. Several of the veterans interviewed had been clerks before the war and were made company clerks. Having a particular trade or talent did not necessarily guarantee a special position in the army, however. Nor did the lack of a particular skill always matter. William Grubb and another soldier were made company buglers, though neither had ever played the instrument. Grubb recalled: "I didn't even know the music, and he didn't either. We got instructed, and we would go down in the pines and practice. We had to learn the manual of arms—now we didn't play it perfect, don't misunderstand—but we did know it."[53]

The transformation from civilian to soldier is evident in these photographs of Guy Earl Wise of Stanly County. As a civilian, he stands relaxed and wears a suit, as most men did when they reported for military duty. As a new soldier, dressed in a summer-issue uniform, Wise stands stiff and straight. Photographs courtesy of Raymond M. Wise.

When reveille sounded, every soldier was expected to be ready for the daily routine of work and drill. Horton Hall remembered how each day began: "When reveille was called our captain was out there ready to lead us. We went on a mile run to a tree every morning, and we went around that tree and back to camp. The next thing we did was to go into our barracks, wash our faces, shave, and were marched out to the kitchen to breakfast."[54] Luther P. Hall of Surry County remembered the morning run and how it affected some of the men: "We would get up at daylight, and the first thing we would do was to run in that sand four to six hundred yards. A lot of them would fall out. I've seen them fall out and their faces go right into that sand."[55] Smith C. Cable of Watauga County recalled that men at Fort Bliss, Texas, often passed out during training because it was "as hot as the dickens."[56] James V. Covington, a native of Stokes County, said that when soldiers were on the drill field at Camp Wadsworth, South Carolina, the officers "worked them like horses."[57] Covington was spared this, however. Even though the average training period was usually six months, Covington was shipped out after only a week in camp when a departing company required a few more men.[58]

"Well, I'll tell you, I went out and drilled many a morning on syrup and bread; now that's the truth," so declared William Crouse.[59] This fortunately was not typical of the food served in training camps. When asked about the food at Camp Jackson, David Edwards sang this song in response:

> Are you from Jackson, I said Camp Jackson
> Where the damned old food comes
>   up to your neck?
> I'm glad to see you, I'm going to feed you
> On all the hash that's been through a wreck.
> Right about and left about or as you were,
> Gosh, you've earned your dollar per.
> Are you from Jackson, I said Camp Jackson,
> Well, I'm from Jackson too.[60]

Edwards added that the food at Camp Jackson "wasn't outstanding."[61] Camp food in general, however, was not judged so harshly by most of the men who were interviewed. Roby G. Yarborough of the Thirtieth Division observed that outstanding food or not, the men at Camp Sevier "rushed up to get served" any time the field kitchen opened.[62]

The kinds of food served in the different training camps varied little, and many of the men had good memories about what was served. Smith Cable was served "rough vegetables . . . some meat, and a lot of beans" at Fort Bliss, Texas.[63] Noah Whicker of the Eighty-first Division recalled that at Camp Jackson most meals consisted of "taters and beef, and bread."[64] To drink, Guy

Soon to be "spread out like a covey of quails," Clarence Cicero Moore and other draftees stand in front of the courthouse in Winston-Salem on April 1, 1918. Moore, standing second from the right, second row from the rear, appears to be holding a cigar. Moore was assigned to the Thirtieth Division and with little training was sent to France in less than two months. Photograph courtesy of Mrs. Jean Moore Jones.

Wise explained, "you had your choice: coffee, tea, or water," but he was not a coffee drinker and chose water instead of tea because "the tea we had back then wasn't fit for anything."[65] Horton Hall had no objections to the kind or amount of food served at Camp Jackson. The food, as he remembered, was good: "We had beef stew, bacon and eggs for breakfast; beef stew and other vegetables for supper."[66] Beef stew seems to have been the mainstay in camp, but this did not bother Hall, who added, "If we didn't get enough the first time we could go around through the line again and get seconds, which we always did, including me."[67] Once he got to the front in France, he did not have a chance for seconds and sometimes went hungry because of a complete lack of food.

While soldiers were naturally concerned about the comforts of camp life, their primary purpose in being there was to learn to fight. "If a man could not learn to shoot a rifle, he wasn't any good in the infantry," according to Horton Hall, who was assigned to be a machine gunner and spent hours learning to fire his weapon.[68] Any private who could qualify as a marksman received an additional two dollars to supplement his thirteen dollar monthly salary.[69]

The physical demands of training gave the new recruits big appetites, and they ate almost anything that was served. The veterans remembered that the camp food was generally good, especially when compared to that served on the voyage to Europe and on the front. Photograph from a scrapbook in the Robert R. Bridgers Papers, Private Collections, State Archives, Division of Archives and History, Raleigh.

Qualifying as a marksman was difficult, however, especially when trying to hit a target without the benefit of a rifle. Noah Whicker found himself in that situation at Camp Jackson: "When we started off we didn't have any guns; we started by having sticks with a piece with a hole in it. You had to sight through the hole to get it on the target, and when you got it where you wanted it you would say so, and they would mark it. That was our first training with the guns—with sticks."[70]

In addition to target shooting, real or imagined, the recruits also had bayonet practice. Archie Ingram, a newly promoted sergeant, was assigned to be an instructor. "I asked, 'What do you want me to do,' and they said, 'Don't stop for anything!' " Ingram also recalled that "they made dummies out of sticks and hung them up, and we poked at them with our rifles."[71]

Soldiers were also trained to protect themselves from poison gas, a weapon used for the first time during World War I. Each man was given a gas mask, either in the United States or upon arrival overseas, and taught how to use it. Carl W. Clodfelter, a private in the Thirtieth Division, received his

Learning to use the bayonet was an important part of basic training. Noah Whicker (right), a veteran interviewed for this book, is shown practicing at Camp Jackson, South Carolina. Whicker recalled having to start his training with sticks until rifles were found for the troops. Photograph courtesy of Katherine Whicker Linville.

training at Camp Sevier. "They took us out through the woods and fired shots," he recalled. "They said it was gas, but I didn't think it was because you could hear traffic on the highway. But that's what they claimed, and we had to put on gas masks to protect us. It was a mask, and you clamped your nose so you had to breath through your mouth through chemicals in your mask, and it kept the gas from getting in your lungs. It was hot, and they carried us down into the woods, and it was rough."[72] The two-day routine proved to be too severe for Clodfelter, who "got sick, fainted, and fell backwards standing at attention."[73] He was loaded in a truck and sent back to camp that afternoon when he could not keep up with the men who were returning on foot.

Artillery regiments had as much trouble finding training equipment as their infantry counterparts. In many of the camps, field guns were not to be found, and the men had to use logs placed on wheels or on wooden forks stuck

Because of a lack of weapons, artillery units often had to train with log guns. Members of the 113th Field Artillery are shown drilling at Camp Sevier, South Carolina. Soldiers in U.S. training camps were taught to fire the American three-inch fieldpiece, but because of shortages, none of these weapons were sent to France. American artillerymen had to be retrained with French guns once the troops arrived overseas. Photograph from A. L. Fletcher, *History of the 113th Field Artillery, 30th Division* (Raleigh: History Committee of the 113th F.A., 1920), 25.

in the ground.[74] Whether or not artillery pieces could be found, the soldiers were taught to work with the horses and mules that were used in the artillery units. In El Paso, Texas, Smith Cable was made a wagoner. "We trained with rifles, and we trained with our horses," he remembered. "The men who didn't know how to ride learned to ride. I knew myself; I was brought up with stock."[75] Joe W. Thompson was also assigned a wagon and a team of horses. He recalled: "I already knew how to drive because I came off a farm. I knew how to handle stock with no trouble at all."[76] Robert F. Gaither, a private at Camp Jackson, had been brought up with stock on his farm in Davie County, but he still had problems with the horses used in the artillery because they were too big to mount. "We were taking those exercises—we were riding— and that big old horse they would give me, I couldn't jump up there and get on him and never could. You had to jump up far enough to get on him and then throw your leg over. I couldn't quite make it, and they were waiting on me. So the fellow next to me, he was already on his, he said, 'Here, you can put your foot on mine and get up on there.' And those old horses had sharp backbones, and they wore the skin off my back end."[77]

Generally, officers were patient with new recruits and left a favorable impression, according to the veterans. This is not to say, however, that the officers were always quiet or good natured. Robert Gaither remembered his first day in camp and the officers he encountered: "Those officers took charge and said, 'Get up those steps. They aren't going to fall in on you!' They were talking like that. I hadn't ever been talked to like that before. I knew I was in for it then."[78] At the Marine Corps training camp at Parris Island, South Carolina, Wade Marshall was also surprised by the rough handling from the noncommissioned officers. In a letter to his mother from May 1918, he wrote: "I thought and still think that this is the worst place for bad language I ever saw. . . . The first day I was here I thought the cursing was awful. . . . Understand, no one has cursed me but everyone seems bent on excelling the other. But now they have taken a back seat for we had a lieutenant come down, and he lectured us. He gave the non-coms the very devil, so things have gotten mighty quiet."[79]

Occasionally a soldier would gamble that an officer would be lenient in correcting an offense. John Collins took such a chance when he stayed home in Surry County on leave five days on a thirty-six-hour pass. When he returned to camp, he was sent to his captain: "I went to see the captain and knocked, and he said, 'Come in.' He was sitting there with his back to me, putting his boots on. I said, 'Private Collins reporting.' He said, 'You're back are you.' I said, 'Yep.' He said, 'Private Collins, don't you appreciate a pass when you get one?' I said, 'Yes siree, I did that one.' He was tough [but] I saw him grin from behind his ears, but he never looked at me. He told me to go back out, and he would put up on the bulletin board what he was going to do

Wade Latimer Marshall, a twenty-year-old volunteer from Forsyth County, followed two older brothers into service in May 1918. He joined the Marine Corps and was assigned to the First Marine Aviation Force. In October, he arrived in Europe as part of a bomber squadron. The photograph on the left was taken at Parris Island, South Carolina, in May 1918; the one on the right was taken ca. 1955. Photographs courtesy of the Wade L. Marshall family.

with me. I went on back out, and I went and looked up on the bulletin board and there was, 'Twenty days confined to company streets.' They gave me the detail work all the time, and I got tired of that."[80]

At one point, Collins thought he was going to be caught during his "absence without leave." When he got off the train at a station, a guard approached him: "The guard called me and asked me if I had a pass. I told him yes. I looked at him, and he was in the same fix I was in—he couldn't even read nor write. I showed him [my pass], and he said, 'Go ahead.' "[81]

During World War I, illiteracy was common among the soldiers. When these men were brought into service, the army tried to teach them at least the basics in reading and writing. Sergeant Roby Yarborough was assigned to teach soldiers at Camp Sevier: "Very few of us had finished high school, and quite a few could not read nor write. We had some mountain boys brought into the company, and I was called in by the YMCA secretary to go to the "Y" building and try to teach these fellows to write their names so they could stand the payroll. Some of them were not lacking in intelligence, but they were just illiterate. They could not help from being illiterate because they came from back up in the mountains in the western part of the state where they didn't have any schools to go to up there."[82]

The YMCA buildings, such as the one in which Sergeant Yarborough taught, were established in all of the military camps. The YMCA had been adopted by the government and authorized by President Wilson in April 1917 to promote "the social, physical, intellectual, and moral welfare of enlisted men" in the training centers around the nation.[83] At the "Y" soldiers were subjected to lectures, enjoyed moving-picture shows, and gathered to pass the time. In addition to the YMCA, other organizations served the soldiers, including the Red Cross, Knights of Columbus, and Salvation Army.[84]

The government took additional steps to protect the morals of the soldiers. At no time was a soldier allowed to gamble, and the Army Bill of May 18, 1917, prohibited the sale of liquor to anyone in uniform and required communities to clean up "red light" districts.[85] The bill's prohibition against the sale of drink to soldiers apparently included cola, a new beverage of questionable characteristics. Otho Offman of the Eighty-first Division explained how he got around the law: "When I was at Camp Jackson it was against the law to sell Coca-Cola. If you wanted Coca-Cola you went to a restaurant over in Columbia, and the man would sell you one for a nickel, and you would drink it out of a teacup."[86] No doubt soldiers could find ways to circumvent any law and do far more than sneak a sip of cola, but then that was part of learning to be a soldier.

There were legal diversions for the men in camp. World War I was perhaps the last American war in which soldiers went into the fight with a song on their lips. Horton B. Hall remembered the group singing at Camp Jackson: "At night we would gather in our barracks and there was always somebody in our group who could sing and play the piano. . . . We would just have a big time."[87] Veterans remembered such songs as "Over There," "It's A Long, Long Way to Tipperary," "Good-bye Broadway, Hello France," "K-K-K-Katy," "Lilli Marlene," "Dixie," and "The Star-Spangled Banner." In camp these songs helped to offset the drudgery and keep the soldiers' spirits high against the reality of war.

In addition to the singing, there were trips into town, visits from family members, and the highly prized letters from home. These letters kept the soldiers informed of the latest gossip, farm news, and family situations. They also gave the men encouragement to endure the trials that were before them. Private Matt M. Strader received a letter from his aunt in Winston-Salem in the summer of 1918 that read: "There were special services in the churches here Thursday for humiliation and prayer for you boys and for righteous peace that will last forever and ever. I went to two of the services and there were earnest prayers for you all. I am so weak this morning that I know if I had to keep the Kaiser away he would have been here long ago. . . . I pity the poor boys in France that are in the front of the terrible Hun."[88] Certainly, by the summer of 1918 news was beginning to arrive of the first American battle engagements. Shortly after receiving this letter, Private Strader started his journey to France with the Eighty-first Division. Ultimately, he would be in "front of the terrible Hun," where the American Expeditionary Force had been fighting for months.

Notes

1. Otho Fredrick Offman, interview with author, Greensboro, N.C., January 12, 1984.
2. Guy Earl Wise, interview with author, Greensboro, N.C., January 5, 1984.
3. Wise, interview, January 5, 1984.
4. George H. Allen et al., eds., *The Wavering Balance of Forces*, vol. 4 of *The Great War* (Philadelphia: George Barrie's Sons, 1919), 473.
5. Alex Mathews Arnett, *Claude Kitchin and the Wilson War Policies* (Boston: Little, Brown and Company, 1937), 227-240; Alex Mathews Arnett, "Claude Kitchin Versus the Patrioteers," *North Carolina Historical Review* 14 (January 1937): 29-30.
6. John J. Pershing, *My Experiences in the World War*, 2 vols. (New York: Fredrick A. Stokes Company, 1931), 1:8.
7. Offman, interview, January 12, 1984.
8. Allen et al., *Balance of Forces*, 472.
9. Santford Martin, comp., and R. B. House, ed., *Public Letters and Papers of Thomas Walter Bickett, Governor of North Carolina, 1917-1921* (Raleigh: Edwards and Broughton Printing Company, 1923), 83.
10. Martin and House, *Public Letters*, 161-162.
11. Sarah McCulloh Lemmon, *North Carolina's Role in the First World War* (Raleigh: State Department of Archives and History, 1966), 16-17.
12. Nelson Lloyd, *How We Went to War* (New York: Charles Scribner's Sons, 1919), 23; Leonard P. Ayres, *The War with Germany: A Statistical Summary* (Washington, D.C.: Government Printing Office, 1919), 16; Thomas G. Frothingham, *The American Reinforcement in the World War* (New York: Doubleday, Page and Company, 1927), 67.
13. Lloyd, *How We Went*, 43.
14. Brockman, interview, January 5, 1984.
15. William Carloe Grubb, interview with author, Greensboro, N.C., January 5, 1984.
16. Marion Alvin Andrews, interview with author, Winston-Salem, N.C., October 30, 1981.
17. A. L. Fletcher, *History of the 113th Field Artillery, 30th Division* (Raleigh: History Committee of 113th F.A., 1920), 11, 13.
18. Roy Jackson Marshall, interview with author, Forsyth County, N.C., September 21, 1976.

19. Frothingham, *American Reinforcement*, 50; James G. Harbord, *The American Army in France, 1917-1918* (Boston: Little, Brown and Company, 1936), 26; Lloyd, *How We Went*, 51.

20. Lloyd, *How We Went*, 51; Allen et al., *Balance of Forces*, 474-475.

21. Ayres, *War with Germany*, 17; Lloyd, *How We Went*, 47.

22. Arnett, *Claude Kitchin*, 244-248; Harbord, *American Army*, 26.

23. Lemmon, *North Carolina's Role*, 53.

24. Lemmon, *North Carolina's Role*, 53.

25. R. D. W. Connor, *North Carolina: Rebuilding an Ancient Commonwealth, 1584-1925*, vol. 2 (New York: American Historical Commission, 1929), 544.

26. A. L. Fletcher, *Ashe County: A History* (Jefferson, N.C.: Ashe County Research Association, 1963), 145.

27. Lloyd, *How We Went*, 65.

28. Clarke, interview, January 4, 1984.

29. Daniel Harvey Hill, *Young People's History of North Carolina*, rev. ed. (Raleigh: Alfred Williams and Company, 1923), 412.

30. Elmer A. Murphy and Robert S. Thomas, *The Thirtieth Division in the World War* (Lepanto, Ark.: Old Hickory Publishing Company, 1936), 24; L. D. Tyson, "The Breaking of the Hindenburg Line at the St. Quentin Canal," in *Proceedings of the State Literary and Historical Association of North Carolina*, comp. R. D. W. Connor (Raleigh: Edwards and Broughton Printing Company, 1920), 46.

31. Murphy and Thomas, *Thirtieth Division*, 24.

32. Murphy and Thomas, *Thirtieth Division*, 24; Tyson, "Hindenburg Line," 46.

33. Laurence Stallings, *The Doughboys: The Story of the AEF, 1917-1919* (New York: Harper and Row, 1963), 258.

34. Clarence Walton Johnson, *The History of the 321st Infantry: With a Brief Historical Sketch of the 81st Division* (Columbia, S.C.: R. L. Bryan Company, 1919), 3, 133, 8.

35. Noah Lester Whicker, interview with author, Forsyth County, N.C., September 21, 1983.

36. Felix E. Brockman, *Here, There, and Back* (Greensboro: Felix E. Brockman, 1925), 3-4; Lemmon, *North Carolina's Role*, 52; Johnson, *321st Infantry*, 147-201.

37. Brockman, *Here, There, and Back*, 2.

38. Robert Franklin Gaither, interview with author, Forsyth County, N.C., October 3, 1983.

39. William Morris, interview with author, Walnut Cove, N.C., February 2, 1984.

40. John Flem Adams, interview with author, Winston-Salem, N.C., November 7, 1981.

41. David Nesbit Edwards, interview with author, Winston-Salem, N.C., October 5, 1983.

42. Grubb, interview, January 5, 1984.

43. Horton Bower Hall, interview with author, Winston-Salem, N.C., November 3, 1981.

44. Ayres, *War with Germany*, 20.
45. Brockman, *Here, There, and Back*, 6.
46. H. B. Hall, interview, November 3, 1981.
47. Lloyd, *How We Went*, 49; Frothingham, *American Reinforcement*, 117; Harbord, *American Army*, 31.
48. Archie Clifford Ingram, interview with author, High Point, N.C., April 10, 1984.
49. William Foster Crouse, interview with author, Forsyth County, N.C., September 22, 1983.
50. Clarence Cicero Moore, interview with author, Winston-Salem, N.C., November 5, 1981.
51. John Henry Collins, interview with author, Guilford County, N.C., April 12, 1984.
52. Moore, interview, November 5, 1981.
53. Grubb, interview, January 5, 1984.
54. H. B. Hall, interview, November 3, 1981.
55. Luther Pinkney Hall, interview with author, High Point, N.C., April 10, 1984.
56. Smith Coy Cable, interview with author, Winston-Salem, N.C., September 16, 1983.
57. James Vance Covington, interview with author, Forsyth County, N.C., September 19, 1983.
58. Covington, interview, September 19, 1983.
59. Crouse, interview, September 22, 1983.
60. Edwards, interview, October 5, 1983.
61. Edwards, interview, October 5, 1983.
62. Roby Gray Yarborough, interview with author, High Point, N.C., April 19, 1984.
63. Cable, interview, September 16, 1983.
64. Whicker, interview, September 21, 1983.
65. Wise, interview, January 5, 1984.
66. H. B. Hall, interview, November 3, 1981.
67. H. B. Hall, interview, November 3, 1981.
68. H. B. Hall, interview, November 3, 1981.
69. Catlin, *"With the Help,"* 289.
70. Whicker, interview, September 21, 1983.
71. Ingram, interview, April 10, 1984.
72. Carl William Clodfelter, interview with author, Forsyth County, N.C., September 19, 1983.
73. Clodfelter, interview, September 19, 1983.
74. Fletcher, *113th Field Artillery*, 26.
75. Cable, interview, September 16, 1983.
76. Joe Willoughby Thompson, interview with author, Raleigh, N.C., December 19, 1985.
77. Gaither, interview, October 3, 1983.

78. Gaither, interview, October 3, 1983.
79. Wade Latimer Marshall to his mother, May 1918, manuscript in private possession.
80. Collins, interview, April 12, 1984.
81. Collins, interview, April 12, 1984.
82. Yarborough, interview, April 19, 1984.
83. William Howard Taft et al., eds., *Service with the Fighting Men: An Account of the Work of the American Young Men's Christian Associations in the World War*, 2 vols. (New York: Association Press, 1922), 1:214.
84. Pershing, *My Experiences*, 1:108.
85. Taft et al., *Service*, 1:116.
86. Offman, interview, January 12, 1984.
87. H. B. Hall, interview, November 3, 1981.
88. Carrie Marshall Ford to Matt Marshall Strader, June 1918, manuscript in private possession.

Chapter Two
Off to Whip the Kaiser:
Troop Transport and Combat Training

Once training was completed, the men shipped out. The train trip northward from the training camps and the voyage overseas were experiences shared by all of the North Carolina doughboys. The soldiers were packed into troop trains, night and day, rain or shine. Many of the soldiers passed through their home state on the journey north, and for some it was painful and frustrating. Wade Marshall, a homesick, nineteen-year-old volunteer in the marines, realized that his train was going to pass within a mile of his homeplace in September 1918. Knowing that the train would not stop at his small-town station, he wrote a note to his mother saying, "so close, yet so far," tied it to a rock, and waited for the train to near his home. When the train passed the station, he threw the rock out of the window. The note was found and taken to his mother, who was heartbroken that she had missed him as he passed by.[1]

The troop trains were bound for harbors in New Jersey and New York for the most part, although some of the men departed from Boston, Norfolk, or Montreal. For most of the men, this was their first trip so far north. Carl Clodfelter said, "It was the first time I had ever crossed the Potomac."[2] David Edwards was the second soldier in his family to cross the Potomac River. His father, Joseph Thomas Edwards, had crossed while serving in the Army of Northern Virginia during the Civil War.

Fifty percent of the American soldiers were transported to France in British-controlled ships, 45 percent in American ships, and the remainder in French or Italian transports.[3] Most of the veterans interviewed were shipped to Europe in steamers of the British Empire. During the war the United States paid approximately $50 per man for the Atlantic voyage, and Britain made about $170,000,000 for shipping American soldiers to Europe.[4] None of the North Carolina doughboys who were interviewed had favorable memories of the voyage. Seasickness was expected, but the poor sleeping quarters and the terrible British food made the trip even more of an ordeal.

Because of the lack of passenger liners and the pressing need for American soldiers on the western front, the British used old cattle boats to ship the soldiers. Otho Offman of the Eighty-first Division boarded such a steamer in

David Nesbit Edwards, a Wilkes County native, was a recent graduate of the University of North Carolina when he was drafted in April 1918. He was assigned to the 306th Ammunition Train, Eighty-first Division, as a private. The patch on his shoulder bears the symbol of the Eighty-first Division, which was known as the "Wildcat" division. Photograph courtesy of David N. Edwards Jr.

Hoboken, New Jersey. He remembered that it "was an English cattle boat, and the cattle hadn't been taken out very long before we went in. It was not a very savory odor."[5] In Boston, Roby Yarborough of the Thirtieth Division had a similar experience: "It was a cattle boat, and when we went aboard the ship, being Company A, the first in line in the column, we were put to the lowest deck that could be used. There we found the remains of what the livestock had left. We had the unpleasant job of trying to clean up these decks."[6]

On some boats the doughboys were given bunks or cots, but many were assigned hammocks, or "those swinging things," as Clarence Moore remembered them.[7] Isham B. Hudson of the Eighty-first Division was given a hammock when he boarded an English ship. "The ship was crowded, of course, and there were no bunks to sleep in," he recalled, "but you were supplied a hammock. When you left your hammock in the morning you put it in a container. Some of the hammocks had short ropes on one side, and if you did not get one of those—the ship would be tilted from the waves—you would roll out of your hammock on top of the dining room table, which I did one night."[8]

When Corpsman Charles H. Gibson of Winston-Salem boarded his ship in August 1918, he and others with him were assigned bunks some thirty feet below water level, much to Gibson's chagrin. At night he and a friend, Charlie Sherrill, also from Winston-Salem, would slip up on deck and sleep in the open air. When challenged by guards, they would explain that they too were guards, just off duty, and were allowed to sleep anywhere they wished. Gibson was unconcerned about the deception. Like most soldiers, he viewed it as a survival technique. "It was kind of in order of taking care of yourself," he said.[9]

What soldiers found most objectionable about their Atlantic voyage was the poor quality of food served aboard ship. Isaac E. Winfrey recalled quite clearly that the food was "rotten—it was English food."[10] Luther Hall described it as "slop, about what you would feed the hogs."[11] Horton Hall had an even lower opinion—"The food on the *Melita* was typical English food, and it wasn't even fit for a hog to eat, if you want to know the truth about it." He went on to say that the soldiers were not always sure what they were eating because "it was an English ship [and] you didn't know what it was, but we ate the food because we had to or starve."[12] For some, hunger was a real concern. William Morris recalled that his group "didn't get enough food going over . . . so we stayed pretty hungry."[13] John Adams agreed, and added, "I stayed hungry all the time, so I would eat anything they brought out."[14]

The food prepared by the British cooks varied from day to day and from ship to ship. Generally, the soldiers were served a meal twice a day of stew, hard bread, beans, tea or coffee, and some type of meat. Many times the meat was mutton or beef, both of which the soldiers believed to be horsemeat because of its tough texture and poor taste. Sometimes rabbit was served. As

Isham Hudson recalled, "They would take these rabbits that had been frozen down in the hold of the ship and pile them on the deck with the hides on them [to thaw], so when you went to eat dinner there was about so much rabbit fur in the stew as there was rabbit."[15] Eggs and orange marmalade were also served, both of which the Americans found distasteful. Robert C. Hamlin remembered that he "broke eggs that had feathers in them," and Noah Whicker was served boiled eggs in which "the yellow in them would be black."[16] Orange marmalade, an English favorite, was sometimes served three times a day but generally was thrown overboard because, as Isham Hudson said, "it was full of orange peelings and was bitter."[17] Even after the war, Hudson and other veterans who were interviewed refused to eat orange marmalade.

William Grubb, a corpsman with the Eighty-first Division, described the consequences of eating bad food on a ship in rough waters: "I never did get sick, real sick, but I did get woozy a couple of times. This one boy one morning came out with his mess kit and turned as white as a sheet. He said, 'I would give five thousand dollars if this boat would stop just five minutes. . . .' I don't care how big a man you were, if you were plumbed to be seasick you would be seasick."[18]

Most soldiers got seasick, at least on the first day or so on the open sea. Ernest James, who made the voyage in September 1918, described a typical experience in his diary: "I was seasick all day [Monday]. I managed to get my breakfast, but did not get back for mess until Tuesday dinner. I thought I would not get there then."[19] Guy Wise, who also crossed in September 1918, was caught in a storm that lasted six days. "It got so rough one night," he said, "that the water came in over the top deck and down through the [hatchway]. The next morning there was water in the section where I was, about six or eight inches deep. When the boat rocked from one side to the other everything you had laying under the bunks would move all around, mess kits and everything. The boys got so sick they would try to eat, and you would see them umm—and they would start vomiting right there in their mess kits."[20] While the voyage must have been miserable for many soldiers, Robert Gaither recalled that it was not without some humor. Gaither remembered: "The sergeant said, 'If anybody gets seasick, come and report it.' So, I got seasick and went and told him, and do you know what he said? 'Feed the fishes!' "[21] Many doughboys did just that.

Some of the doughboys got sick on the first day out and remained sick until they died or completed the voyage, whichever came first. Otho Offman recalled the near loss of one man in his outfit: "We had one boy with us, a little fellow, and he got sick the hour we got on the boat, and we were nine days crossing. He never ate a bite or got off of his bed. Captain Rosenbaum went down to the storage and forced them to give him every lemon they had to keep the boy alive."[22] The soldier survived the voyage, but only because his captain forced the Englishmen aside to find something the sick man could eat. Others were not so lucky. Several men remembered burials at sea, and even though the cause of death in each case was probably influenza, it was easy for the survivors to blame the English and their food. Ernest L. James, who remembered that "the boys always grumbled about what they had to eat—just beans and slop," thought that the English were trying to make a profit from the United States government, and for this reason, "they wouldn't give us the best food they had."[23] The doughboys in one company of the old Third North Carolina Infantry confronted their captain about the poor food and gave him an ultimatum. John Collins told the story: "It was bad the first few days—the first week. We all got together and told our captain if he didn't put some other cooks in there we were going to throw them [the English] over in the sea. It wasn't long before we had our own cooks; then we had good food."[24]

While the common soldiers grumbled about their food, the officers apparently fared much better. Felix Brockman had the opportunity to observe the officers' mess: "Several times, by chance, I was in the cabin which was right over our officers dining hall [and] it was quite appetizing for me to look down on our officers eating. . . . For breakfast, first, a nice piece of grapefruit, then eggs, steak or ham, biscuits and coffee."[25] What Felix Brockman saw, Charles Gibson actually tasted. Gibson and his buddy, Charlie Sherrill, became waiters in the officers' mess, and after each meal they ate the leftovers. Following evening meals the two of them would linger and "would sit down on those nice seats and look at the moving-picture show" with the officers.[26] Then, as if to press their luck, Gibson and Sherrill stole sandwiches and gave them to other enlisted men. Gibson remembered that they "got credit for being right good thieves."[27]

In addition to enduring the lack of creature comforts on board ship, the soldiers had to contend with the tedium and dangers of the journey. Frank L. Devane of Wilmington remembered that the ship he was on "was the slowest boat you ever saw."[28] On average the transport ships took about two weeks to make the voyage to Europe. The soldiers, when not sick or sleeping, passed the time by exercising on deck, standing guard duty, and looking for the feared German submarines. Clarence Moore, like many of the doughboys, was "afraid all the time that a submarine might get us."[29] William Grubb recalled the same concern. He remembered feeling particularly vulnerable on one occasion when his ship's engines had stopped. "Oh, it was terrible," he said. "We got out there, and something went wrong with the ship's motors, and we ended up in the middle of the Atlantic Ocean floating around. There were twenty-five ships in the convoy, and you couldn't even see a ship. I told the boys, 'If I see a submarine coming I'm going to get the biggest weight I can find and tie it around my neck and jump in.' I wasn't about to have that ship shot out from under me."[30] As it turned out, however, the soldiers had little to fear. Not a single American troop transport was lost on the voyage to France.[31]

Almost half of the American soldiers sent to Europe, including those in the Thirtieth and Eighty-first Divisions, landed initially in an English port. Liverpool received the greatest number of troops, about 884,000 men.[32] After the ships docked and the soldiers disembarked, the men marched to rest camps where they were given a good meal and a bath. Archie Ingram remembered being tired of the mutton served on his ship and after landing in Liverpool being given "English food, which was for the common folks—beef and vegetables. It wasn't too bad, better than that durn goat food."[33] A good bath was also a much-welcomed relief. Noah Whicker described that happy event: "We were all dirty dogs. I hadn't had a bath in eleven days. They sent us to a bathroom when we got off the ship, handed us some soap and a rag, and we took our bath. It was so hot in there you would sweat enough to bathe; you could bathe yourself with it. Then as you came out the door a man was standing there with a bucket of cold water, and he would throw it on you. There was some hollering and squealing going on."[34]

The rest at the English camps lasted only a few days. On occasion some of the men were given passes to leave camp and see the surrounding countryside or nearest town. Gladney Clarke, a soldier from Greensboro, remembered seeing Winchester Cathedral. "You've heard this Winchester Cathedral song," he said. "Well, I've been through that cathedral, and I don't see why in the world they would write a song about it."[35] Perhaps being tossed about in an English ship and having to eat bad English food for two weeks colored his opinion. At any rate, such leisure hours were short-lived. Before the men could get settled in their new surroundings, they were loaded onto trains and sent southward to the English Channel ports. Horton Hall thought the trip in the English trains, which took a day and a night to complete, was "about like riding on a log wagon in this country."[36]

The voyage across the English Channel was made at night. The soldiers usually left from Southampton, loaded on an assortment of transport vessels. Horton Hall was surprised at the type of ship he found tied at the dock: "Our battalion had to travel on an old-timey side-wheeler. It was a very big ship, but it was a side-wheeler, built like a riverboat, except it was built big enough for ocean travel."[37] Carl Clodfelter made the crossing in the same type of ship. "We got on an old boat to cross the English Channel that was driven by two big wheels with a shaft in the middle," Clodfelter recalled. "They ran those two wheels on the outside edge, and oh Lord, was it rough. That was about the roughest night we ever spent. . . . We got out about midway, and the Germans came over with an air raid, and they stopped and stayed out there a while. If you went down in the ship it was so hot you couldn't hardly stand it, and if you went out on deck it was so cold you couldn't hardly stand it. There were boys in and out, lying all over the floor sick."[38]

On the other side of the rough, choppy water was the coast of France and the war-weary British and French veterans. For them the war was three years old and the casualties were high, but for the young doughboys the fight was only beginning. The war had not gone well for the Allies in 1917. In April, the month the United States entered the war, French and British armies launched new assaults on the German lines. The French offensive was a disaster, while the British made slight gains but incurred heavy casualties. The French assault, called the Second Battle of the Aisne, collapsed into confusion on the first day, but the French commander, General Robert Nivelle, refused to admit defeat and ordered repeated attacks. Alarmed at the growing casualty lists, the government in Paris temporarily halted the offensive, only to permit Nivelle to renew the futile assaults in May. Open mutiny broke out in the French army, leaving only two dependable divisions on the front defending Paris. As a result of this catastrophe, Nivelle was replaced by General Henri Philippe Pétain, and the offensive was ended. French casualties numbered 187,000.[39] Of the 28,385 French soldiers found guilty of mutiny, 55 were executed.[40] While Pétain had quelled the mutinies, the French army was not what it had been before the Nivelle debacle. The general mood of the French soldiers was that they would defend their lines but would not attack the German positions. By 1918, the French infantry divisions were half their 1914 strength, down to about six thousand men.[41] This was one-fourth the size of an American infantry division. Because of the depletion of men of military age in France, many of the soldiers were either very old or very young.[42] Julius F. Dillon of Forsyth County saw what the war had done to the male population of France: "In France there were not any men, there were old men and young ones. They would take them sixteen and sixty-five years old into the army. The womenfolk even worked on the railroads over in France. I've seen them out there with picks and shovels working on the railroad. None of the menfolk [were] there; they were all in the army."[43]

The British Expeditionary Force (BEF) had also suffered in 1917. As part of Nivelle's overall war plan, Field Marshal Sir Douglas Haig initiated an offensive in April 1917 as a diversion to draw the Germans away from the French front. In the month-long Battle of Arras, the BEF made little gain after they captured Vimy Ridge and lost about 158,000 men. Haig continued the British drive against the enemy in two additional offensives, the Battle of Passchendaele (July-November) and the Battle of Cambrai (November-December). These resulted in no advantage at a cost of about 290,000 more casualties. Because of the high losses and poor results, British prime minister Lloyd George refused to send any replacements to Field Marshall Haig. In

Julius Franklin Dillon, a Forsyth County draftee, served in the medical detachment of the Forty-sixth Engineer Regiment and worked in a camp hospital in France. As a corpsman, Dillon was constantly reminded of the cost of war and of the severity of the influenza epidemic, which took the life of a friend and nearly killed him. Photograph courtesy of the Julius Dillon family.

fact, the prime minister withdrew troops from the western front and sent them to bolster the Allied forces in Italy, while holding over 600,000 soldiers inactive in England.[44] Consequently, it appeared to many that while the French army was struggling with a collapse in morale, the British army was facing slow attrition, partly at the hands of its own government.

The American Expeditionary Force under General John J. Pershing had little to offer to offset the French and British casualties in 1917. Pershing arrived in France on June 13, 1917, and was followed by the First Division, Regular Army, the same month. The Second and Fourth Divisions did not arrive until fall and the Twenty-sixth until December.[45] The mobilization in France proceeded slowly. The total number of American troops amounted to no more than 176,655 by the end of December, not nearly enough to replace the Allied losses for the year.[46] During the same period, Germany moved combat divisions to the western front from the east after the collapse of Russia, bringing the total in the west to 155 divisions.[47] The majority of American troops would not arrive in Europe until 1918, and the Germans planned to win the war before the Americans could be mobilized.

The European Allies and General Pershing disagreed on how the U.S. troops should be used. The European leaders repeatedly asked that the American soldiers be placed in French and British divisions to serve under French and British commanders. Pershing adamantly refused to hand over his men and insisted on an independent American army, as did Secretary of War Newton Baker. The British and French pressure persisted, however, and the debate continued into 1918. Though Pershing relented on occasion and sent some divisions to other Allied armies to bolster their strength, he did not lose sight of creating his own army.[48]

Pershing also differed with British and French leaders on how the war should be fought. After years of trying to end trench warfare, most Allied leaders believed that the war would never break out of the trenches. Pershing, however, was determined to drive the enemy from the trenches and fight in the open. American military leaders believed that the Allies had lost their aggressive spirit after three years of stalemate on the western front. While admitting that the American army could learn much from the British and French about trench warfare, Pershing took exception to the Allied fixation on merely fighting from trench to trench and training new recruits only for that type of combat. He also firmly believed that the Allied troops no longer had the zeal and basic skills they needed as individual soldiers. He was determined to train his men to be proficient with the rifle and to promote an aggressive attitude among his officers and men. Certain Allied tactical applications were adopted in Pershing's army, but the overall training emphasis was on the importance of the individual soldier fighting in the open. This was the philosophy instilled in American soldiers by their combat officers before they were turned over to the British and French training instructors and after they returned.[49]

Training centers were established across France to receive the Americans. The French and British each considered their training methods to be superior to the other, while the American officers, at the encouragement of their commander, knew that their methods were the best. Despite the seeming cross-purposes in training emphasis, the American soldiers did benefit from the additional instruction received overseas, which on average lasted two to three months. Horton Hall was placed under the tutelage of the French and, as he recalled, was "taught how to go in and out of trenches, ditches they fought in, and how to prepare for it and how to survive."[50] Carl Clodfelter, like most Americans who trained with the English, was more reluctant to credit the instructors for what was learned. Clodfelter said, "We didn't get any training from the English. All they did was pretend to feed us."[51]

Because of a shortage of American weapons, the first American divisions to arrive in France were supplied with either the French Hotchkiss or British Vickers heavy machine gun, and the French Chauchat automatic rifle. The British Lewis light machine gun was used by Americans serving with the British armies but was not adopted by the other American divisions because of its tendency to jam. The superior American-made Browning automatic rifle and heavy machine gun were not obtainable for combat until near the end of the war.[52] The Ninety-second Division was one of the American units to

James Vance Covington, a Stokes County native, is shown here holding the basic combat weapon, a rifle with a fixed bayonet. General John J. Pershing believed that a well-trained army could drive the kaiser's armies out of Belgium and France, and carry the war into Germany. To that end, Pershing demanded that every American soldier be taught how to shoot a rifle and be proficient as an individual fighter. Photograph courtesy of the James Vance Covington family.

receive the Chauchat automatic rifle. A member of that division, William Morris, recalled: "I went to a French school over there to learn to use that French Chauchat. I was a trainer after I went to the school, a trainer for the company, with five or six men from the company. . . . [The Chauchat] had a clip shaped like a half moon. . . . When you raised it, the legs would fold down from the gun and would stick out in the ground. The legs folded up on the side when you carried it. Three was a team—one loading it, the other carrying ammunition, [and] I was the gunner."[53] In most American squads there were two such gunners, and they were to support the movement of the infantry in battle.

The U.S. Army never used American artillery pieces during World War I. The American three-inch field guns were not taken to France because they were in limited supply and there was a concern about the availability of ammunition and parts.[54] Instead, the American divisions were equipped with French weapons, which were regarded as some of the best produced during the war. On the western front these French-made fieldpieces could be more easily supplied. Each American division had one brigade of artillery, consisting of three regiments. Two of the regiments had twenty-four French 75mm light guns each, and the third regiment had twenty-four French Schneider 155mm howitzers.[55] The only complication arising from the use of these French guns was that American artillery personnel could not be trained to use them until the men had arrived in France. The artillery barracks at Valahoun, France, which had been abandoned for two years, were reopened as a training facility for the Americans. In the fall of 1917, the First Division artillery regiments were the first Americans to train there.[56]

Smith Cable, a private in Battery C, Fifth Artillery Regiment, was among the first Americans to arrive at Valahoun. His regiment was assigned the 155mm guns, and he was designated as a wagoner. "We took the train there to Valahoun," he said, "and we got all of our equipment right there, horses and everything. . . . This was a regular training camp where we were then. [We learned] the working of the guns, the hauling of the ammunition. These shells that these guns shot weighed ninety pounds. [We] worked with them loading and unloading them, and when we got into the war we hauled them to the front."[57]

While some men learned to shoot and supply the guns, others were trained as signalmen to assist in directing the artillery fire. Jack Marshall, Battery A, Fifteenth Artillery Regiment, Second Division, was trained as a signalman at Valahoun during the winter of 1917-1918. One day while serving as a forward observer, he witnessed the effects of the battery fire directed by his captain. "We had a captain once," he recalled, "who was the best at directing fire. I've seen times during practice rounds that he would pick out a tree on the other end of a field and within three shots cut it down."[58] After

Once American troops arrived in France, they received combat training from French or British instructors. The British refused to accept African American troops, however. As a result, they remained with General Pershing or were assigned to assist the French. Here African American infantrymen are being trained to fire the French 8mm Hotchkiss machine gun. Photograph from the files of the Division of Archives and History.

about two months of practice, his captain was trying to cut down more than trees; in mid-March 1918, Marshall's regiment was moved to the front.

At that time the German army, under the command of General Erich Ludendorff, included 205 infantry divisions and numbered over a million men. They were opposed by about 764,000 British, 682,000 French, and 30,000 Belgian troops.[59] At the end of March, the American Expeditionary Force numbered only 287,500 men.[60]

With the hope of winning the war during the spring of 1918, the Germans launched an offensive on the morning of March 21. Seventy well-trained German divisions were massed against the twenty-nine divisions of the British Third and Fifth Armies. More than half of the German divisions were grouped against the fifteen divisions of the British Fifth Army.[61] By April 4, the Germans had driven the British back over thirty-seven miles on a fifty-mile front and were within twelve miles of the British supply center at Amiens. Though Ludendorff had planned to capture Amiens in this drive, thus dividing the French and British armies, the effort fell short. The offensive was a great tactical success for the Germans, however. The British Fifth Army was annihilated and was officially abolished on March 28, 1918, even before the German drive ended.[62] Total casualties for the BEF for only sixteen days of fighting numbered 163,493 men, and Ludendorff was still determined to destroy the British forces.[63]

The French 75mm fieldpiece, shown here, was thought by many to have been the best produced during the war. American artillery units in France were trained to use the French 75mm and 155mm French cannons because the United States could not supply its army with artillery pieces. Photograph from A. L. Fletcher, *History of the 113th Field Artillery, 30th Division* (Raleigh: History Committee of the 113th F.A., 1920), 71.

In response to the German offensive, more American soldiers were sent to the front to aid the hard-pressed Allies. "Do not be uneasy about us, for our dugouts are fairly deep and safe and of course, bomb proof until hit by a bomb, or shell, then not always destroyed." Matt Marshall tried to reassure his sister with these words in a letter written from the Troyon sector of the French lines on March 26.[64] Marshall, along with other members of the Second Division, had been sent forward in mid-March to relieve the French. In a diary entry on April 2, Marshall noted: "I made my second trip to the front. Someone in C.O.'s office blundered; we had to make two trips in broad day light over a shelled road. This flirting with death does not make one feel any too comfortable."[65] Matt's younger brother, Jack Marshall, was more upbeat about the future. On April 1, he wrote home, "We are not bothered by the Huns, but let 'em come; we are ready."[66]

The British, farther to the north, were not as confident as young Marshall. The last thing they needed was another German offensive. Prepared or not, the second Ludendorff offensive was initiated in the fields of Flanders against the British First and Second Armies on April 9. On the first day of the attack, a Portuguese division, trying to hold an area in the British line previously held by two divisions, was routed. By mid-day the Germans had passed through the

Jack Marshall, a 1917 volunteer, exemplified the youth and optimism in General "Black Jack" Pershing's army. Marshall's first letters home conveyed the confidence he had in himself and in the American war effort. A year later, after being wounded and seeing the horrors of numerous battles, his outlook changed. Photograph courtesy of the R. Jack Marshall family.

entire British trench system.[67] On April 10, the same day the city of Armentières fell, the British commander, Field Marshal Haig, issued the following order: "Every position must be held to the last man. There must be no retiring. With our backs to the wall, and believing in the justice of our cause, each one of us must fight to the end."[68] By April 29, when the Battle of the Lys ended, the BEF had sustained about 170,300 additional casualties.[69]

As a result of the terrible losses incurred in the German Somme and Lys offensives and because of the shortage of reinforcements, ten British divisions had to be disbanded.[70] Just as the 1917 Nivelle disaster had shaken the morale of the French, the near destruction of the British armies in the spring of 1918 brought on a sense of disillusionment among British civilians and soldiers. British veterans told arriving American soldiers that they had arrived too late to change the course of the war.[71] Clarence Moore of Winston-Salem was serving with the Thirtieth Division and was training in the British camps at this time. "They were nice looking soldiers," Moore said of the British, "but they had been in that war for so long that they had gotten stupid. They were afraid of everything. . . . Our boys didn't think too much of them."[72]

First impressions of the Germans were entirely different. Smith Cable, a First Division soldier, saw imprisoned enemy soldiers when he first stepped off the docks at St. Nazaire in August 1917. For Cable and many of the other newly recruited Americans, the German prisoners looked intimidating: "They

In the eyes of Americans, Kaiser Wilhelm II, ruler of the German empire, became the symbol of military aggression during World War I. American soldiers personalized their hatred of Germany and the war through "Kaiser Bill." Portrait from Francis J. Reynolds, Allen L. Churchill, and Francis Trevelyan Miller, eds., *The Story of the Great War*, vol. 2 (New York: P. F. Collier and Son, 1916), facing 206.

had I don't know how many—a few thousand—but they were big men. They were some of the first men of the Germans who had been captured, and they were big jokers, I can tell you that. They looked like they were really bigger than we were. . . .They were as big as elephants, [and] they looked tough, they sure did."[73]

While several American divisions were serving on the front lines with the French, and a few had fought in some minor engagements, such as the Twenty-sixth Division at Seicheprey, many Allied leaders were beginning to believe that the Americans had indeed arrived too late. In a meeting on April 27 during the Battle of the Lys, Marshal Ferdinand Foch, supreme Allied commander, spoke to Pershing of a potential disaster.[74] Pershing was more optimistic. In May alone, an additional eleven American divisions arrived in France, and though they would need extensive training, Pershing believed that they would be ready when called into combat. The American doughboy shared this confident outlook. Jack Marshall in a letter to his father on May 26, 1918, inquired about the farm and added: "Well, we will have old Kaiser Bill whipped by fall; then we will be at home to help you."[75] The next day Ludendorff opened his third offensive against the Allies.

Notes

1. Mrs. Wade Marshall, letter to author, March 27, 1984.
2. Clodfelter, interview, September 19, 1983.
3. Ayres, *War with Germany*, 43.
4. Frederick E. Drinker, ed., "America's Part in the War," in *The World War for Liberty*, ed. Francis Rolt-Wheeler and Frederick E. Drinker (n.p.: National Publishing Company, 1919), 462.
5. Offman, interview, January 12, 1984.
6. Yarborough, interview, April 19, 1984.
7. Moore, interview, November 5, 1981.
8. Isham Barney Hudson, interview with author, Winston-Salem, N.C., October 27, 1981.
9. Charles Herbert Gibson, interview with author, Winston-Salem, N.C., November 2, 1981.
10. Isaac Enos Winfrey, interview with author, Walnut Cove, N.C., September 15, 1983.
11. L. P. Hall, interview, April 10, 1984.
12. H. B. Hall, interview, November 3, 1981.
13. Morris, interview, February 2, 1984.
14. Adams, interview, November 7, 1981.
15. Hudson, interview, October 27, 1981.

16. Robert Colon Hamlin, interview with author, Greensboro, N.C., January 13, 1984; Whicker, interview, September 21, 1983.

17. Hudson, interview, October 27, 1981.

18. Grubb, interview, January 5, 1984.

19. Diary of Ernest Luther James, September 15, 1918, manuscript in private possession.

20. Wise, interview, January 5, 1984.

21. Gaither, interview, October 3, 1983.

22. Offman, interview, January 12, 1984.

23. Ernest Luther James, interview with author, Forsyth County, N.C., January 19, 1984.

24. Collins, interview, April 12, 1984.

25. Brockman, *Here, There, and Back*, 13.

26. Gibson, interview, November 2, 1981.

27. Gibson, interview, November 2, 1981.

28. Frank Lewis Devane, interview with author, Greensboro, N.C., January 4, 1984.

29. Moore, interview, November 5, 1981.

30. Grubb, interview, January 5, 1984.

31. Ayres, *War with Germany*, 47.

32. Ayres, *War with Germany*, 42.

33. Ingram, interview, April 10, 1984.

34. Whicker, interview, September 21, 1983.

35. Clarke, interview, January 4, 1984.

36. H. B. Hall, interview, November 3, 1981.

37. H. B. Hall, interview, November 3, 1981.

38. Clodfelter, interview, September 19, 1983.

39. John Terraine, *The Great War, 1914-1918: A Pictorial History* (Garden City, N.Y.: Doubleday and Company, 1965), 296-297; Cyril Falls, "Western Front, 1915-17: Stalemate," in *A Concise History of World War I*, ed. Vincent J. Esposito (New York: Frederick A. Praeger, 1964), 93-94; Frank H. Simonds, *History of the World War*, 5 vols. (Garden City, N.Y.: Doubleday, Page and Company for the Review of Reviews Company, 1917-1920), 4:153.

40. Falls, "Western Front," 94.

41. Terraine, *Great War*, 297, 325.

42. Vincent J. Esposito, "Western Front, 1918: The Year of Decision," in *A Concise History of World War I*, ed. Vincent J. Esposito (New York: Frederick A. Praeger, 1964), 103.

43. Julius Franklin Dillon, interview with author, Forsyth County, N.C., September 29, 1983.

44. Terraine, *Great War*, 299, 314, 318, 325-326; Winston S. Churchill, *The World Crisis: 1916-1918*, vol. 2 (New York: Charles Scribner's Sons, 1927), 52-53.

45. *Division Insignia: The Insignia of Pershing's Crusaders with a Brief History of Each Unit* (Camp Dix, N. J.: I. L. Cochrane, n.d.), 4-12.

46. American Battle Monuments Commission, *A Guide to the American Battle Fields in Europe* (Washington, D.C.: U.S. Government Printing Office, 1927), 16.

47. George H. Allen et al., *The Triumph of Democracy*, vol. 5 of *The Great War* (Philadelphia: George Barrie's Sons, 1921), 274.

48. [Oliver Lyman Spaulding and John Womack Wright], *The Second Division, American Expeditionary Force, in France , 1917-1919* (New York: Hillman Press and Historical Committee, Second Division Association, 1937), 11; Pershing, *My Experiences*, 1:33, 38; Frothingham, *American Reinforcement*, 270-275; Harbord, *American Army*, 185-191, 256-262.

49. Pershing, *My Experiences*, 1:151-155.

50. H. B. Hall, interview, November 3, 1981.

51. Clodfelter, interview, September 19, 1983.

52. Ayres, *War with Germany*, 66.

53. Morris, interview, February 2, 1984.

54. Ayres, *War with Germany*, 73.

55. Allen et al., *Triumph*, 180.

56. Floyd Gibbons, *"And They Thought We Wouldn't Fight"* (New York: George H. Doran Company, 1918), 96.

57. Cable, interview, September 16, 1983.

58. R. J. Marshall, interview, September 21, 1976.

59. Allen et al., *Triumph*, 274; Simonds, *World War*, 5:13.

60. American Battle Monuments Commission, *American Battle Fields*, 17.

61. Esposito, "Western Front," 108.

62. Allen et al., *Triumph*, 284.

63. Terraine, *Great War*, 335.

64. James Madison Marshall to his sister, March 26, 1918, manuscript in private possession.

65. Diary of James Madison Marshall, April 2, 1918, manuscript in private possession.

66. Roy Jackson Marshall to home folks, April 1, 1918, manuscript in private possession.

67. Esposito, "Western Front," 111; Churchill, *World Crisis: 1916-1918*, 2:151-152, 430.

68. F. A. March, *A History of the World War*, vol. 5 (New York: Leslie-Judge Company, 1918), 58-59.

69. Simonds, *World War*, 5:93.

70. George Aston, *The Biography of the Late Marshal Foch* (New York: Macmillan Company, 1929), 295.

71. Pershing, *My Experiences*, 2:105.

72. Moore, interview, November 5, 1981.

73. Cable, interview, September 16, 1983.

74. Pershing, *My Experiences*, 2:13.

75. Roy Jackson Marshall to his father, May 26, 1918, manuscript in private possession.

Chapter Three
"They Were Shooting at Me": Château-Thierry, Second Marne, and Ypres

The German offensive that began on May 27, 1918, struck the French front between the cities of Soissons and Rheims. In this third great drive, Ludendorff planned to force the French to fall back and to pull their reserve divisions from the British lines. Once this was accomplished, Ludendorff intended to try again to destroy the entire British force. The German drive against the French lines was even more successful than Ludendorff had anticipated. By the evening of the first day of fighting, the French Sixth Army was overwhelmed and driven thirteen miles from its morning position. The following day the French continued their retreat, and except for a small, isolated incident, the Germans pushed on successfully with their march.[1]

That incident, mentioned only briefly in German reports, was the loss of the village of Cantigny to American soldiers. This, the first significant attack by Americans in the war, was made by the First Division of the regular infantry. Smith Cable, a twenty-one-year-old Watauga County native, remembered that fight as "a right smart skirmish."[2] The Germans could not retake Cantigny, though they tried repeatedly for three days.[3]

The rest of the Allied line, however, did not hold. During the same three days, the Germans, keeping a pace of about six miles a day, drove the French closer to Paris.[4] The French generals, lacking sufficient reserves to stem the retreat, asked General Pershing on May 30 to send his untried divisions forward. Even as these American troops made their way to the front, the French government continued its plan to abandon the capital.[5]

By May 31, the Germans had captured Soissons and were trying to force a crossing at Château-Thierry on the Marne River. They were only thirty-seven miles from Paris, a distance equal to that already covered by their attack since May 27, but at Château-Thierry the French line held. Elements of the American Third Division had reinforced the weary French soldiers and had stopped the enemy at two key river crossings. Meanwhile, the American Second Division, made up of infantry and marines, rushed to the front north of Château-Thierry. As they moved along the road to the front, they encountered a tangle of French troops and civilians falling

American troops, with the support of French tanks, attack German positions at Cantigny, France. On May 28, 1918, the American First Division drove the Germans out of the village of Cantigny and then for several days held the high ground around the village against German counterattacks. Photograph from a scrapbook in the Robert R. Bridgers Papers, Private Collections, State Archives, Division of Archives and History, Raleigh.

back in disorder. The retreating French soldiers warned the Americans that the situation was hopeless.[6] After the war the French would deny that their army had been forced to fall back in utter despair and defeat, but to the Americans who were on the Paris-Metz Highway struggling to pass the refugees, the rout seemed complete. General Pershing wrote, "I have heard this retirement referred to as a masterly strategic retreat, but it was nothing of the kind."[7]

Amid the chaos the Second Division was deployed in a line across the highway in support of the French. On the evening of June 2, great numbers of French soldiers passed through the American line in retreat, and by the evening of the following day, the French had completely abandoned the front. The Americans suddenly found themselves on the battle lines and under attack from the advancing Germans. At one point, a French officer ordered the Second Battalion, Sixth Marine Regiment, to fall back, but the Americans refused. They held their ground, as did all of the soldiers of the Second Division, and the Germans were stopped by the American fire. On the afternoon of June 3, the Second Artillery Brigade arrived and went into position: the Twelfth Field Artillery Regiment in support of the marines, the Fifteenth in support of the infantry, and the Seventeenth in general support.

The Twelfth and Fifteenth Field Artillery fired 75mm guns, while the Seventeenth Field Artillery used 155mm howitzers. The Germans saw some of these guns put into position, and from a body taken from the battlefield, they learned that the stubborn resistance that they had encountered was American.[8]

By June 4, 1918, the Germans had brought up their artillery and for the next several days subjected the Americans to a terrific bombardment. Despite this fire, the Fifth and Sixth Marine Regiments of the Second Division attacked the German lines. On June 6, they assaulted Belleau Wood, a strongly held enemy position, and suffered terrible casualties. By the end of the next day, the marines had captured the village of Bouresches and had penetrated Belleau Wood, but could not drive out the Germans. While this fight raged, the artillery duel continued between American and German gunners. Most of the shelling was directed toward the support areas and against enemy artillery positions.[9] On June 7, three German shells crashed through the trees and exploded above the sleeping men and tethered horses of Battery A of the Fifteenth Field Artillery Regiment. Jack Marshall remembered the incident: "We had worked all day running [telephone] wire for six miles. By the time we got finished we got the command that we were at the wrong village. . . . We were behind the battery sleeping in the leaves on the ground. Three shells fell and killed eleven horses. After it was over we found [Private First Class] Leroy Hill lying on his left side like he was still asleep. He was still in his blanket. We rolled him over and saw that he had been hit in the chest."[10] Hill died shortly afterward, the first of thirteen members of the Fifteenth Field Artillery Regiment killed or mortally wounded in the fighting around Belleau Wood.[11]

On June 9, the marines withdrew from the entanglements of Belleau Wood so that the American and French artillery could try to reduce the German stronghold. For two days the Allied guns pounded the woods with more than five thousand explosive and gas shells, leaving the forest a twisted and broken wreck.[12] Following the bombardment the marines reentered the woods and continued their struggle to capture it. The Germans responded with an artillery barrage of their own. From June 21 to June 24, they swept the American lines continually with gas and shrapnel shells. The Third Infantry Brigade alone suffered over four hundred poison-gas casualties in one night; one infantry company lost 170 of some 250 men during the three-day bombardment.[13]

The infantry did not suffer alone. During the same period, the Fifteenth Field Artillery Regiment lost six men killed or mortally wounded, while many more fell wounded. Jack Marshall, who served in that regiment, remembered: "Every few days there would be a casualty. You got so you wouldn't be scared. You just took the chance."[14] On June 22, as the artillerymen ate their meal, they saw Corporal Harry Gale killed by shellfire. "He was sort of a chowhound,"

47

German troops (above) advance near Belleau Wood, north of Château-Thierry. Note the shell craters behind the soldiers. American soldiers (below) rest in Belleau Wood. On June 3, 1918, American marines and infantry of the Second Division stopped the Germans near Belleau Wood. Three days later, the marines attacked the forest, resulting in the bloodiest battle the Americans had experienced up to that point in the war. After weeks of fighting, the marines captured the position. Photographs from a scrapbook in the Robert R. Bridgers Papers, Private Collections, State Archives, Division of Archives and History, Raleigh.

Marshall recalled. "He finished up early and said, 'Boys, I'm going for seconds.' So, he went for seconds, and he caught it in the neck. Up in the woods we had a dugout covered with logs where we were then. We had no place to bury him, so we just rolled him up in a blanket; all we had were blankets. He was just as well off as the rest of us."[15]

On June 25, the marines finally cleared the Germans from Belleau Wood. Between Belleau Wood and Château-Thierry the Germans held the village of Vaux, and the U.S. Second Division was assigned to take it. On the morning of July 1, American artillery opened fire on the village, reducing it to rubble. That evening the Third Infantry Brigade captured the ruins and over the following few days held the position against several enemy counterattacks. On the night of July 9, the Second Division was relieved by other American troops after more than a month of fighting. The Germans had not only failed to push the American marines and infantry aside, they had also lost ground to what the Germans classified as "shock troops." The Second Division had won respect from the enemy and praise from the French, but at a high price—7,860 casualties, 29 percent of its strength.[16]

As the Second Division fought the enemy to a standstill around Belleau Wood, the Germans initiated their fourth great offensive against the French. In the face of this drive, the French were forced to yield ground, including an additional thirteen miles west of Soissons. The French finally halted the German advance on June 13, 1918.[17]

The fifth German drive, called the Champagne-Marne offensive, began July 15 and was an attempt to capture the city of Rheims. This effort collapsed three days later, and on July 18 Marshal Foch responded with the Allied Aisne-Marne offensive. Together these two July offensives are referred to as the Second Battle of the Marne. On the same day the Germans started their drive on Rheims, the artillery of the Second Division was moved toward Soissons to join the French Tenth Army. A few days later the infantry of the First and Second Divisions arrived on the front just south of Soissons and prepared to attack the German positions. Farther south, three additional American divisions were deployed with the French armies for the assault, the first major Allied offensive of the year.[18]

Without the customary artillery preparation, the American First and Second Divisions, on either side of the French Moroccan Division, began the attack on the morning of July 18. The artillery fired a rolling barrage just in front of the infantry advance, then limbered up, and with their batteries of light 75mm guns, followed the soldiers. Jack Marshall was assigned as the battery operator of the guns in Battery A, Fifteenth Field Artillery, and was responsible for relaying to the gunners the signals sent from the forward observers. He recalled: "It was all we could do to keep up with the infantry, they were moving so fast. [We] expected to march into the Germans around

James Madison "Matt" Marshall had already seen the world as a merchant marine before the war. In 1917, at the age of thirty-two, he volunteered for military service at the urging of his younger brother Jack. In this new adventure, Matt Marshall almost lost his life several times, including once in the Soissons attack and later in the Meuse-Argonne offensive. Photograph courtesy of the R. Jack Marshall family.

every bend in the road."[19] At one point the Germans disappeared behind the hills, followed by the American doughboys. While the artillerymen waited with the guns, three observers were sent ahead to find the range of the enemy. Jack Marshall watched the three men cross the battlefield, one of whom was his older brother Matt. "He went over to a hill with an officer and another signalman to relay back the German position," Jack Marshall said. "They were using semaphore flags, and the Germans got their range. From where we were it looked like the whole top of the hill exploded, just blown off completely. We thought they were all dead. The dirt and dust covered the hilltop. We had gotten their replacements when they came back covered in dust but all right. They had lived; I don't know how. The Germans had just missed them."[20] For its accomplishments during this battle, the Fifteenth Field Artillery Regiment was awarded a citation for "the greatest audacity and remarkable skill" in supporting the advance of the infantry and for "inflicting on the enemy the heaviest losses."[21]

Less than five miles to the north, Smith Cable of the First Division encouraged his team of horses over the bodies of the dead for two miles in order to bring ammunition to the 155mm guns.[22] He was a teamster with Battery C, Fifth Field Artillery Regiment, and spent several days hauling shells. On one of the trips, the three men working the six horses on his wagon took a short break. Cable climbed a hill above the road to get into the warm sunlight, and he saw a German observation balloon. Then the shells began to fall. "I know they were shooting at me," he said. "I was on one of the ridges walking around. A shell came over and fell, and when they did that I got out of sight. I know they were shooting at me because when I did get out of sight they quit shooting."[23]

According to Jack Marshall, German shells gave plenty of warning: "The Germans had a shell, their 77mm, that made the loudest screaming. You could hear it coming, duck down so it wouldn't hit you in the head, and then about that time hear it explode behind you."[24] Due to German shellfire and machine guns, the First and Second Divisions were soon shot away. By nightfall on July 19, after two days of constantly being on the attack, their drive slowed to a halt. The Second Division was pulled out of the line before dawn on July 20. The First Division remained in line until being relieved on the night of July 23.[25]

To the south, above Château-Thierry, six American divisions continued the fight. The combat veterans of the Fourth Division, who had been dispersed and mixed with French divisions, were reunited and on August 2 sent forward against the German line. Several days would pass before the artillery brigade would catch up with the rest of the division and assist in the attack. Nineteen-year-old Marion Andrews, a volunteer from Forsyth County, went forward with the Thirteenth Field Artillery Regiment of the Fourth Artillery Brigade. From what he saw, he knew that "the Second Battle of the Marne was [a] toughie," because up and down the roads "wagons were scattered all over everywhere."[26] By the time the Fourth Artillery Brigade reached the American lines on August 6, the Germans had retired across the Vesle River and had entrenched on the heights overlooking the river. Every time the Americans tried to cross the Vesle they were met by heavy fire from the heights and by counterattacks.[27] The Americans were unable to move the Germans.

"Our infantry never had to charge much after Soissons," according to Jack Marshall. "The Germans after that were running too fast to charge them outright."[28] This remark exemplifies the pride felt throughout the American forces following the Second Battle of the Marne. In fighting that lasted about a month, the combined French and American divisions drove back the

Germans more than twenty-five miles. Despite Marshall's comment, the enemy was never routed. The Allied soldiers had to fight for every mile of ground. The casualties for the eight American divisions numbered about 45,000. The First Division lost 7,870 men. The Second Division added 3,792 casualties in two days of fighting to the number lost earlier near Château-Thierry. The Fourth Division lost 6,154 men in its first engagement. The remainder came from the American Third, Twenty-sixth, Twenty-eighth, Thirty-second, and Forty-second Divisions.[29]

Carl Clodfelter, a twenty-five year old from Davidson County, learned of the severity of American losses firsthand. He arrived in France on June 28 and, after traveling two hundred miles by railway, went into training. On July 19, he was traveling once again. "They came down there with trucks when the Germans made that big drive on Paris," he said. "They had so many wounded they couldn't take care of them, and they wanted about five hundred men."[30] Two companies of infantry were loaded onto the trucks and taken to Evacuation Hospital No. 7 at Callimers. When they arrived on July 20, the Second Battle of the Marne had been raging for five days, and Clodfelter and the others were immediately put to work. "What we did when we first got there," he said, "was to unload ambulances and trucks. It was a great big hospital, but it was full. We laid them on the ground. I expect we had an acre covered with litters with wounded boys on them. Most of them were Americans and Germans; they brought the Germans back too. There were a lot of them. They didn't have ambulances to carry them, so they had these big trucks. They would lay the bottom full of litters. I believe there were eight or twelve in there crossways with the handles on the sides of the truck."[31]

For the next several weeks Clodfelter unloaded wounded soldiers brought from the battlefield. He recalled that the doctors could not possibly care for all of them, and because "there were so many wounded, they would wait on the ones who were seriously wounded, and the others we would load on the trains and send on to the base hospitals."[32] The German wounded, "big old fellows, most of them," did not receive any attention until after the Americans were seen by the medical staff, and at one point ambulances carrying German wounded were turned away by the doctors.[33] Clodfelter spent the last several days of his service at Evacuation Hospital No. 7 carrying the wounded in and out of the operating room. On August 10, he was transferred to another hospital.

While Carl Clodfelter bound the wounds of Americans on the battlefields near Paris, his fellow North Carolinians continued the fight in the trenches near Ypres, Belgium. The Thirtieth Division had arrived in France on May 24, 1918, and was immediately sent into British training camps. In June, the Twenty-seventh and Thirtieth Divisions were combined to form the American Second Corps, but at the insistence of the British, General Pershing detached

Carl William Clodfelter of Davidson County was drafted in March 1918, given a few months of infantry training, and sent to France in June. Within a month of his arrival in France, he was reassigned to a hospital to help handle truckloads of battlefield casualties. He never forgot how overwhelmed he felt at that time or the horrific scenes of suffering and death. The photograph on the left was taken at Camp Sevier, South Carolina, in 1918; the one on the right was taken in 1980. Photographs courtesy of the Carl William Clodfelter family.

the corps from the American First Army and left it to serve with the British. After about a month of training, both divisions were sent to the British Second Army: the Twenty-seventh to the British Nineteenth Corps and the Thirtieth to the British Second Corps. On July 2, 1918, these two American divisions were sent into the trenches at Ypres.[34]

The Ypres front gave the young soldiers of the Thirtieth Division their first impressions of the realities of war. Joe Thompson of Smithfield was a wagoner in the 119th Infantry Regiment. His nightly trips to the front to deliver supplies were nightmarish and surrealistic. "There was a graveyard as big as Raleigh," he recalled. "The English had lost a million soldiers. Canadians, New Zealanders, South Africans, West Indians, and Australians were all buried there; it was a big graveyard. When we were on that hill there and looked down, there was the valley of Belgium near the French-Belgium line. There was a smoke haze in the air from the gunpowder, and there were observation balloons in the air looking for targets, and that cemetery. You were going down through the valley of the shadow of death, that's what it was, the jaws of hell, to tell you the truth. That was Ypres, Belgium."[35]

Initially, the Thirtieth Division held the trenches in a relatively quiet sector but on July 16 was sent to the support lines of two British divisions south of Ypres. Their trenches were in poor condition. Private Isaac Winfrey, a twenty-three year old from Winston-Salem, was put to work with the others in his regiment rebuilding the old lines. "Those old trenches were built in 1914," he said, "and they were all torn up. The water was knee deep. We had to take boards and crawl up on them to walk on."[36] To the new soldiers, it seemed to rain every day, even in the summer. As a result, they had to get used to the ubiquitous mud and standing water.

Having to rebuild the poorly kept British trenches annoyed the Americans. The doughboys thought it was a waste of time to dig here and there, especially for the British, when their real purpose was to fight the Germans. The British, however, went to great lengths to discourage the Americans from shooting at the enemy. According to Private Winfrey, the British, "well, they were soft [and said], 'Don't shoot; if we don't shoot, they don't shoot.' "[37] This rule was also drilled into the head of Archie Ingram when he first met the British soldiers. The Buncombe County native remembered that at "Ypres they had trenches and there was a standoff—'Don't shoot at us, and we won't shoot at you.' If somebody shot a rifle all heck would break loose."[38] After the doughboys arrived in the trenches, this arrangement was often broken. The British, nevertheless, continued to impress upon the individual soldiers the need to try to abide by the unspoken agreement. The Americans on the whole, however, were not intent on maintaining the stalemate.

While the soldiers of the Thirtieth Division held the trenches at Ypres, the Allied commanders decided, even before the Second Battle of the Marne was won, to initiate a great offensive against the German lines with the hope of winning the war before the end of 1918. The presence of the Americans and their contribution to stopping the German drives against the French and British had improved Allied morale. At the same time, German morale was at an all-time low. The Germans realized that with the failure of the Ludendorff offensives and the involvement of the United States in the war, a victory for the kaiser was unlikely. On August 8, 1918, the day Ludendorff called the "black day of the German army," the demoralization was fully evident when the Germans were routed on the first day of the Battle of Amiens. By August 11, more than 29,000 Germans had surrendered and 46,000 were killed or wounded. The British lost 22,000 men and the French some 24,000.[39] To redouble the Allied effort to take advantage of the German

Archie Clifford Ingram, a Buncombe County native, was a member of the 119th Infantry Regiment, Thirtieth Division. On arriving at Ypres, he was unimpressed with the passive behavior of the British soldiers. Ingram, like General Pershing and other American soladiers, wanted to get on with the fighting. Hundreds of thousands of casualties since 1914 had destroyed the same aggressive spirit in the British army long before the Americans had arrived. Photograph courtesy of Norris Ingram, Ila Mae Canter, and Kenneth Ingram.

collapse, the British initiated a campaign near Ypres on August 19, 1918, called the Ypres-Lys offensive. In this drive the American Thirtieth Division was brought to the front and sent into its first battle.

The Thirtieth Division, after only a month in the trenches, relieved the weary British Thirty-third Division and was in position the day before the Ypres-Lys offensive began. The Sixtieth Infantry Brigade, which included the 119th and 120th Infantry Regiments, was placed in the front lines and remained there until September 4. The German infantry slowly abandoned their forward lines, including the high ground of Mont Kemmel. On the evening of August 30, the British commanders believed that the Germans were withdrawing from the lines in front of the Thirtieth Division. To be certain, on August 31 patrols were dispatched from the Sixtieth Infantry Brigade to reconnoiter.[40]

At dawn on August 31, Private Isaac Winfrey was pulled from the ranks of regular infantry. "They put me in a machine-gun squad," he remembered, "and I didn't know a thing. I told them I wasn't trained for that, but they told me to go along and tote the ammunition."[41] He was told that he was replacing a man who had a toothache, but the reason mattered little to him. He was more concerned with what he was supposed to do in a machine-gun squad. By midmorning they were sent over the top toward the German lines. According to an official report: "About 10:30 a.m. combat patrols of one platoon each were sent out toward the village ruins of Voormezeele from the front line battalions of the 119th Infantry. Before they had advanced 200 meters they encountered stiff resistance."[42] The Germans had not withdrawn from the front of the Thirtieth Division and were determined to hold their position.

The "stiff resistance" encountered by Winfrey's squad was their undoing. Winfrey remembered: "We got out there in those trenches built by the Germans. There was this blockhouse, and we had orders to go over and run them out. We got right close to them, but the Germans ran out the back door. I saw some Germans run down into this trench, and I was the first to yell, 'There's the Germans now!' We were all lying down except the sergeant [Lorraine P. Benton]. He grabbed the machine gun from the one carrying it and said, 'Give me that machine gun—I'll knock them down!' He fired one shot, and they shot him."[43]

Unfortunately for the sergeant and his men, their machine gun, a Lewis .303, had jammed. The sergeant was wounded in the right forearm and went back to the American lines, leaving his corporal in command of the squad. They set up the gun and took turns trying to repair it. Then the young soldiers began to fall, one by one. "There was a sniper back in some trees picking them off as fast as they could man the gun. He would shoot, and some one would fall." Winfrey continued, "I tried my best to find where the bullets were coming from, but I couldn't see a thing."[44] He never located the sniper.

Winfrey, who was unfamiliar with the workings of a machine gun, moved behind some bushes and let the others work in the exposed position. Within a matter of minutes, he and only one other soldier remained. All of the other squad members were casualties of the sniper, except for Private First Class Lindo S. Kinney, who had carried a wounded man to the rear. Stretcher-bearers came forward to remove another one of the wounded, and while they were there, Winfrey witnessed the death of the last machine gunner, Private First Class Herbert S. Turrentine. "It was stuck," Winfrey said, "and he couldn't get it to work. He was sitting on his knees working on the gun. I was sitting behind some bushes behind him. I told him, 'They've got the rest of you, and they're going to see you and kill you.' He said, 'I reckon not.' And then he was shot by one shot through his head, and he fell right over. You could see his brains. He only took a few breaths and died." When the two stretcher-bearers saw what had happened, they suggested to Winfrey that he "might as well get out," which he did.[45] For his ill-fated effort, Turrentine, a Winston-Salem native, was posthumously awarded a Distinguished Service Cross.[46]

On his scramble back to the American lines, Winfrey saw "a little old plane circle around two or three times."[47] He thought about shooting at it, but

Soldiers of the Thirtieth Division serving with the British army were equipped with the British .303 Lewis light machine gun, one of the best weapons on the western front. The Lewis gun could fire up to forty-seven rounds within seconds but was prone to jamming, especially in muddy conditions. Photograph from the files of the Division of Archives and History.

believing the plane to be a spotter for German artillery, he returned as quickly as possible to his own lines to avoid the anticipated shelling. As Winfrey reached the trenches, the German airplane turned and flew away, and as expected, the German artillery began firing. Winfrey was put on a fire step, up on a wooden platform, as a guard. While the shells fell on the American position, Winfrey saw Lindo S. Kinney, the friend from Winston-Salem who had carried back a casualty of the sniper attack. Kinney and Winfrey were the only members of their squad not killed or wounded on the morning patrol. Winfrey recalled that Kinney stepped up to him and said, "Winfrey, you come down here and stay down in the trench, and I'll take over your place." Winfrey sought rest in a "funk-hole," a burrow cut in the side of the trench wall that was large enough for one man. Just as Winfrey got settled, he heard shellfire come nearer. "I heard one shell fall," Winfrey said. "They usually shot three shells [at a time], and one usually falls short. I thought, 'I reckon I'll be safe here,' and then I felt myself going up."[48]

Kinney and Winfrey's position had received a direct hit from a German 5.9-inch howitzer shell. Kinney, who only moments before had taken

Winfrey's position on the fire step, was hit by a shell fragment in the stomach and fell over into the trench. As the smoke and dust cleared, Captain Lawrence Bradshaw rushed up with several men. The captain pointed at Kinney and said, "Just leave him, he's already dead," and seeing that Winfrey was still conscious but badly wounded, Bradshaw told the men to "bring four stretcher-bearers [and] take Winfrey back!"[49]

Winfrey was taken to the British Tenth Casualty Clearing Station, where he was given a shot to ease the pain from his numerous wounds. The English doctor who examined Winfrey found that shell fragments had shattered his right wrist and left arm between the shoulder and elbow. In addition, he had cuts on the right side of his head and a cut over his heart. A steel mirror in Winfrey's breast pocket, pierced by shell fragments, had prevented an even more serious injury.[50] Winfrey never forgot that night: "This English doctor came, and he told me, 'I've got to dress your wounds.' I said, 'You'll take my arm off.' But he said, 'Not if I can help it.' He gave me a shot, and when I woke up my arm was gone."[51] Winfrey's left arm was amputated at the shoulder. The doctors managed to repair most of the damage done to his right wrist, and after a few days of recovery, he was sent first to a Canadian hospital in France and then to American Base Hospital No. 37 in England. He remained there until he was sent back to the United States in October 1918.[52]

Just before he was wounded, Winfrey saw a German reconnaissance plane. German aircraft were a common sight on the Ypres front. At times these enemy planes dropped bombs, but usually they were spotters for artillery. During the day the airplanes, and even the pilots and observers, were easy to spot because they flew so close to the ground. Although the Americans were ordered not to fire on hostile aircraft in order to avoid attracting attention, the temptation was sometimes too great. John Collins, a member of the 120th Infantry Regiment, remembered such an occasion: "Me and this other boy, they put us down on guard duty at the officer's quarters, way down in the ground. We had to stay up on top. An old German airplane came over. It came around two or three times, and every time he came around he came a little lower. This boy, [Private] Ed Gore from Tennessee was working his nose like a squirrel. He said, 'If that thing comes around again I'm going to take a shot at him.' I said, 'You better not.' It came around and he raised his rifle, and when he pulled the trigger I saw one of them fall over in the airplane. The captain came out there, and he said, 'Who's that doing that shooting?' Well, I just pointed my thumb at him. [The captain] said, 'We told you not to shoot at anything.' Gore said, 'Yes, I know you did, but he came over so low I just had to shoot at him.' "[53] The German airplane did not return.

At night the soldiers learned to distinguish the sounds made by the different aircraft. Archie Ingram knew just what to listen for: "You could recognize the German planes because they went whoo-whoo-whoo-whoo. I always knew when they were up, and everybody else did. We would put out the lights and have a hole handy."[54] Sometimes a foxhole provided little protection from the enemy shellfire that often followed the sighting of an airplane, but to be caught out in the open was far worse. "We were hit by artillery fire," recalled Frank Devane of the 115th Machine Gun Battalion, "and two or three started running from their positions to get further back. One fellow passed by, and you could see his brains where he was hit. He ran about fifty yards before he fell."[55] Fortunately for the common infantry soldier in the frontline trenches, most of the shelling dropped behind the lines in the support areas.

As Isaac Winfrey lay on the operating table with the doctors trying to save his life, various officers of the Thirtieth Division discussed the results of the August 31 fighting. They were not satisfied. The combat patrols of the 119th Infantry Regiment, Winfrey's outfit, remained in no-man's-land, scattered and disorganized. The patrols of the 120th Infantry Regiment had started toward the German lines at 3:50 in the afternoon, about the same time Winfrey was wounded, but by dark they had to retreat in the face of German fire.[56] The officers decided that even though the Germans had not withdrawn, efforts to move forward should continue through the night, followed by a general advance by both regiments the next morning.

Twenty-three-year-old John Collins was in one of the frontline battalions that was ordered to attack on the morning of September 1. Having heard that the Germans had abandoned Mont Kemmel, to the southwest of the Thirtieth Division, Collins thought that they were going to occupy its heights. What he did not know was that the British had already retaken the mountain and that the ground he was to cross was still occupied by the enemy. At about 7:30 A.M. two infantry battalions of the 120th Infantry Regiment were ordered out of the trenches and into no-man's-land. Their objective was the German position around the Lankhof farm.[57] The Americans did not advance far before encountering the enemy. When they came under fire, Collins took it personally: "They turned a machine gun loose on me, and there was a ditch [so] I fell down in that. They were shooting at me all the time and knocking dirt in my face. Somebody told me, 'Keep your head down!' I looked up to see who it was, but I didn't see anybody. Every once in a while he said, 'Keep your head down!' Well, I slid on my stomach [about twenty-five yards] so I could get out of the reach of them, and I went back."[58] John Collins had had enough for one day. He returned to the American lines and was put on guard duty by one of his lieutenants. Later the same day a shell exploded a few yards from where he was posted and threw dirt all over him. "The captain came out and said, 'Are you all right?' I said, 'Yes, that one didn't have my name on it.' " Collins went on to tell the captain, "There's somebody looking after me more so than you are, sir."[59]

Isaac Enos Winfrey, a native of Davie County, was severely wounded near Ypres on August 31, 1918. As a result of the wounds, Winfrey's left arm was amputated. Winfrey was also hit in the chest and right arm by shell fragments. He was saved by a steel mirror in his left breast pocket. The damaged mirror, shell fragments, and Winfrey's bloodied dog tags are shown on the opposite page. On this page, the photograph in the upper left corner was taken in 1918; the photograph in the lower right was taken in 1983. Photographs courtesy of the Winfrey family and the author.

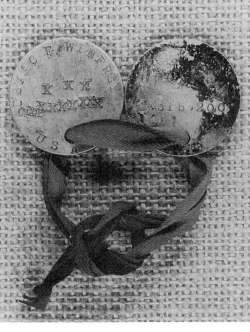

By the evening of September 1, elements of the two regiments, having reached the objectives outlined in their orders, held a new line. The 119th Infantry Regiment had a better day than the 120th and had captured several German positions, including the town of Voormezeele. After dark, efforts were made to strengthen the lines, and much of that work fell to the division's engineers. William Crouse of the 105th Engineer Regiment remembered going out into no-man's-land: "Well, it was rough. We had to go out and put up barbed-wire entanglements. They had iron stakes that screwed into the ground, [and] you would screw some here and stretch the barbed wire."[60] Six men were used to wire each twenty-five-yard section, a task that had to be done while lying on the ground because of enemy fire. Under the cover of darkness, it was relatively safe to move about and work, but, according to Crouse, "when they [the Germans] shot up those flare lights you had better be lying in that mud. You had better not be up. They would shoot up those flare lights and open a machine gun on you."[61] The work to improve the defensive lines continued through the night, with engineers and infantry laboring side by side.

Even though no further advance was scheduled for the Thirtieth Division, the officers were worried about the strength and exact location of the Germans across no-man's-land, as well as the possibility of a counterattack the next

John Henry Collins was drafted off of a Surry County farm in October 1917. He was sent to Belgium and France in 1918 and had more than one brush with death in combat. Collins escaped injury while in battle near Ypres and later in the attack on the Hindenburg Line. His luck ran out, however, on October 10, 1918, when he was wounded in the left elbow by an exploding shell that killed several of his comrades. Photograph courtesy of the John H. Collins family.

morning. As a result, patrols were sent out during the night to gather information. One of these patrols included Private Luther Hall, a twenty-two year old from Surry County. "I was attached to the [First] Battalion Headquarters temporarily with the battalion intelligence section," he said. "This one night we went out on patrol because a good many men had been picked off [by enemy fire]; that's what they told us. It seemed like the middle of the night when we went out. . . . There were twenty-three of us who went out that night on a fighting patrol. We carried hand grenades [and] two machine guns within the bunch. I had my rifle and hand grenades. . . . The patrol that night was to find out the distance between us and the enemy. . . . We crawled through barbed-wire entanglements and went, it seemed, a mile, but we never did contact the enemy. But in the meantime there were always bullets flying. I was hit in the [upper] right [arm] muscle by a bullet. . . . I thought when I got shot—I felt the sting—that it was a barbed-wire scratch, [but] when [the Germans] sent up a flare I saw the blood running off my fingers."[62]

Hall was the only one of the twenty-three in the group who was wounded, but that was sufficient for the lieutenant in charge to order the patrol to return to the American lines. The officer bandaged Hall's wound, and several men had to help the injured soldier get across no-man's-land and back to the trenches. Hall had become weak from loss of blood, and after reaching the trenches and a doctor, he passed out.[63] For the next few weeks, he stayed in a British hospital but returned with his arm in a sling at the end of September in time for the Somme offensive and the assault on the Hindenburg Line.

With a fierce counterattack, the Germans tried unsuccessfully to force the 120th Infantry Regiment out of its lines early on the morning of September 2. The same day the division received word that it was to be replaced by British troops. The 119th Infantry was pulled out of the lines on the night of September 3-4; the 120th Infantry was replaced the night of September 4-5.[64] The transfer went about as smoothly as could be expected but not without cost. German shells fell on the Allied lines throughout both nights, inflicting casualties. One shell found wagoner Joe Thompson of the 119th Infantry Regiment: "We were bringing the boys out of the lines—the English were relieving the American soldiers. We were a quarter of a mile from the frontline trenches, and of course, the German army had good intelligence so they knew what we were doing, and the shells were falling like raindrops. I don't know how many got killed, but I can hear them hollering now. I will never forget the sound. It was dark and it was raining, and I got hit in the left leg. Frank Powell from Indiana was with me. He was my brakeman, my helper, and I told him I was shot. He said, 'Like hell you are!' He cussed like a sailor. I said, 'Yes I am, come around here!' He put his hand on my leg, and it was like it burned his hand. He said, 'You are!' So I got off (the mule), and he helped me onto the wagon. We came on about a quarter of a mile from there. He and Roscoe

Holland helped me into the house where the doctor was. He pulled the shrapnel out of my leg. My shoe was full of blood. I told them good-bye and I'd see them in a few days. The doctor said, 'Well it's nice to have that friendship, but if they don't go to England with you, you won't see them for a long time because I've seen so many holes just like that, just exactly like yours, and it takes a long time to heal up.' "[65]

The doctor sent Thompson to a field hospital for treatment. When he arrived he was shocked by what he saw: "I raised up on my elbows to see just what was in there, and I never saw the likes of stretchers like mine. The whole floor was just covered with wounded soldiers; it was surprising how many could be there. Up on the operating table was a boy wounded up in his breast, and he was gagging. Then they came and picked me up and took me into an operating room, and there were a dozen operating tables in that room, two doctors, and two nurses."[66] Before the operation, a nurse asked Thompson to give her his false teeth because many of the British soldiers that they treated had them, but Thompson still had his original teeth. After giving Thompson ether, the doctor operated on his leg to remove bone splinters and repair the damage. Thompson's wound was slow to heal, as the first doctor had predicted. He did not return to his unit until December, after the war was over.

From its arrival on the Ypres front in July until its departure in September, the Thirtieth Division lost 777 men. The 119th and 120th Infantry Regiments, both North Carolina National Guard regiments before the war, suffered far more casualties than any other regiments in the division. The 119th (2nd N.C.) Infantry sustained 296 casualties and the 120th (3rd N.C.) 269 from July 11 to September 6, 1918.[67] In most accounts of the activities of the Thirtieth Division, the Ypres front is not mentioned, or at most, briefly discussed. The losses in the trenches on the Ypres front, however, were significant, especially for men such as Isaac Winfrey.

Notes

1. Esposito, "Western Front," 112-113.
2. Cable, interview, September 16, 1983.
3. Allen et al., *Triumph*, 292; Stallings, *Doughboys*, 63-74.
4. Drinker, "America's Part," 481.
5. Pershing, *My Experiences*, 2:89.
6. Esposito, "Western Front," 113; Pershing, *My Experiences*, 2:63; Catlin, *"With the Help,"* 87.
7. Pershing, *My Experiences*, 2:61.

8. [Spaulding and Wright], *Second Division*, 46-47.
9. [Spaulding and Wright], *Second Division*, 52-55; Harbord, *American Army*, 290.
10. R. J. Marshall, interview, July 7, 1978.
11. [Spaulding and Wright], *Second Division*, 410.
12. Francis J. Reynolds, Allen L. Churchill, and Francis Trevelyan Miller, eds., *The Story of the Great War*, 8 vols. (New York: P. F. Collier and Son, 1916-1920), 7:387.
13. [Spaulding and Wright], *Second Division*, 71.
14. R. J. Marshall, interview, December 18, 1979.
15. R. J. Marshall, interview, December 18, 1979; [Spaulding and Wright], *Second Division*, 410.
16. Simonds, *World War*, 5:191.
17. Esposito, "Western Front," 114.
18. Esposito, "Western Front," 114-118; Stallings, *Doughboys*, 146-149.
19. R. J. Marshall, interview, September 21, 1976.
20. R. J. Marshall, interview, September 21, 1976.
21. [Spaulding and Wright], *Second Division*, 299.
22. Cable, interview, September 16, 1983.
23. Cable, interview, September 16, 1983.
24. R. J. Marshall, interview, September 21, 1976.
25. Harbord, *American Army*, 335-336.
26. Andrews, interview, October 30, 1981.
27. *Brief History of the 4th Division* (Germany: Fourth Division Headquarters, 1919), 2.
28. R. J. Marshall, interview, September 21, 1976.
29. Simonds, *World War*, 5:197-200.
30. Clodfelter, interview, September 19, 1983.
31. Clodfelter, interview, September 19, 1983.
32. Clodfelter, interview, September 19, 1983.
33. Clodfelter, interview, September 19, 1983.
34. Tyson, "Hindenburg Line," 46.
35. Thompson, interview, December 19, 1985.
36. Winfrey, interview, September 15, 1983.
37. Winfrey, interview, September 15, 1983.
38. Ingram, interview, April 10, 1984.
39. David Shermer, *World War I* (London: Octopus Books, 1975), 209, 211.
40. American Battle Monuments Commission, *30th Division: Summary of Operations in the World War* (Washington, D.C.: U.S. Government Printing Office, 1944), 8.
41. Winfrey, interview, September 15, 1983.
42. American Battle Monuments Commission, *30th Division*, 8; Murphy and Thomas, *Thirtieth Division*, 82.

43. Winfrey, interview, September 15, 1983, and January 27, 1984; Memorandum to the Division Surgeon, August 31, 1918, Military Collection, World War I Papers, Private Collections, John Van B. Metts, State Archives, Division of Archives and History, Raleigh.
44. Winfrey, interview, September 15, 1983, and January 27, 1984.
45. Winfrey, interview, September 15, 1983, and January 27, 1984; Murphy and Thomas, *Thirtieth Division*, 264.
46. Murphy and Thomas, *Thirtieth Division*, 264.
47. Winfrey, interview, January 27, 1984.
48. Winfrey, interview, January 27, 1984.
49. Winfrey, interview, January 27, 1984.
50. Winfrey, interview, September 15, 1983.
51. Winfrey, interview, January 27, 1984.
52. Winfrey, interview, September 15, 1983.
53. Collins, interview, April 12, 1984.
54. Ingram, interview, April 10, 1984.
55. Devane, interview, January 4, 1984.
56. American Battle Monuments Commission, *30th Division*, 8.
57. Murphy and Thomas, *Thirtieth Division*, 83; John O. Walker, William A. Graham, and Thomas Fauntleroy, *Official History of the 120th Infantry* (Lynchburg, Va.: J. P. Bell Company, n.d.), 17.
58. Collins, interview, April 12, 1984.
59. Collins, interview, April 12, 1984.
60. Crouse, interview, September 22, 1983.
61. Crouse, interview, September 22, 1983.
62. L. P. Hall, interview, April 10, 1984.
63. L. P. Hall, interview, April 10, 1984.
64. Murphy and Thomas, *Thirtieth Division*, 84-85.
65. Thompson, interview, December 19, 1985.
66. Thompson, interview, December 19, 1985.
67. American Battle Monuments Commission, *30th Division*, 10.

Chapter Four
Bully Beef, Cooties, and Rest Camps:
The Discomforts of War

Jack Marshall was left behind. The master sergeant and a corporal of artillery had ridden off, leaving him on his own. Marshall always remembered the frustration he felt that day: "All of us had a horse, and we rode hard all day, but my horse gave out. . . . I don't know why that horse gave out the way he did. He was big and should have been stronger. . . . He couldn't gallop or canter, not even trot; he could just walk."[1] Though Marshall eventually made it back to his outfit and traded his animal for one in better condition, he never forgot that forsaken and isolated feeling of being left alone. While such personal tribulations were important to the individual soldiers, they are usually not included in histories of the war. To the common soldier, however, these daily trials were as significant as the great battles. The terrible memories of combat, of course, remained foremost in veterans' minds, but the battle experiences were, nevertheless, relatively brief moments in the overall war experience. During the course of the interviews with the veterans, once the reminiscences of battle were told, each old doughboy turned to the topic of personal comfort, or lack thereof, and the personal battle against hunger, lice, and sleeplessness. An awareness of the daily adversities endured by the soldiers is necessary for a full understanding of World War I.

Without a doubt, the doughboy's biggest concerns were when was the next meal and would it be edible. When a soldier was hungry, all other physical discomforts seemed magnified. The first meals in France were often served while the soldiers were in transit. Following the voyage to France in British cattle boats, with the memories of British food and seasickness still fresh, every American soldier upon arrival was loaded into a French railroad cattle car and transported to some unknown location. Horton Hall remembered: "We went to a railroad siding where we boarded freight trains . . . about forty men to the car. . . . You had to keep your packs with you to sit on or lean back against. If you were traveling overnight you slept on your pack. Our field kitchen had to travel on the same train, but they couldn't serve us because they couldn't cook on the train. They had the stations along the way where the train stopped long enough for us to get out and take a thirty-minute exercise and get our meals."[2]

Felix Brockman, another doughboy with the Eighty-first "Wildcat" Division, crossed France by train and remembered the food served at the various stations as being " 'corn willie' [canned corn beef], canned tomatoes, and hard bread." He said that the soldiers were given hot, strong coffee to drink, even at "about ten or eleven o'clock at night—just at the time we didn't want the stuff."[3]

Once the trains delivered the soldiers, either to the camps or to the front, the company cooks fired up the field kitchens. Officers ate far better than the men they commanded. Judging from the ledger kept for the 120th Infantry Regiment, the officers were well fed. They enjoyed a diet of fresh vegetables, such as asparagus, cauliflower, cabbage, beans, peas, radishes, turnips, potatoes, and onions; fresh or canned fruit, including apricots, oranges, pears, peaches, plums, strawberries, and cherries; meats, including chicken, fish, and pork; and such wartime delicacies as milk, eggs, butter, custard cream, chocolate, and jam. During and after their meals, officers drank wine and smoked cigars.[4] Most of the time the enlisted men were served "slumgullian," sometimes called "slum" or "slumgully." According to William Crouse, a doughboy from Forsyth County, "slumgully [was] beef, taters, and stuff like that," including anything else the cooks could find to mix into some sort of stew.[5] Otho Offman also remembered slumgullian: "When we got to France we didn't have much. I remember one rainy night in the fall of the year when the stove came up with the mess sergeant and the cooks. We took out our mess kits, and they put in some slum and put a couple of Irish potatoes on top. They were not peeled, and one of them I had was about half rotten. Well, I just cut that off and ate the rest of it."[6]

Slumgullian was not the only impromptu concoction put together by the cooks. Many times the necessary but varied ingredients could not be found, so the soldiers were served whatever might be on hand. In April 1918, Jack Marshall wrote in his diary: "About 7 o'clock a.m. we started for chow. Well, we walked and walked—through the mud all the time—but finally found the cook shack and chowed up very well on tea, syrup, butter, corn beef hash, and punk—even got seconds."[7] Sometimes the men did not want a second portion; the first was bad enough. Clarence Moore recalled: "The worst mess we got into was in Belgium. We had to eat horsemeat up there. It was so coarse it was sort of like eating shoestrings. That was all the meat we had—well no—they had those old Belgium rabbits, and they were just about as bad as the horsemeat."[8]

When the soldiers were on the front lines, either in the trenches or on the move, the availability and quality of food was a major concern. Soldiers knew that the cooks would not spend much time preparing a good meal when the shells were falling too close to the kitchens. Noah Whicker remembered one hastily prepared meal delivered to the trenches. "We were in dugouts," he said,

These soldiers anxiously wait for the hot meal that is cooking before them. The food in the pot might well be a concoction the soldiers called "slumgullian," a mixture of beef, potatoes, and some vegetables cooked in a stew. Photograph from a scrapbook in the Robert R. Bridgers Papers, Private Collections, State Archives, Division of Archives and History, Raleigh.

"and the Germans were throwing shells over us. We were on [the back side of] a hillside, and the Germans would shoot, but the shells would go over and bust. . . . While we were there the kitchen was behind us, and we sent for our meals. [They served] beans, and they would pour them out [into the mess kits], and they would rattle. We used to say, 'I wish a shell would fall on that kitchen if they couldn't cook beans any better than that.' "[9]

In most cases, the soldiers would try to eat what was offered, particularly if they had not eaten for a long time. John Collins remembered that "sometimes they would bring Irish potatoes in bags, with the peelings on them, [but] we didn't even peel them. We ate peelings and all, lint and everything."[10] From experience, Sergeant Whicker also knew to be thankful for any food that arrived. "While I was up there in the trenches," he recalled, "they brought up a bucket full of fatback. It was supposed to have been fried, but I think they threw it in there and took it out. It would crack when you would bite it. We would reach in there with dirty hands and get some to eat, and would be glad to get it."[11]

Like Whicker and Collins, the average doughboy ate almost anything, whenever it was served, but sometimes food and water were not available.

Luther Hall, a private in the Thirtieth Division remembered such hardships: "Out on the line at Ypres one time I went without a drink of water for two days and nights. I needed a drink of water. I didn't think about food. You would run across water, but you were not allowed to drink it because it was poisoned."[12] Clarence Moore, also a private in the Thirtieth Division, recalled being without food: "The longest our company went without food was about three days. . . . The boys come across a turnip patch, and they ate those turnips, leaves and all. . . . It made the difference."[13] Occasionally food was unavailable because the field kitchen personnel had gotten lost. Horton Hall wrote that in October 1918 "our ration wagon, drawn by four mules, took a wrong turn and went about ten miles in the wrong direction. It took our captain on horseback about twelve hours to find the ration wagon and get it back in the right direction. During the next twenty-four hours we were without food."[14]

At other times the field kitchens did not have food to serve because of breakdowns in the supply organization. The soldiers then went hungry or had to open their emergency rations, if they had them. Most infantrymen carried these rations in their field packs, while artillerymen carried them in their saddlebags on their horses. Emergency rations usually consisted of hardtack and some type of canned meat, which as Horton Hall recalled, was "packed in a tin can so hard you couldn't hardly gouge it out with the point of a knife."[15] The meat was called "corn willie" or "bully beef," to name two of the more pleasant of many labels. According to Luther Hall, the hardtack "was so hard you couldn't even break it," and as for the bully beef, "it tasted pretty good sometimes, after you would go without [food] for two or three days."[16] But as Gladney Clarke said, "It may not have been the most desirable stuff, but it was something to keep you from starving to death."[17]

Hunger was not the doughboy's only worry. In addition to waging war against the soldiers of the kaiser, American soldiers fought an equally arduous battle against the terrible "cootie." Cooties, the soldiers' name for lice, were the vermin that made every doughboy's life miserable and, like the rainy weather, seemed to be ever present. James Covington of the Fifty-sixth Pioneer Regiment never forgot the trouble he had with the irascible little creatures. "I never did see one," he said, "but I could feel them walk. After I got home if somebody said cootie, I could feel them walk then."[18] Probably every man on the front, officer and private alike, at one time or another was infested with cooties. "You didn't lose any status in World War I because you were lousy, because thousands of others were also lousy," Isham Hudson said.[19]

Many of the veterans remembered their first contact with the persistent little bugs. Otho Offman stated: "I remember the night we first got them. We came to a little place where the French had driven the Germans out, and it looked like a good barrack. There was straw in there so everybody stayed in there that night. The next morning when everybody woke up, they were full of cooties. The Germans left them there."[20] Offman was not the only one to blame the Germans for the cooties. Isham B. Hudson also held the enemy responsible: "We went to this abandoned barracks we had captured from the Germans and got some straw mattresses and took [them] out to where we had [dug] our holes to sleep in. This wasn't a very wise move because there were a lot of lice in these mattresses . . . and when we lay in the holes with wet mud in them, we got up the next morning with a good dose of army lice." Hudson had to live with the torment for the next few months because, as he recalled, "you couldn't change your clothes for weeks and weeks and weeks."[21]

Not all of the doughboys blamed the Germans for the terrible cooties. Some blamed the French. In a letter sent home in the spring of 1918, Matt Marshall wrote, "We know now what cooties really are and are having some more of rotten French sanitation. We have been in many of their camps and none are good."[22] Just as Marshall condemned the French, another soldier blamed the British. Clarence Moore, a private in the Thirtieth Division, had arrived at a British training camp with his friends. "I never will forget it," he said. "Our company commander told us, 'I got news for you boys, you are going to get lousy tonight.' And sure enough, the place was just full of lice, and we did get lousy. The place was called 'Dirty Bucket.' That was the name of the camp, 'Dirty Bucket.' "[23]

No matter where a soldier was when first infested or who was blamed for the pest, once introduced the cooties were impossible to exterminate as long as the man remained at the front. Frank Devane recalled that "as long as you were active you didn't notice them, but if you would sit down to rest or lie down that's when they went to work on you, [and] they would keep you awake."[24] Jack Marshall also remembered the aggravation they caused. He often had to sit in the sun as a forward observer for the Fifteenth Field Artillery Regiment and that is when the cooties began to move about. He said: "Many times it got so hot—there were no trees or you just had to stay out—but you could pull back the cloth covering your shirt buttons and see lice eggs up and down your shirt. When you got really hot the cooties would crawl out of your shirt and onto your neck."[25]

These insects stayed in clothing, and the only way for a soldier to avoid being bitten was to remove every stitch of cloth from his body. John Collins recalled taking off his sweater, hanging it in a tree, and seeing the sweater quiver with activity. To him it looked like there was "a bug in every hole."[26] The vermin were impossible to avoid while on the front, so it was best to try to live with the torment. Yet some doughboys, such as Gladney Clarke, said that they were not bothered very much. "The cooties, I think, picked out the fellows who looked a little bit better to eat than me," Clarke said.[27]

The veterans, in addition to complaining about the cooties, condemned the consistently bad weather in France for adding to the misery of war. Marion Andrews, who was a wagoner in the Thirteenth Field Artillery Regiment, gave this advice: "No matter who you ask about the weather, if he doesn't tell you it was cloudy and rainy all the time, he wasn't over there."[28] Henry C. Holt was introduced to the poor weather soon after he landed in Brest, France. Holt and his fellow soldiers were assigned pup tents just prior to a rainstorm. "It poured down rain while we were there," he said, "and we couldn't keep those little pup tents staked down, and they would blow up. We had a pretty rough time there for a few days."[29] Every soldier carried half of a pup tent when on the march, and at the end of the day the men would pair off to sleep together. The tents did not necessarily keep the men dry, however, and many times the tents were not used at all.

Many of the doughboys remembered sleeping in water at one time or another. Smith Cable, a volunteer from Watauga County, recalled: "It rained a lot over there. In a lot of places we had to cut bushes and small limbs to put our blankets on to keep us out of the water."[30] Robert Hamlin recollected

Near the battle lines where dugouts were not available, soldiers had to sleep on the open ground. These men have set up their "dog tents" near Château-Thierry as shelter from the hot July sun. Each man carried a shelter half, one of two parts of the tent, which could be used separately, if necessary. Photograph from a scrapbook in the Robert R. Bridgers Papers, Private Collections, State Archives, Division of Archives and History, Raleigh.

similar conditions on a trip he made with the 306th Ammunition Train: "On one of our trips to the front we stopped at a village not far away from the artillery range, and when those shells came over it sounded like freight trains. We were in an old church, partly destroyed, so I went up on the hillside and got in an old trench. I went to sleep and when I woke up there was about six inches of water in the trench. . . . I could sleep most anywhere, of course. I was raised on a farm."[31] Noah Whicker, who went so far as to say that the war improved his health, recalled an example of how he overcame adverse conditions: "I'll tell you about one of the best nights we had. There had been corn or something planted there in rows, and weeds had grown up. I pulled up weeds and made me a bed on top of one of those ridges. I hadn't had any sleep in two or three nights. I lay down on one of those ridges and slept, and when I woke up the next morning there was water standing."[32] Not once during the night did the cold rain wake Sergeant Whicker. Sheer exhaustion overcame discomfort.

Trench warfare was commonplace during World War I, and in the trenches the cooties and bad weather were joined by boredom, mud, and rats. As already noted, General Pershing was determined to prevent American forces from being bogged down in the endless fighting of trench warfare. Nevertheless, most American soldiers spent some time in the trenches, even if it was for a short stay. At best, the first nights in the trenches were unpleasant, and among all other aspects of trench life, nothing caused as much anxiety among the new recruits as the rats. The rats far outnumbered the soldiers and grew to enormous proportions from feeding on the battlefield dead. They were known to burrow into the corpses to eat, then later crawl under the blankets or run across the faces of sleeping soldiers. Jack Marshall wrote this description in his diary: "April 1918: My first 24 hours on the Western Front. Arrived about 11 o'clock p.m. muddy and tired. It was raining and had been so for many days. Mud was nearly knee deep. . . . We finally found our dugout after walking miles it seemed [with] full pack, so slipping and sliding we went in the dugout. It had mud all over the floor and a big pool of water under the boards. . . . After unpacking we went to bed or rather got on a bunk. Well, when the candle went out and all was still we got introduced to the trench rats and oh what a welcome they gave us. Never will I forget it or them."[33] The rats moved boldly in and out of the dugouts and trenches day and night. One of these trench rats saved the life of Clarence Moore. As Moore recalled: "I was in a trench about waist high—a little more than that— and this old rat ran across there, and as he did I ducked down, and as I did a machine gun just mowed that whole [spot] up around me. . . . That rat saved me."[34]

The terrible weather in France was almost as common as the vermin, and with each rainstorm the trenches increasingly became quagmires. Jack

Marshall wrote home in April 1918: "We are having good weather, but the last few days it rains about 40 times a day, so we have plenty of mud. We all have oil skin trousers, coats, and hats so with the hip boots we don't mind the rain and mud so long as it is not so cold."[35] Oil slickers and trousers did not keep a man clean, even if they did help keep him dry. Near the end of the war, Noah Whicker and other soldiers in the 321st Infantry Regiment took position in an old trench with unpleasant results. "If you could have smelled me . . . in this old trench we were in," he said. "When we went up there it was dark as pitch, and you couldn't go out to use the toilet. You had to use the trench. The boys had been in there no telling how many times, different bunches. I pulled my pack off when I got there and sat down to rest, and I got that stuff all over me, and you talk about a stink."[36]

Once soiled with the filth of war, the doughboy had no choice but to remain that way until pulled from the front. On the front removing one's shoes, much less any clothing, was rare. The muddy clothes remained muddy, and the cooties continued to bite. Even in the best of circumstances, finding water for shaving was difficult. "You would go to the [field] kitchen and get a cup of coffee, drink part of it, and use the last part of it to shave with. . . . I did that several times," recalled Otho Offman.[37] Jack Marshall remembered: "If you had a cup of water you could do a lot—shave and wash your face and neck. Now, if you had a bucket of water, well, two or three, could take a bath."[38]

After spending weeks at the front fighting against the Germans and the elements, the doughboys welcomed the order to return to camp. This gave the soldiers an opportunity to get the rest they needed and the officers the chance to reorganize units and bring in replacements for men lost in battle. Many times thousands of replacements were required for a division just pulled from the firing line. For the veterans, however, the rest camp was a place to try to remove the stench of war, catch up on the news from home, and generally just relax. Horton Hall recalled one occasion when he returned to camp from the front: "Only when we would get back to a rest station did we get a chance to clean up. We all had problems with lice. There were lice in all the trenches, and I don't think there was a man over there who didn't get them in his clothes. When we would get back to a rest camp we would take care of that, [take] steam baths, wash our clothes, clean up, and get our hair cut."[39]

A soldier's ability to get clean varied drastically from camp to camp. Fortunate soldiers were sent to camps with a delousing operation and the steam baths that Horton Hall noted. The "decootieizing devices" were steam pressure tanks in which infested clothing was placed. By the time the men had completed bathing elsewhere, the vermin in their clothes would be thoroughly destroyed. Unfortunately, the clothes might also be destroyed in the process. Otho Offman related the results of one delousing operation: "I got a pair of gloves back you couldn't put on a two-year-old boy. My belt was drawn up so

Opportunities to bathe and have uniforms steamed to kill the "cooties" were rare once soldiers were at the front. These men of the Eighty-first Division stand near a Red Cross bathhouse waiting for their turn to wash. Many of them are holding a change of clean underwear. Photograph from the Military Collection, World War I, State Archives, Division of Archives and History, Raleigh.

that I had to tie a string to the buckle to get it around me. My pants were so tight I couldn't get in them."[40]

There were times when the ravages of war or the delouser necessitated the replacement of clothing. When men were pulled from the front and sent to rest camps, they were supposed to receive new clothing.[41] According to the Quartermaster Department, from June to November 1918 each enlisted man received on average: a slicker and overcoat every five months; a blanket, flannel shirt, and breeches every two months; a coat every seventy-nine days; a pair of shoes and puttees every fifty-one days; a pair of drawers and an undershirt every thirty-four days; and a pair of woolen socks every twenty-three days.[42] This is a statistical average, however, and does not describe the experience of all soldiers, some of whom went without proper clothing for long periods of time.

Often when the doughboys arrived at the rest camp there was no exchange of clothing, and the men had to continue to wear the soiled and torn uniforms from the previous months. This was the case soon after the United States entered the war, and the situation did not improve significantly after a year of fighting. Another clothing problem concerned seasonal uniforms. Most of the soldiers who arrived before December 1917, almost 176,665 men, wore

Members of the Quartermaster Department prepare to issue clothing and boots. Despite the impression of plenty given in this photograph, securing replacement uniforms was often difficult for the doughboys. Many soldiers had to wear light summer uniforms in the winter or heavy woolens in the summer, and their clothes were frequently dirty and torn. Photograph from a scrapbook in the Robert R. Bridgers Papers, Private Collections, State Archives, Division of Archives and History, Raleigh.

summer uniforms, and by the winter of 1917-1918, these uniforms had not been exchanged for wool, much to General Pershing's displeasure.[43]

Most of the men received wool uniforms eventually, but some of the soldiers remembered having to wear wool as late as July or August before being reissued summer uniforms. By then the winter issue was worn to shreds.

Officers and enlisted men were acutely aware of clothing problems. Jack Marshall remembered that his uniform was in terrible condition when he was admitted into a hospital after being wounded. As he recalled: "The nurse undressed me, went through the pockets and got out anything worth anything, rolled my clothes in a bundle, tied my belt around them, and threw them on the floor. She told me they were going to the incinerator."[44] Colonel Joseph Pratt of the 105th Engineer Regiment, Thirtieth Division, was appalled by the appearance of his men in September 1918 and wrote in his diary: "The U.S. troops are by far the poorest dressed troops over here. It is disgraceful the way they look, and yet we are unable to send them the clothes they need. Nearly all the uniforms and shoes issued to our supply officer for our troops are second hand and of little value. Our boys are not complaining, but they are disgusted with the way the clothes are issued."[45] From accounts such as these, it seems that the doughboy looked more like a ragamuffin than a crusader.

Typically rest camps did not have delousers and steam baths, and in such cases the soldiers had to invent ways to bathe, clean their clothes, and kill lice. In the absence of steam baths, the local stream would serve the dirty soldiers, or as Carl Clodfelter remembered, the men would devise a bathing contraption: "While we were there [Faye Billet] we hadn't had a bath lately. There was a big old stream up above us there, and I don't know where they got it, but they had a trough made of wood. They ran it up to the stream, and they drilled holes in it so the water would sprinkle out. Some of the boys would go up to the spring and pour the water in there, and the rest of them would get down there under it and take a bath right there with that water sprinkling down, and that water was cold."[46]

Cleaning filthy clothing and exterminating cooties were more difficult than finding a stream for bathing. If a soldier had to put a dirty, lice-infested uniform back on, bathing was pointless. For this reason the doughboys quickly devised their own delousing methods. Roby Yarborough told of how he and his friends got rid of cooties: "In many cases where we stayed in billets we used candles, and we would take our shirts off and literally singe the lice out of the seams on the insides of our shirts. We called that 'reading the shirt.' "[47]

After singeing the lice from their uniforms, the soldiers would force themselves to wash their clothing. Months of grime was not easily removed. Yarborough explained that because of the shortage of supplies, each soldier had but one shirt and the only way to clean it "was to take it off, wash it, hang it up to let it dry, and hope it would be dry enough to put back on before he was called back into the ranks."[48] When possible the Americans would hire French or Belgian women to do their laundry. Clarence Moore was in a rest camp behind the British lines in Belgium and remembered that "the old women would wash our clothes there, beat the dirt out of them with a stick, and when you got your clothes back they would be as clean as they could be."[49] Carl Clodfelter recalled that in France the women provided the same service: "We were right on the river bank, and the French did all our washing on the river bank. They had those washboards that stuck down in the river. They sat on their knees, and they would raise it up and down at the water level. They would wash for us if we gave them a cake of soap. They didn't have any soap."[50]

Dirty laundry was not the only thing over which the Americans and French negotiated. After arriving in rest camps, most doughboys wanted a break from the field kitchen routine of bully beef and slumgullian, and so supplemented their diets with purchases from the local people. Jack Marshall wrote home about the food that he and his brother had acquired: "We both are feeling good and eat everything eatable in camp—no end to our appetite.

We bought eggs for three francs per dozen and butter for four per pound. Four of us boys bought a frying pan, so eggs fried in butter don't eat as bad as you might think. Although the [artillery] battery feeds very well, on the long lonesome nights we get hungry a bit."[51]

Other doughboys were not so lucky in their attempts to cook for themselves. Lawrence A. Crawford recalled: "Several of us got together and bought a goose from this Frenchman. We finally got it fixed . . . and we cooked and cooked and cooked that old goose. That fire went out so we borrowed some more wood and kept cooking. That old goose must have been fifty years old. We never did get anything off that goose. We just couldn't cook it, and we never did get it so we could eat it."[52]

Long, lonesome nights and tough old geese surely made the doughboy yearn for home—for the good meals and conversation. News from North Carolina or from anywhere in the United States was difficult to obtain, however. Private Henry Holt, a Randolph County native, recalled that for "two or three months I didn't get a thing. I would send my address home, and by the time my mail would get there I would be transferred somewhere else."[53] Horton Hall said that he received very few letters when he was in France. He recollected: "Sometimes on the front we wouldn't get one for a month. When we were on those hikes marching back, we didn't get any mail sometimes for six weeks, but the mail would be at our next stop when we got there."[54] Guy Wise, who served behind the lines with the engineers, had a better chance than most to keep up with the news, but he never really knew what was happening, even concerning the war. "We didn't know much about what was going on," he said. "We would get a *Stars and Stripes* and read it, but people over in the States knew more about it than we did."[55]

The home folks may have had some idea of how the war was going for the Allies, but few of them received news about their family members in the service overseas. From the first card stating, "I have arrived safely overseas," to the continuous "Somewhere in France" return address, the families received incomplete information because all of the soldiers' mail was censored. As Archie Ingram recalled, "We couldn't tell them where we were, what we were doing, or anything."[56] Guy Wise explained that they were told to write in their letters that "we were always getting along well or satisfactory."[57]

In a letter sent home in the spring of 1918, Jack Marshall wrote: "Hope you can read this but don't see how you can. Three of us boys are writing on a wrickety [sic] table with one candle so don't be surprised at the writing. We are lucky to get a table and have a light at night now."[58] Finding the time and the materials to write was difficult. Since it was almost impossible to write while at the front, the doughboy usually had to wait until he arrived at a rest camp to put pen to paper. Horton Hall recollected that "the YMCA., the Knights of Columbus, and the Salvation Army all had their own camps set up behind every front at the rest stations, and they furnished us with envelopes, paper, and pencils, and would do our mailing for us."[59] The stationery provided by these groups usually had the organization's logo at the top of each sheet.

Getting news about the war from French soldiers and civilians was difficult because of the language barrier. Isham Hudson had studied French for a year in high school, but he discovered that his "high school French was not very adequate when talking to a Frenchman."[60] When Guy Wise billeted in one town "every day some fellow would come out on the street corner and read the news," but none of the men with Wise could understand a word, and this went on every day for weeks.[61] The Frenchman, no doubt, thought he was doing the Americans a favor, and apparently they continued to let him think so.

The Americans in the rest camps usually got along well with the French but not with the English. American officers found their English counterparts "unbearably egotistical, blind to everything save their own national greatness, stubbornly opinionated, and vain beyond description," or in the words of one

The YMCA, Knights of Columbus, and Salvation Army established facilities in France to offer aid to the doughboys. They provided coffee, stationery, and a quiet place for the men to gather. These men are setting up a YMCA in Rambervillers, France, in October 1918 to serve the Eighty-first Division. Photograph from the Military Collection, World War I, State Archives, Division of Archives and History, Raleigh.

North Carolina soldier, "the British seemed to know it all, and you knew nothing."[62] The prevailing sentiment among Americans was that the British were not going to win the war, so it was time for them to get out of the way and let Pershing's army get the job done.

The friction between American and English soldiers occasionally erupted into brawls. William Crouse, who remembered the English as "the sorriest, no good people ever I met," recalled a run-in he and some friends had with a group of British Tommies: "We couldn't get along with the British, no, no. . . . I didn't have any use for the British, [and] nobody in my company had any use for them. . . . I was on a bridge over there one night with one of our boys. His name was Cub Wright, [and] he couldn't even write his own name. This Britisher [said], 'Ehh, you Yankees come here and you think you know how to fight!' Cub looked at his feet like he was marking a line. Cub had half a bottle of cognac in his hand, and he hit him with it, and the fight started."[63]

The Americans did not brawl exclusively with the English, for the English had many other nationalities fighting the war with them, including Scots, New Zealanders, Australians, and South Africans. In another incident, a group of South Africans and some North Carolina members of the 119th Infantry Regiment tangled. According to Isaac Winfrey: "They were about seven feet tall, dressed in British uniforms, with big brass buttons shining. . . . I reckon they were pretty tough. We were back in the rest camp in Belgium, and they had a dance hall down there. A bunch of the boys went down there and wanted to dance with the young women. The South Africans said they were as good as we were. . . . We went out and started to throw rocks through there, but they [the military police] stopped us and wouldn't let us go back."[64]

For the most part the Scottish and Australian soldiers were held in high esteem by the Americans. Archie Ingram remembered only one grievance he had about the Scots: "Those bagpipes were all around up there. I didn't think much of the bagpipes. I didn't like the music."[65] Music aside, Frank Devane thought that "the Scots were more cordial and better to get along with than the English."[66] As for the Australians, Archie Ingram found them to be "happy-go-lucky," an opinion shared by many Americans.[67] William Crouse also thought highly of the Australians. About thirty-two Australians were attached to Crouse's engineer company, and he remembered that they "were the finest men I ran into while I was over there. They were fine looking people. They didn't wear those tin hats up there; they wore those big hats with the flap up on the side."[68] When the Australians went to the front they did put on helmets and earned the reputation of being very good fighters, or as Roby Yarborough put it, "real scrappers, they were good."[69]

For most soldiers the stay at the rest camp was never long enough, and the amount of rest was never sufficient. Matt Marshall wrote his family: "We are back of the front quite a ways in what is sometimes called a rest camp,

American soldiers interacted with Allied soldiers from a variety of nations, sometimes with happy results, sometimes not. Harvey C. Maness (right) and John C. Hoosey became good friends and exchanged uniforms for this photograph, which was taken in Watou, Belgium, in 1918. Corporal Hoosey was from Glasgow, Scotland, and had survived the 1915 battles of Second Ypres and Loos. Maness noted that Hoosey, "one of the Ladies from Hell," was an orphan of sorts because his Highland Division was nearly wiped out in 1915 by poison gas. Photograph courtesy of the Harvey C. Maness family.

but there is no such animal over here. It's drive, drive, all the time until men and horses are worn to a frazzel [*sic*], then you drop out, someone else takes your place, and on things go."[70] Isham Hudson and his companions in the Forty-second Division did not believe there was such a thing as a rest camp either. Hudson recalled: "They would tell you in the Army that after an attack you would go back to a rest camp. We would come by these cemeteries, where the soldiers were buried, and we always said, 'There's the rest camp.' So, if we ever had a rest camp that we went to, I never did get to one of them."[71]

The opinions of Marshall and Hudson may have been shared by most American soldiers. With a war to fight, any amount of rest must have seemed too little. All men in uniform, however, had to return to the trenches and face the dangers of combat against the kaiser's forces. They hoped to return to the temporary rest camp eventually, but not to the permanent ones Hudson and his friends passed so frequently.

Notes

1. R. J. Marshall, interview, September 21, 1976.
2. H. B. Hall, interview, November 3, 1981.
3. Brockman, *Here, There, and Back*, 15.
4. "Cash paid out for the officers' mess," June-November 1918, Ledger for the 120th Infantry, manuscript in private possession.
5. Crouse, interview, September 22, 1983.
6. Offman, interview, January 12, 1984.
7. Diary of Roy Jackson Marshall, April 1918, manuscript in private possession.
8. Moore, interview, November 5, 1981.
9. Whicker, interview, September 21, 1983.
10. Collins, interview, April 12, 1984.
11. Whicker, interview, September 21, 1983.
12. L. P. Hall, interview, April 10, 1984.
13. Moore, interview, November 5, 1981.
14. Horton Bower Hall, "Memoirs of H. B. Hall," manuscript in private possession.
15. H. B. Hall, interview, November 3, 1981.
16. L. P. Hall, interview, April 10, 1984.
17. Clarke, interview, January 4, 1984.
18. Covington, interview, September 19, 1983.
19. Hudson, interview, October 27, 1983.
20. Offman, interview, January 12, 1984.
21. Hudson, interview, October 27, 1981.
22. James Madison Marshall to his sister, March 26, 1918, manuscript in private possession.

23. Moore, interview, November 5, 1981.
24. Devane, interview, January 4, 1984.
25. R. J. Marshall, interview, September 21, 1976.
26. Collins, interview, April 12, 1984.
27. Clarke, interview, January 4, 1984.
28. Andrews, interview, October 30, 1981.
29. Henry Clyde Holt, interview with author, Greensboro, N.C., January 6, 1984.
30. Cable, interview, September 16, 1983.
31. Hamlin, interview, January 13, 1984.
32. Whicker, interview, September 21, 1983.
33. Diary of Roy Jackson Marshall, April 1918, manuscript in private possession.
34. Moore, interview, November 5, 1981.
35. Roy Jackson Marshall to his family, April 1, 1918, manuscript in private possession.
36. Whicker, interview, September 21, 1983.
37. Offman, interview, January 12, 1984.
38. R. J. Marshall, interview, September 21, 1976.
39. H. B. Hall, interview, November 3, 1981.
40. Offman, interview, January 12, 1984.
41. Pershing, *My Experiences*, 1:345.
42. Ayres, *War with Germany*, 61.
43. Pershing, *My Experiences*, 1:201-202.
44. R. J. Marshall, interview, September 21, 1976.
45. Joseph H. Pratt, "Diary of Hyde Pratt, Commanding 105th Engineers, A.E.F.," part 4, *North Carolina Historical Review* 1 (October 1924): 531.
46. Clodfelter, interview, September 19, 1983.
47. Yarborough, interview, April 19, 1984.
48. Yarborough, interview, April 19, 1984.
49. Moore, interview, November 5, 1981.
50. Clodfelter, interview, September 19, 1983.
51. Roy Jackson Marshall to his family, April 1, 1918, manuscript in private possession.
52. Lawrence Alyette Crawford, interview with author, Greensboro, April 1, 1918.
53. Holt, interview, January 6, 1984.
54. H. B. Hall, interview, November 3, 1981.
55. Wise, interview, January 5, 1984.
56. Ingram, interview, April 10, 1984.
57. Wise, interview, January 5, 1984.
58. Roy Jackson Marshall to his family, April 1, 1918, manuscript in private possession.
59. H. B. Hall, interview, November 3, 1981.
60. Hudson, interview, October 27, 1981.

61. Wise, interview, January 5, 1984.
62. Fletcher, *113th Field Artillery*, 46; H. B. Hall, interview, November 3, 1981.
63. Crouse, interview, September 22, 1983.
64. Winfrey, interview, September 15, 1983.
65. Ingram, interview, April 10, 1984.
66. Devane, interview, January 4, 1984.
67. Ingram, interview, April 10, 1984.
68. Crouse, interview, September 22, 1983.
69. Yarborough, interview, May 8, 1984.
70. James Madison Marshall to his family, May 26, 1918, manuscript in private possession.
71. Hudson, interview, October 27, 1981.

Chapter Five
"Root Hog or Die":
St. Mihiel and the Hindenburg Line

In September 1918, the Allies initiated several offensives that would help bring about an end to the war, including the battles of St. Mihiel and the Hindenburg Line. The Battle of St. Mihiel was a significant Allied victory and the first major battle organized and fought by a united American army. The Hindenburg Line battle was fought primarily by the British. North Carolinians of the Thirtieth Division were credited with being the first troops to breach the Hindenburg Line at the village of Bellicourt and the St. Quentin Canal. At St. Mihiel and Bellicourt, North Carolina soldiers assaulted well-established German positions in the classic World War I wave formation. The losses suffered, especially at Bellicourt, proved again the high cost of using this type of assault against machine guns, a lesson seemingly ignored from 1914 to 1917. In 1918, however, the German lines crumbled under the weight of the surge of Allied soldiers.

On August 30, 1918, General Pershing met with the supreme Allied commander, Marshal Foch, supposedly to discuss plans for the American St. Mihiel offensive. Foch, however, proposed limiting the St. Mihiel offensive and breaking up the newly created American First Army. The French were planning offensives on the Aisne River and the Meuse-Argonne front, and Foch wanted to intersperse the American divisions with those of the French. Pershing protested that this was contrary to what Foch had promised in several previous conferences. Foch insisted, however, pointing out that Americans had fought well under French direction in the Second Battle of the Marne and would do so again. Pershing had no intention of dividing the American forces, especially since they had only recently been united, nor did he approve of placing Americans under the command of French generals, particularly Jean Marie Degoutte. Many American officers believed that Degoutte's directives during the Second Battle of the Marne had needlessly cost the lives of Americans in his command.[1] Pershing declined to accept Foch's plan, and with a few exceptions, American soldiers remained under American commanders.

General John J. Pershing (left), commander of the American Expeditionary Force, and Marshal Ferdinand Foch, Allied supreme commander, often disagreed on how American troops should be used. Pershing wanted to keep U.S. forces united under his command. Foch wanted to disperse American units among the other Allied forces. A compromise was reached, by which a few U.S. divisions were loaned to European generals, while a strong American army served under Pershing's direct control. Photograph of Pershing from the Library of Congress, reproduced from *Dictionary of American Portraits* (New York: Dover Publications Inc., 1967), 484; photograph of Foch courtesy of the author.

While the commanders argued over grand strategy, the common soldiers prepared for the next conflict, wherever it might be. In mid-August 1918, the Eighty-first Division arrived in France and went into training. Many of the soldiers in the "Wildcat" Division were North Carolinians, including Isham Hudson, a Sampson County native. One Sunday afternoon, following a meal of "sour wine and some raw eggs" with a French family, Hudson returned to camp to find a surprise waiting. "When I came back from this meal at this Frenchman's house on Sunday," Hudson said, "I was told by some of the other soldiers: 'Your name is posted on the bulletin board. You're one of the thirty-six to be transferred tomorrow, and to give you the company news, where you are going the average life of a man is thirty days.' I had rather of not known that." The next morning Hudson and the other transferees boarded a truck for a twenty-four-hour ride, during which they would have nothing to eat and little sleep.[2]

When the truck reached its destination, Hudson was taken to the camp of Company M, 168th Infantry Regiment (Iowa National Guard), Forty-second Division. The company commander, Captain John C. Christopher, met Hudson and a few of the other new men. He welcomed them to the camp and told them to make themselves comfortable. Christopher, as it was later learned, was a humane and understanding officer. For example, some of the veterans told Hudson that once when an enlisted man tore his pants on barbed wire, the "captain unrolled his roll of clothing and gave this boy, this soldier, a new pair of pants from his own private roll."[3] Christopher, who already had been awarded a Distinguished Service Cross, and his men were survivors of the Second Battle of the Marne, in which the Forty-second Division lost fifty-five hundred men in only eleven days.[4] Isham Hudson was a replacement.

Unlike their captain, the veteran enlisted men of the 168th Infantry Regiment caused problems for Hudson during his first days in camp. Someone stole his mess kit, an essential piece of equipment for the soldier. Hudson initially went to his first sergeant about the matter, but the sergeant told him, "Dammit, steal somebody else's!" Hudson decided to take the matter into his own hands. He went to the front of the chow line during mess call and confronted the entire company, but no one confessed. Later, a soldier came forward with Hudson's mess kit but claimed that he did not steal it. Hudson traded a clean pair of socks for his own mess kit but never learned the thief's identity.[5] Within a few weeks, Hudson and his new companions were moved into the line on the St. Mihiel front.

On September 12, 1918, Private Hudson received his baptism of fire in the Battle of St. Mihiel, less than three weeks after being transferred to the Forty-second Division and only four months from the day he left home. The Germans had won the St. Mihiel salient in their 1914 drive to capture Verdun and held it against French assaults in 1915.[6] The Germans had cut several important railroads at St. Mihiel, and the very location of the salient weakened the Verdun defenses and threatened the stability of the Allied front.[7] Foch determined that before any overall Allied offensive could begin in 1918, this salient had to be reduced, and Pershing was given that task.

For this battle Pershing brought together 550,000 soldiers from the American First Army and 110,000 troops from the French Second Colonial Corps.[8] Eight American divisions were brought to the front lines. Seven were placed on the southern face of the salient: the 2nd, 5th, 82nd, and 90th divisions of the American First Corps and the 1st, 42nd, and 89th divisions of the American Third Corps. The American Twenty-sixth Division was positioned on the northern face of the salient. Three French divisions, two of infantry and one of dismounted cavalry, were placed facing the center of the salient between the two groups of Americans.[9] While the French Colonials engaged the Germans at the point of the salient, the Americans to the south of the salient were to launch the principal assault into the heart of the German position, there to link up with the Twenty-sixth Division and cut off the enemy's line of retreat.[10]

As it was later learned, the Germans expected an Allied attack to be made on the St. Mihiel salient at the end of September and had just begun to withdraw when the Allies launched their assault.[11] At 1 A.M. on September 12, almost three thousand American and French artillery pieces opened a four-hour bombardment of the German position.[12] Just prior to and during the bombardment, the American infantry was deployed in the frontline trenches and readied for the attack, which was to commence at 5 A.M. For Private Hudson and the other soldiers of the Forty-second Division, the march to the front started before sundown on September 11. Pounding rain, darkness, and enemy shelling made the journey difficult.[13] Hudson remembered that once at the front "the sky was lit with cannon fire. It was tremendous. You would have thought the world was coming to an end."[14]

Once they reached their position in the water-filled frontline trenches, the weary soldiers tried to rest and prepare themselves for the upcoming attack. The 168th Infantry Regiment, which was Hudson's unit, and the 167th Infantry Regiment—together forming the Eighty-fourth Infantry Brigade—were placed in the forward lines of the Forty-second Division for the assault. The brigade was commanded by Brigadier General Douglas MacArthur. Their initial objective for the attack was to pass through the German trench lines and capture Sonnard Woods, near the center of the southern face of the salient.[15]

After four long hours of waiting under the terrible roar of artillery fire, the signal was given at 5 A.M. to go "over the top." The two leading infantry companies, including Captain Christopher's Company M, poured out of their trenches and moved forward in the darkness. Private Hudson recalled that when they got to their own wire only one hole had been cut through it for his company and that he and the others had to follow a guide wire in order not to get lost in the entanglements.[16] Because he was an ammunition carrier for an automatic rifleman in his squad, Hudson also had to worry about staying close to his gunner. Hudson had to carry almost three hundred rounds for the gunner's French Chauchat automatic rifle, as well as one hundred rounds of ammunition for his own Springfield rifle.[17]

Once through their own wire, the first two infantry companies quickly moved forward toward the German trenches in two waves, followed by three additional companies in support.[18] Captain Christopher led Company M across no-man's-land behind a rolling artillery barrage and into the German wire entanglements. There, Private Hudson remembered, men with heavy wire cutters cleared paths through the wire "and the men would come through the openings in the barbed wire and then spread out in a wave line maybe five or six feet apart."[19] The Americans were then between the German wire and enemy-held trenches. Hudson described what happened next: "The Germans knew from the cannonading that we were going to attack, and when we got out pretty well through the wire, they shot up flares . . . which showed exactly where we were. We were sitting ducks, and they mowed our men down like grass."[20] Hudson and the other men in Company M were caught out in the open: "The people who had gotten through the wire were just clear shooting, and they [the Germans] used their machine guns very effectively, and a great number of our men were killed or wounded."[21]

Within minutes Captain Christopher fell wounded, and his second in command, First Lieutenant John M. Currie, was killed. Then Second Lieutenants Frank W. Weiner and Charles A. Gibbons were wounded, leaving Company M leaderless and pinned down under enemy fire.[22] Hudson's platoon sergeant was also killed, and half of his eight-member squad were casualties, two dead and two wounded.[23] Under such deadly fire the survivors could do little but run for cover. Hudson recalled: "I jumped into this shell hole and got myself wet. The machine-gun bullets were just clipping right through the top of this loose dirt and coming in right in on top of me. Two bullets passed through my clothes, but I didn't know it at the time."[24] Minutes later Hudson looked out of the shell hole to see waves of Americans falling behind him under German fire, and off to the side, a fellow squad member lying on his back, shot through the head. Hudson and the others were frustrated because they could not return fire. As Hudson recalled, "We had our own rifles, but we did not even get a chance to use them because we didn't even know where the Germans were, except that they were right close."[25]

Hudson and the others who were pinned down could not move forward until MacArthur flanked the Germans in Sonnard Woods. Once the woods were cleared the infantry of the Forty-second Division advanced and within a few hours captured the towns of Essey and Pannes.[26] Leaving behind the company's casualties from the early morning attack was difficult for Private Hudson. He remembered that "one poor lad came to me, soaking wet and limping holding one puttee in his hand. He had a bullet through the shinbone. Though frightened, I did the best I could in the way of binding his wound, and found a place where the water was not standing so deep in the trench, and asked him to wait there for the stretcher bearers."[27]

Hudson moved on with the remainder of his company and continued until nightfall. At one point during the day, he stopped for a rest with about twenty other soldiers from his company to recount the morning attack and exchange information about what had happened. Hudson recalled: "One boy said, 'Well, I wasn't touched.' And I said, 'Well, I wasn't touched.' A fellow looked up on my blouse, and he said, 'Yes you were too, look at that button on your coat.'

As it turned out, a machine-gun bullet had smashed the top button on my coat, and another bullet went in above the [left breast] pocket and came out from the seam of my coat."[28] Another member of his squad had a bullet hole through the back of his coat but, like Hudson, was not wounded.[29]

All across the American forty-mile front the German line collapsed, and by 10 A.M. on September 12, just five hours after the attack began, the village of Thiaucourt fell to the Americans, thus cutting the enemy's supply line.[30] The attackers on the southern side of the salient had achieved the day's objectives by the afternoon and by the end of the day had accomplished the following day's goals.[31] Before dawn on September 13, the soldiers of the First Division, driving from the south, and the Twenty-sixth Division, advancing from the north, linked up at the town of Vigneulles, closing off the German retreat and trapping the enemy in a pocket.[32] According to Smith Cable, it was then that the Battle of St. Mihiel was won. The salient "was loaded with Germans," he said. "We killed the most of them and drove them out of there."[33]

German resistance stiffened once the salient was reduced. The American infantry attacks subsided as their objectives were won, and the battle became primarily an artillery duel. German guns pounded American lines to discourage further advances, and the American guns returned fire in earnest. The artillery bombardments would last several more weeks before action shifted to the Meuse-Argonne front in October. Henry Holt from Randolph County was a new replacement thrown into the artillery battle. He had arrived in France in late August 1918 and had been transferred here and there until finally being assigned to the 341st Field Artillery Regiment, Eighty-ninth Division, in September. When he arrived on the St. Mihiel front he had received no training and had never even seen a battlefield, much less served on one. He was promptly assigned to a 75mm fieldpiece and had to learn his responsibilities quickly as the battle was raging all around. "My duty was to shove the shell into the gun," he recalled. "We were working down in the gun pit. There were four men—one man punched the fuse into the end of the shell and handed it to me, another man opened the breach, and I shoved it in, and he closed the breach. Then another one would pull the lanyard and fire it."[34] Holt maintained this routine night and day, it seemed, and not once did his regiment change position. Holt added: "I did a whole lot of shoving in shells, that was my job. I had never seen a gun fired in my life, of course. That wasn't much to learn, shoving in shells."[35]

Behind the artillery positions, in what were once the German lines, the Americans were surprised by the elaborate trench installations that they had recently captured. Since 1914 the enemy had constructed seemingly permanent and unusually comfortable dugouts, especially for the officers. Some of the shelters had electricity, running water, and elegant furnishings.[36] One such

Isham Barney Hudson of the 168th Infantry Regiment, Forty-second Division, experienced two close calls during the Battle of St. Mihiel. One bullet creased the top button of his uniform, while another passed through his coat. Hudson, however, was untouched. The photograph of Hudson, wearing the damaged uniform, was taken in 1919. The dented button is from the coat Hudson wore at St. Mihiel. Photographs courtesy of Mrs. Catherine Hudson Smith.

Henry Clyde Holt arrived in France in mid-August 1918 and was sent to the 341st Field Artillery Regiment, which was already engaged in the Battle of St. Mihiel. He was assigned to a 75mm fieldpiece, though he had never had any training as a member of a gun crew. He later served in the Meuse-Argonne offensive and in the Army of Occupation. The photograph was taken in 1919 and provided courtesy of the Henry Clyde Holt family.

dugout was discovered one evening by members of the Fifteenth Artillery Regiment. These men had not eaten in two days, and though they were warned not to eat any food left by the enemy, their hunger got the best of them. Jack Marshall remembered that "it was an officers' dugout. There was carpet on the floor and a piano. We found plenty of food—cabbage, meat, and potatoes—and we fixed it up and ate all we wanted."[37] For once the common soldiers ate like officers, even if they were enemy officers.

At St. Mihiel the spoils of victory were impressive. Approximately 16,000 German and Austrian soldiers were taken prisoner, including an entire German infantry regiment. In addition to the prisoners, 443 pieces of artillery were taken, and in one depot alone 4,000 77mm shells, 350,000 rifle cartridges, 200 machine guns, 30,000 hand grenades, 42 trench mortars, and an assortment of wagons and railway cars were captured.[38] Jack Marshall remembered one prisoner taken by his outfit, a horse they called "Blinkey." "I believe it was at St. Mihiel. . . .We had one horse we got from the Germans. He was blind in one eye, you see. He had been hit above the eye socket, and the bone had been pushed down over his eye. The driver called him 'Blinkey' and used to hitch him up so his blind side was next to the carriage tongue, his good eye outside where he could see. He was a big German horse and a good one. We never could tell if he was really blind in that bad eye."[39]

By September 16, 1918, the victory at St. Mihiel salient was complete. In addition to the capture of a large number of German prisoners and vast stores of equipment, some two hundred square miles of French soil were liberated.[40] The cost of the victory was slight, considering what was accomplished. Only seven thousand American casualties were sustained during the five-day battle, a much smaller number than expected.[41] General MacArthur's Eighty-fourth Infantry Brigade lost 528 men, of which 100 came from the 250 men in Captain Christopher's Company M of the 168th Infantry Regiment.[42] As ordered, the captain had led Isham Hudson and the other men in the frontal assault on the morning of September 12. There, on the open ground just short of the German trenches, most of the casualties of Company M remained at the end of the day. After the attack the first lieutenant and Hudson's platoon sergeant were dead, and the captain and two second lieutenants were wounded. Private Hudson had seen many of the officers and men fall and had witnessed a member of his own squad tremble and quiver on the ground as he died.[43] These terrible memories were not forgotten by the Sampson County native. On the day following the attack Hudson wrote in his diary, "May God refuse to me seeing ever another battle."[44]

Only a week after Pershing pulled his victorious troops from the front at St. Mihiel, the detached American Second Corps, serving with the British, was placed in the frontline trenches facing the Hindenburg Line in preparation for battle. Since early September, when their role at Ypres ended, the Twenty-seventh and Thirtieth Divisions had been undergoing additional training in preparation for the continued Allied offensive. On September 23, 1918, the two American divisions were sent to the British Fourth Army, which was under the command of General Sir Henry Rawlinson. By the next morning, they had replaced English and Australian troops on the front line. The Thirtieth Division relieved the First Australian Division in the trenches in front of the Hindenburg Line at the German-held towns of Bellicourt and Nauroy. This section of the German permanent trench system, located between the cities of Cambrai and St. Quentin, was considered the most formidable part of the German defenses.[45] The heavy losses suffered by the First Australian Division were proof of this. When the Americans went to the front, they found that one American company could relieve an Australian battalion containing four companies of infantry.[46]

On the night of September 26, the preliminary artillery bombardment and infantry attack opened against the German line. To provide a better "jumping off" position for the main attack on September 29, the two American divisions each sent forward a regiment to assault the enemy outpost line. From the Thirtieth Division, the South Carolinians of the 118th Infantry Regiment pushed the Germans back five hundred yards, but the soldiers of the Twenty-seventh Division failed to gain their objective. For the next few days the Germans attempted to restore their line and attacked the Americans repeatedly. These attacks prevented the Twenty-seventh Division from any further advance but could not force back the Thirtieth Division. Meanwhile the British and Australian artillery increased the bombardment on the Hindenburg Line by firing some thirty thousand mustard-gas shells, followed by high explosive and shrapnel shells. The bombardment continued without interruption for two days.[47]

During this bombardment and the continuous back-and-forth infantry fighting, the engineers of the Thirtieth Division erected and repaired barbed-wire entanglements in no-man's-land. This work began on September 22, even before the American infantry was in position in the trenches. Under the direction of thirty-two Australian engineers, doughboys from Company E, 105th Engineer Regiment, worked on roads and crawled between the lines for several nights preparing defenses. William Crouse of Forsyth County was one of these soldiers, and he remembered the difficult nights in no-man's-land: "When those boys got killed on the front putting up barbed wire we had to go out on the next night and hunt them. . . . They would get up too high. Some of the boys would holler 'Stay down!' but they would get up, they wouldn't listen. We didn't actually lose but four men, outside of the wounded—we had a lot of them wounded."[48] Making a fatal mistake working in no-man's-land was easy, especially, as Crouse recalled, when crawling up to the enemy positions. On one occasion he was "so close to them we could hear the Germans talking in their trenches," which made him wonder if he was "going to get back or not."[49]

Crouse remembered that when the Allied bombardment began it looked like "a blaze of fire for miles and miles."[50] When Private Luther Hall came to the frontline trenches with the 119th Infantry Regiment, he thought it sounded like "all hell broke loose. The artillery barrage they were putting over was terrific; [it would] just shake your head, sometimes just jar you to death."[51] The 118th Infantry Regiment was replaced by the 119th and 120th Infantry Regiments on the night of September 27. These two regiments were to lead the assault on the Hindenburg Line, followed by the 117th Infantry and then the 118th, if necessary.[52] To support the infantry the British sent forward thirty-four Mark V tanks, twelve each to the 117th and 119th regiments and ten to the 120th.[53]

William Foster Crouse (back row, left) of Winston-Salem served in the First North Carolina Infantry, a national guard unit, which became the 105th Engineer Regiment, Thirtieth Division. He is shown with other youthful trainees at Camp Sevier, South Carolina, in 1917. Crouse saw his most dangerous action at Ypres and in the attack on the Hindenburg Line. Photograph courtesy of Carl R. Crouse.

As the infantry gathered in the trenches the night before the attack, the machine-gun battalions prepared to provide support during the battle. To cover the infantry advance, the 114th and 115th Machine-Gun Battalions were placed in key positions along the American trench lines to fire initially on the Hindenburg Line and then on the St. Quentin Tunnel.[54] Frank Devane of Wilmington was responsible for three .303 Vickers heavy machine guns in the 115th Battalion, and he had them set up well before the attack. Because of the endless roar of artillery and the anticipation of battle, Devane could not sleep on the night of September 28. "You didn't know what was going to happen, sort of like quail hunting, you don't sleep much," Devane said. "You're thinking mostly of living if you can and doing what you're supposed to do."[55]

While Frank Devane stayed awake listening to the thunder of artillery, the 105th Engineer Regiment was sent one last time into no-man's-land. The engineers opened holes in the wire entanglements so the infantry could pass, and along the entire Thirtieth Division trench line they placed a white "jumping off tape." This one-inch-wide tape was stretched along the ground several yards in front of the advance trench line. The zigzag formation of the trench system made it impossible for the attacking infantry to form a uniform line and advance in an organized wave. The white tape, therefore, was placed where the men were to line up after being ordered over the top but before being ordered to move toward the enemy position.[56] With this task completed the attack was ready to begin.

"Zero Hour" was set for 5:50 A.M. on September 29, 1918. At that moment the Allied artillery opened with a rolling barrage, starting on a fixed line near the American trenches for four minutes and then advancing one hundred yards every four minutes toward, and then into, the Hindenburg Line positions.[57] Behind this creeping barrage the infantry stood in front of their trenches along the white tape waiting for orders to advance. Luther Hall, who had only recently returned from the hospital after being wounded at Ypres, was one of many North Carolinians standing behind the artillery storm. He and the others in the 119th Infantry Regiment were standing "a little more than an arm's length away from each other, four or six feet apart," when the orders to advance were "passed right on down the line."[58]

The Allied artillery and machine-gun barrage did not prevent the Germans from returning fire. The enemy shellfire struck the American troops as they were organizing for the attack, causing confusion and death. John Collins of the 120th Infantry Regiment was with his company in a support trench when ordered to advance. Before he and the others could climb from the trench, German shells hit their position. Collins vividly remembered the panic and chaos caused by the exploding shells: "The captain hollered, 'Advance!' I said, 'Captain, they're all knocked out here but me! I'm still living, but the rest of them are dead or wounded!' He said, 'Private, take charge!'

I said, 'I don't know your orders! I can't take care of them. I don't know your orders!' He said, 'No, they will stay right there. You follow me!' "[59] Amid the shellfire and into the dense fog and smoke the 119th and 120th Infantry Regiments, both formerly North Carolina National Guard units, began the attack on the Hindenburg Line.

Moving toward the enemy line was difficult. The terrain was broken by water-filled shell holes, tangled wire, debris, and deep mud. The rainy weather had created a thick fog that, combined with the smoke from the artillery, severely limited visibility.[60] Luther Hall recalled that the smoke was so thick that "you could hardly see your hand before you."[61] Under these circumstances the Americans were soon divided into small bands. Lost, confused, and separated from their officers, they stumbled their way into three belts of German barbed wire and against the enemy trenches.[62] Hall said, it "was root hog or die, you had to go and do the best you [could]."[63]

The attack was a completely confusing experience for two soldiers in the 120th Infantry Regiment. Platoon Sergeant Roby Yarborough went forward with his company in a wave formation, but the line disintegrated in the smoke. "We were supposed to have a solid front to move forward at the same time," he said, "but it didn't last. . . . The air was filled with smoke and dust and fog to where you didn't have much chance to keep your sense of direction. I think that partially accounts for the disorder we had within the ranks. A few of us could stay together, but if we got maybe forty feet away from the other men, we couldn't see those men. . . . We got scattered."[64] John Collins of Company C remembered that during the confusing advance "some of the boys were singing, some of them cussing," and many were wounded, including a soldier next to him. Collins stopped to assist his friend, who was wounded badly in the side, and the company moved on and left them behind. "I got lost from the company. Lord, I didn't know which way to go," recalled Collins, who, not knowing what else to do, remained with the wounded man for the rest of the day.[65]

Neither the Allied artillery and machine-gun fire nor the thick smoke hindered the German fire, and many North Carolinians were hit. Roby Yarborough recalled: "On the battlefield a sergeant [William Jarvis Parker] of my company came running up to the captain, and his [Parker's] arm was shot away. He ran up to the captain and asked him to help him take off his pack. I rushed up, and three or four more, half a dozen of us maybe, and the captain [James A. Leonard] turned to us and said, 'Get the hell out of here! Do you want us to all get killed together?' Now that's the kind of man the captain was."[66] Captain Leonard probably saved himself and his men when he told them to disperse. One burst from a machine gun or a single shell could have killed the entire group. The loss of Parker's arm was his second severe wound that morning. Earlier he had been shot in the abdomen but continued to lead his detail another five hundred yards toward the German lines, while carrying trench-mortar ammunition. After the captain removed Parker's pack, the sergeant refused to be carried to the rear on a stretcher, saying it was needed for more severely wounded men. Parker then walked over a mile to a first-aid station. For his actions the Lexington native received the Distinguished Service Cross.[67]

Luther Hall was shocked when dawn broke, and he could see the dead and wounded scattered across no-man's-land. He recalled that "at daylight after the attack, bodies were thrown all over the place; it was an awful mess."[68] Harvey Maness, a stretcher-bearer in the 120th Infantry Regiment, remembered that "when the fog lifted about eleven that morning there was a scene I'll never forget. There were caissons and trucks and wagons and horses and mules and soldiers—some of them hanging on spikes—and rifles and machine-gun nests upset and shell holes. It was just a scene of devastation."[69] Like Maness, the other men assigned to the Medical Corps followed the infantry as closely as possible and collected the wounded as quickly as they could. Clarence Moore, a private in the 117th Infantry Regiment, was detached as a stretcher-bearer on the morning of the attack. He had to search for men and bring them to the ambulances. For Moore it was a horrible experience. "I was a stretcher-bearer in the Hindenburg Line for about a half a day," he said. "We had to step on these dead soldiers to keep from going in the water and mud so deep and throwing the [wounded] off the stretcher. . . . That's unbeliev-able. . . . [People] don't believe you when you tell them."[70] Private Moore performed this task only briefly. Later in the afternoon he was ordered back to his company, which was in reserve waiting to attack the Germans.

Medical corpsmen were not the only soldiers to follow the infantry in the attack. The 105th Engineer Regiment was sent across open ground to investigate enemy dugouts, look for water, inspect roads, and hunt for mines and booby traps left by the Germans.[71] The engineers were in as much danger as the infantry, especially from the German artillery. William Crouse remembered that he "was going to the First Battalion with a message to the captain from headquarters. I was the runner that day, and another boy was going to the Second Battalion. We were going down a road and there was a bank, and he said, 'I'm going to cut across this field.' I said, 'Stay in this road behind this bank, don't go up through that field.' Shells were falling just like hail. He didn't get [fifty yards], and I knew a shell got him. [Robert] Gorrell Tate, he was the first man killed that I knew of, outside of the ones who got killed at night [working in no-man's-land]."[72] Tate was one of fifty-two casualties in Crouse's company that day.[73]

Whether soldiers were behind the lines or attacking the German trenches, most of them feared the random destruction of shellfire far more than rifle or machine-gun fire. Roby Yarborough, who fought his way through no-man's-land, stayed as far away from the British supporting tanks as possible because they drew shellfire. "We considered it a hot spot to be near a tank," he said.[74] Despite the soldiers' desire to avoid them, the tanks assigned to the 120th Infantry Regiment did offer some assistance initially, particularly in clearing wire entanglements. Because of German shelling, deep mud, and mechanical failure, however, the vast majority of the tanks were soon put out of action.[75]

Far to the right, across the wire-entangled battlefield, the 120th Infantry Regiment was actually gaining ground. "We had driven the Germans back some," recalled Roby Yarborough. "Then we came to the trenches that the Germans had been occupying. When we could we would get into these trenches, and if they would lead us where we wanted to go we would follow the trenches."[76] As a platoon sergeant in Company A, 120th Infantry Regiment, Yarborough had managed to gather together a few scattered soldiers and follow the first wave of attacking Americans into the Hindenburg Line. Before 7:30 on the morning of the assault, the doughboys of his regiment had broken into the formidable German position. They were the first troops, not only to penetrate, but to capture the trenches that the Germans thought were insurmountable.[77] Once in the German trench line, Yarborough explained, "we had compasses, and supposedly we had directions. We had been told that there was a railroad that would lead us to a small town that was one of our objectives. . . . The name of the town was Bellicourt."[78]

The village rubble called Bellicourt fell at 9:30 A.M. to the North Carolinians. The remainder of the day was spent mopping up the captured position by killing or forcing the surrender of the remaining Germans and by waiting for the Australians, who were to "leapfrog" the Americans and continue the attack.[79] Roby Yarborough recalled an incident during this mopping-up operation: "This German came out from a culvert along the railroad, and he had his hands up surrendering. The only word I can remember him saying was, 'Kamerad, Kamerad,' meaning he was surrendering. He was going to give up as a prisoner. One of the men in my platoon section who was carrying the Lewis automatic rifle was walking and holding that rifle on his hip. He just squeezed the trigger and put half a dozen bullets into that German. He fell and he died with eyes open, and he had the bluest German eyes you ever saw. I turned to this man—we were standing almost side-by-side when he let the volley loose—and I jumped on him, 'Why did you do it?' He said, 'Well, he dropped his hands to his belt, and he had some grenades there. I thought he was fixing to throw one of them, so I let him have it.' . . . I can well remember that man's name, but I will not call it. . . . He didn't give him a chance."[80]

To the left of the 120th Infantry, the North Carolinians in the 119th Regiment were having much more difficulty capturing the German trenches. They had reached the Hindenburg Line position well ahead of schedule and

Roby Gray Yarborough was talked into volunteering by his older brother, who was already in service. He arrived in France as a supply sergeant in the 120th Infantry Regiment, but after service at Ypres, he requested and received a transfer into the infantry ranks. On September 29, 1918, Yarborough led a platoon during the attack on the Hindenburg Line. This photograph was taken in France in 1919. Photograph courtesy of the Roby G. Yarborough family.

were met with machine-gun fire, not only from the front, which was expected, but also from the left flank where the New Yorkers of the Twenty-seventh Division were supposed to be. The New York division had been stopped by stiff resistance about a half mile behind the Thirtieth Division's line, thus leaving the 119th Infantry's left flank exposed to enfilading fire.[81] To make matters worse, most of the tanks assigned to the regiment did not arrive in time for the battle. By the time the few scattered tanks reached the front, the infantry was already suffering terrible casualties and was no longer able to renew the attack. Many of the North Carolinians felt betrayed by the New York troops and blamed them for the setback. "These boys from New York, they really fell down on us," Harvey Maness said. "We had to stop and let them catch up because they didn't have what it took. They just weren't pure Anglo-Saxon, knock-down, drag-out, country boys born to fight."[82] Late in the afternoon, the 119th Infantry was reinforced by troops from the 117th and 118th Infantry Regiments, who helped cover the exposed left flank.[83]

At 3 P.M. on September 29, the soldiers of the Australian Fifth Division passed through the survivors of the Thirtieth Division and continued to press back the German defenders until after dark.[84] Withdrawing the Americans from the front at that time was impracticable, and the soldiers of the Thirtieth Division held their positions during the night.

For the soldiers who fought their way into the trenches of the Hindenburg Line and survived, the return trip across the battlefield was an equally horrible experience. Roby Yarborough recalled: "When we came out of action I was told that K Company from Asheboro, North Carolina, that had gone into action with 240 men, came out with approximately seventy men. . . . I was within a few feet of where the captain of K Company was killed. I saw him."[85] Yarborough never described the sight of Captain Ben F. Dixon's body, but he said that he always remembered the image. What made some of the American losses even harder for Yarborough and others to bear was the realization that many Americans may have been killed by British, rather than German, artillery fire. This was certainly the cause of Captain Dixon's death. He had been wounded twice by enemy fire but refused to leave his men. In an attempt to stop his company from advancing into their own artillery barrage, Dixon was caught in the shelling and killed by friendly fire.[86] Roby Yarborough explained: "The biggest hazard was from artillery. At one time we believed that we had advanced faster than had been anticipated, which resulted in casualties from our own artillery fire. When that happened you didn't know which way to [go to] protect yourself."[87]

Colonel Joseph H. Pratt, commanding the 105th Engineer Regiment, also walked the battlefield and wrote in his diary: "I was going over the battlefield, which was still being shelled by the Germans, and we were still having casualties. Dead and wounded were on the field, and it was all a realistic picture of the battlefields I had read about. It was a hard experience to see our men lying dead on the field, and while it was expected, it did not ease the pain it caused me."[88]

Brigadier General L. H. Tyson, commander of the Fifty-ninth Brigade, Thirtieth Division, said of the "Old Hickory" soldiers, "No troops ever fought more gallantly nor with greater determination to win at any cost."[89] The battle to break the Hindenburg Line was an impressive victory. In addition to the large amounts of ammunition and equipment captured from the enemy, about 47 German officers and 1,432 enlisted men were taken prisoner from the morning of September 29 to October 2, when the last units of the division were withdrawn from the battle.[90] For these spoils and for the precious three-thousand-yard advance, the division lost 2,494 officers and men. The vast majority of the casualties came from the North Carolina infantry regiments, the 119th, which lost 874 men, and the 120th, which suffered 994 casualties.[91]

The men of the Thirtieth Division were sent briefly to rest stations behind the lines before being called back to the front. While the division had not recovered from the losses suffered during the costly fighting for the Hindenburg Line, the even weaker Second Australian Division needed relief. The German lines were crumbling, and the kaiser's troops were in slow retreat on the British front. The enemy was not yet decisively defeated, however. On the night of October 5, the Thirtieth Division relieved the Australians. The next day was spent preparing for a morning assault scheduled for October 8. The 117th and 118th Infantry Regiments were placed in the forward lines, while the 119th and 120th Regiments were held in reserve.[92]

Almost all of the soldiers of the 117th Infantry were from Tennessee. In Clarence Moore's Company K, all of the officers were originally from the old Third Tennessee Infantry Regiment.[93] The only enlisted men who were not Tennesseans were draftees like Moore, and most of these were from North Carolina. Moore had gotten to know many of the men personally because he had been company barber during training in the United States and France.

The Germans welcomed the Americans to the front on October 6 with the customary shellfire. Hastily made trenches north of the ruined village of Montbrehain were the only shelter available to the men of the 117th Infantry Regiment. The regiment suffered numerous casualties, including forty-one killed. Many men in Moore's Company K were wounded, and four were killed, including Corporal Harry Smith of Knoxville, Tennessee.[94] Smith was a trained automatic rifleman and squad leader for seven inexperienced privates, including Clarence Moore. His death left his squad without a leader before their first battle. As a result, Moore found his first and, as it turned out, his last battle to be a completely confusing and personally disastrous experience.

The front line held by the 117th Infantry Regiment was about one thousand yards behind the designated starting position for the October 8 attack. To secure the proper position, the 117th was ordered to make a preliminary attack on the German lines a day early, at 5:15 A.M., October 7.[95] Unlike the other three regiments in the division, many of the companies in the 117th had never gone "over the top" to lead an attack, no matter how minor. The regiment had been held in reserve for the most part at Ypres and during the September 29 attack at Bellicourt. Despite their inexperience, the men were confident of success. But in their first attack they suffered terribly. At the outset, the British artillery barrage on the German lines was almost totally ineffective. In return, the enemy's heavy fire tore large holes in the advancing American lines. Moore's Company K went into the attack in support of the leading companies. His captain, Amiel W. Brinkley, a Memphis attorney, soon saw a gap torn in the front lines and moved his men forward. German artillery and machine-gun fire became so intense that at one point the division headquarters thought that the regiment had been destroyed. In the severe fighting Captain Brinkley received a painful wound that nearly severed his jaw from his face. He refused to leave his men until he had reorganized them under fire. The captain then turned his command over to Sergeant Marshall B. Dudderar, who was soon killed while leading the men forward. Only darkness brought an end to the fighting, with fifty-nine men in the 117th killed and several hundred wounded.[96]

The next day proved to be even more difficult for the 117th when many more fell, including an additional ninety-five men killed. Private Clarence Moore of Winston-Salem was one of the wounded. While moving forward, Moore and his company came under fire from a hidden machine gun. "I had a razor strop buckled on my back," he said, "and I got three machine-gun bullet holes through that razor strop, and it fell to the ground. I had it buckled on top of the pack. I was on the ground, and that machine gun was sweeping the ground."[97] He was not hurt, however, so he scrambled away from where he believed the machine gun to be. Just at the moment he thought he was safe, he received another machine-gun burst from a second unseen gunner.

Moore was wounded in the shoulder and hip, and he remembered that when he was hit "it felt like a bumblebee sting."[98] He could not move because of the continuous enemy fire. "I lost my rifle," Moore said. "A piece of shrapnel hit my rifle and made splinters out of it."[99] Finally the battle moved on, and the corpsmen came onto the field to search for the wounded. Two stretcher-bearers found Moore, placed him on a litter, and carried him to an ambulance. There he saw that he was to share the ride to the field hospital with Private Lacey Kerr, a friend from Camp Dodge, Iowa. Kerr was thought to be from a wealthy family because he was generous in lending money to others in the company. At first the medics underestimated the severity of Kerr's wounds. Moore remembered that when Kerr was put in the ambulance "they didn't think Lacey was hurt bad, but there was blood on his uniform on

Clarence C. Moore escaped injury in the fighting on October 7, 1918, while many men around him were killed or wounded. The following day Moore was not as lucky. He was pinned down by a German machine gunner, and as he tried to crawl out of the line of fire, he was wounded twice by a second machine gun. Moore survived but never forgot his terrible days of combat on the western front. This 1981 photograph was provided by the author.

the back and the front, and they found out that a piece of shrapnel about two and half inches long went plumb through him—so he died right there before we even got away from the front."[100] The ambulance took Moore and the other wounded men on to the field hospital. From there Moore was transferred to a base hospital with the other wounded survivors.[101] The total casualty count for the 117th Infantry Regiment in the battle fought during October 5-12 was over one thousand, including over two hundred dead.[102]

Notes

1. Pershing, *My Experiences*, 2:245, 247.
2. Hudson, interview, October 27, 1981.
3. Hudson, interview, October 27, 1981.
4. American Battle Monuments Commission, *American Battle Fields*, 29; John H. Taber, *The Story of the 168th Infantry*, vol. 2 (Iowa City, Iowa: State Historical Society of Iowa, 1925), 68.

5. Hudson, interview, October 27, 1981.
6. Reynolds, Churchill, and Miller, *Great War*, 8:183.
7. American Battle Monuments Commission, *American Battle Fields*, 69.
8. Pershing, *My Experiences*, 2:261.
9. American Battle Monuments Commission, *American Battle Fields*, 69.
10. Allen et al., *Triumph*, 333.
11. American Battle Monuments Commission, *American Battle Fields*, 70.
12. Allen et al., *Triumph*, 333.
13. Hudson, interview, October 27, 1981; Isham Barney Hudson, "Going Over at St. Mihiel," *Wake Forest Student* 40 (March 1921): 305; Taber, *Story of the 168th Infantry*, 2:88-89.
14. Hudson, interview, October 27, 1981.
15. D. Clayton James, *The Years of MacArthur*, vol. 1, *1880-1941* (Boston: Houghton Mifflin Company, 1970), 203.
16. Hudson, interview, October 27, 1981.
17. Hudson, "Going Over," 304.
18. Taber, *Story of the 168th Infantry*, 2:89.
19. Hudson, interview, October 27, 1981.
20. Hudson, interview, October 27, 1981.
21. Hudson, interview, October 27, 1981.
22. Taber, *Story of the 168th Infantry*, 2:93, 95.
23. Hudson, "Going Over," 306, 308.
24. Hudson, interview, October 27, 1981.
25. Hudson, interview, October 27, 1981.
26. American Battle Monuments Commission, *American Battle Fields*, 71.
27. Hudson, "Going Over," 307.
28. Hudson, interview, October 27, 1981.
29. Hudson, "Going Over," 307.
30. Allen et al., *Triumph*, 333.
31. Pershing, *My Experiences*, 2:269.
32. American Battle Monuments Commission, *American Battle Fields*, 72.
33. Cable, interview, September 16, 1983.
34. Holt, interview, January 6, 1984.
35. Holt, interview, January 6, 1984.
36. Reynolds, Churchill, and Miller, *Great War*, 8:188.
37. R. J. Marshall, interview, September 21, 1976.
38. Heywood Broun, *Our Army on the Front* (New York: Charles Scribner's Sons, 1919), 274; Reynolds, Churchill, and Miller, *Great War*, 8:188; Allen et al., *Triumph*, 334.
39. R. J. Marshall, interview, July 7, 1978.
40. American Battle Monuments Commission, *American Battle Fields*, 72.
41. Ayres, *War with Germany*, 110.

42. James, *Years of MacArthur*, 1:204; Hudson, "Going Over," 308.

43. Hudson, "Going Over," 307-308.

44. Diary of Isham Barney Hudson, September 13, 1918, manuscript in private possession.

45. Tyson, "Hindenburg Line," 47.

46. Murphy and Thomas, *Thirtieth Division*, 92.

47. Murphy and Thomas, *Thirtieth Division*, 92-93.

48. Crouse, interview, September 22, 1983.

49. Crouse, interview, September 22, 1983.

50. Crouse, interview, September 22, 1983.

51. L. P. Hall, interview, April 10, 1984.

52. American Battle Monuments Commission, *30th Division*, 16.

53. Murphy and Thomas, *Thirtieth Division*, 97.

54. Murphy and Thomas, *Thirtieth Division*, 97.

55. Devane, interview, January 4, 1984.

56. Pratt, "War Diary," part 4, 537.

57. Murphy and Thomas, *Thirtieth Division*, 100.

58. L. P. Hall, interview, April 10, 1984.

59. Collins, interview, April 12, 1984.

60. Murphy and Thomas, *Thirtieth Division*, 100; Walker, Graham, and Fauntleroy, *Official History*, 27; C. B. Conway and George A. Shuford, comps., *History, 119th Infantry, 60th Brigade, 30th Division, U.S.A.: Operations in Belgium and France, 1917-1919* (Wilmington, N.C.: Wilmington Chamber of Commerce, n.d.), 46.

61. L. P. Hall, interview, April 10, 1984.

62. Tyson, "Hindenburg Line," 54; Murphy and Thomas, *Thirtieth Division*, 100-101.

63. L. P. Hall, interview, April 10, 1984.

64. Yarborough, interview, May 8, 1984.

65. Collins, interview, April 12, 1984.

66. Yarborough, interview, April 19, 1984.

67. Murphy and Thomas, *Thirtieth Division*, 258.

68. L. P. Hall, interview, April 10, 1984.

69. Maness, interview, December 19, 1985.

70. Moore, interview, November 5, 1981.

71. Murphy and Thomas, *Thirtieth Division*, 100; Willard P. Sullivan and Harry Tucker, comps., *The History of the 105th Regiment of Engineers* (New York: George H. Doran Company, 1919), 139-151.

72. Crouse, interview, September 22, 1983.

73. Sullivan and Tucker, *History of the 105th Engineers*, 148, 350.

74. Yarborough, interview, May 8, 1984.

75. American Battle Monuments Commission, *American Battle Fields*, 207.

76. Yarborough, interview, May 8, 1984.

77. Tyson, "Hindenburg Line," 55.

78. Yarborough, interview, May 8, 1984.

79. American Battle Monuments Commission, *30th Division*, 17-18.

80. Yarborough, interview, May 8, 1984.

81. "Operations of the Second American Corps Against the Hindenburg Line, September 27-October 1, 1918," in *Source Records of the Great War*, vol. 6, ed. Charles F. Horne (Indianapolis: American Legion, 1930), 307.

82. Maness, interview, December 19, 1985.

83. Murphy and Thomas, *Thirtieth Division*, 104.

84. Murphy and Thomas, *Thirtieth Division*, 104.

85. Yarborough, interview, April 19, 1984.

86. Murphy and Thomas, *Thirtieth Division*, 247.

87. Yarborough, interview, April 19, 1984.

88. Joseph H. Pratt, "Diary of Colonel Joseph Hyde Pratt, Commanding 105th Engineers, A.E.F.," part 5, *North Carolina Historical Review* 2 (January 1925): 119.

89. Tyson, "Hindenburg Line," 57.

90. Murphy and Thomas, *Thirtieth Division*, 104.

91. American Battle Monuments Commission, *30th Division*, 35.

92. Murphy and Thomas, *Thirtieth Division*, 108; American Battle Monuments Commission, *30th Division*, 22.

93. Moore, interview, November 5, 1981.

94. Moore, interview, November 5, 1981; Murphy and Thomas, *Thirtieth Division*, 309.

95. Murphy and Thomas, *Thirtieth Division*, 108; *Operations of the 2d American Corps in the Somme Offensive* (Washington, D.C.: Government Printing Office, 1920), 22.

96. Murphy and Thomas, *Thirtieth Division*, 108, 243, 247, 269.

97. Moore, interview, November 5, 1981.

98. Moore, interview, November 5, 1981.

99. Moore, interview, November 5, 1981.

100. Moore, interview, November 5, 1981.

101. Moore, interview, November 5, 1981.

102. American Battle Monuments Commission, *Thirtieth Division*, 35; Murphy and Thomas, *Thirtieth Division*, 304-310.

Chapter Six
The War behind the Lines

While his friends in the Thirtieth Division were fighting their way through the German lines in France, Joe Thompson was busy behind the lines battling an old enemy. Since being wounded at Ypres in early September, he had been recovering in Base Hospital No. 37 in England, where wounded Americans from the Twenty-seventh and Thirtieth Divisions had been sent. The Twenty-seventh Division was formerly the New York National Guard, while the Thirtieth Division was made up of National Guard units from North Carolina, South Carolina, and Tennessee. It proved to be a bad mix in the hospital wards. The southerners, many of whom were the sons or grandsons of Confederate veterans, did not like the New Yorkers, whom they found to be unbearable. Thompson, the grandson of a soldier in Robert E. Lee's army, had a number of unwanted altercations with the Yankees. As he recalled: "A lot of those boys were from New York, [from] Brooklyn and around there, and they hated the southern boys, and they were always making fun of us. . . . One of them kept after me. I was on crutches and so was he, and every time I got close to him he would pinch me. I asked him, 'Don't do that, quit, let's quit that.' So, we were down in a great room where the toilet was, and he pinched me. I threw a great big porcelain drinking cup, and it grazed his forehead. It knocked a piece of skin off about the size of a penny, and the blood just flew. He grabbed a rag and put it on his head. I said, 'Now, I've asked you to leave me alone, and you won't do it, but the next time I'm going to ram you beside the head with this crutch.' "[1] On another occasion the nineteen-year-old North Carolinian threw a chair at a New York sergeant who kept pushing him around.

Thompson's friends had their fights with the northerners as well. Before long the battle in Thompson's ward reached its climax. Thompson remembered the last fight: "There was another boy who had his arm cut off, who was from New York, about my age, [and] every time I'd pass him he'd pinch me. I had a walking stick. I was on a walking stick at that time. I had asked him several times to quit. Well, when I passed him he pinched me, and just as quick I grabbed my stick, and I started to hit him back of the head. But I knew if I did I'd get in trouble so I got him just below the buttocks with all the power

Joe W. Thompson grew up with stories about the Civil War and Union soldiers visiting his grandfather's farm near Goldsboro in 1865. When World War I began, Confederate veterans were still living in many southern communities. Many young southerners in the American army, like Thompson, were proud of their region and held a lingering hatred of Yankees. The photograph on the left was taken in 1918 in England; the photograph on the right was taken on December 19, 1985. Photographs courtesy of Katherine C. Kinton and the author.

I had. He hit the floor on his knees and then jumped up. We were in a great big room, and most of the boys were southern boys in there. I ran to the wall right quick, and I pushed the cots away and got up next to the wall so [the New Yorkers] couldn't get to me. In the next bed was Robert Stell from Youngsville, North Carolina, [who] was wounded in the hand. Well, he took his pocket-knife out and said, 'Now all you SOBs, come on over! What he don't get with his walking stick I'll get with this pocketknife! You've run all over the southern boys, but these two you can't do nothing with! If you don't quit we're going to hurt you!' They never did do [anything] else to us. That cured them; it did more good than a dose of salts."[2]

Thankfully, most of the Americans behind the lines remained focused on the real enemy, Germany, and worked hard to bring about a successful end to the war. About one-third of the U.S. Army, 644,540 men, worked behind the lines in the Services of Supply organization to keep the war going in the trenches.[3] They were engineers and pioneers, dock workers and railroad men, and they were joined by thousands of troops in the ranks who served as the last link in the supply organization. While these soldiers struggled to keep the combat effort going, the Army Medical Corps had the responsibility to repair

109

the damage to humans caused by the battles. Together, all of these people fought the war from behind the front.

In addition, the American Services of Supply utilized about 31,000 German prisoners. They came from the front to be shuffled away to distant prison camps and to become part of the Allied war effort as laborers in quarries and on roads and as gravediggers in hospital compounds. Sergeant Guy Wise of the 534th Engineer Battalion was responsible for supervising the labor of his men, all African Americans, and German prisoners. Every day Wise took fifty Germans from a camp of twelve hundred and trucked them to a rock quarry. His orders were to return at the end of the day with fifty, "dead or alive." Wise had no trouble with these prisoners, however. He said that "they were just as good as they could be" and that he "wasn't afraid of them."[4]

The German prisoners assisted Wise's small detachment of engineers on the drilling operation and rockcrusher. Wise remembered how the men broke the limestone for road repair and railroad ballast: "We used . . . a churn drill. You put four men on it. That's where my men were working, on that drill. There was a handle on the drill pipe, and you put two [men] on one side and two on the other side, and they would lift that drill and drop it. It was a drop

German prisoners sit along the roadside as American troops pass. Many prisoners were put to work clearing and repairing roads, and as gravediggers at hospitals. As Guy Wise learned, some of the prisoners were happy to be in captivity after years of fighting in the trenches. Photograph from A. L. Fletcher, *History of the 113th Field Artillery, 30th Division* (Raleigh: History Committee of the 113th F.A., 1920), 87.

drill. The stone wasn't too overly hard. We would drill twelve or fifteen feet, load it with TNT powder, and set it off. It would just lay that stone right off, a piece twelve or fifteen feet high. . . . We had big sixteen pound hammers, and the Germans would break the stone up into pieces where they could handle it. We had wheelbarrows and planks where they could roll [the load of rock] to the crusher."[5]

Americans who guarded or worked beside German prisoners usually found the captives to be amiable and were many times sympathetic to their plight. Sergeant Wise recalled: "I was in among the gang [of prisoners], and I heard somebody say in good English, 'I hope this thing will soon be over so I can go back to New York.' I turned around, and I said, 'Now some of you fellows here can speak English—now talk, tell me something!' This fellow told me he was in New York four or five years, but he happened to be back over there [in Germany] at the time the war was declared, and he couldn't get away. He was wanting to get back to the United States."[6] In another situation, Wade Marshall, a marine corporal, was guarding a group of prisoners doing road work. Marshall was standing to the side smoking a cigarette, watching the Germans pass back and forth with wheelbarrows filled with rock. He noticed one German looking at him with longing eyes; the prisoner had spotted the cigarettes. The American gave the German the entire pack. To show his thanks, the prisoner tore an epaulet from his uniform and gave it to Marshall.[7] Had these two men met on the front they would have been mortal enemies; behind the lines they found it easy to be friends.

While prisoners contributed labor, it was the duty of the engineers and pioneers to keep the war effort going behind the lines, just as it was the duty of other soldiers to serve in the front lines. Together these men from the different units worked side by side, each with their respective duties. More than once James Covington and the other men of the Fifty-sixth Pioneer Regiment had to stop their work repairing roads and scramble out of the way of thundering artillery horses, wagons, and guns. As soon as they passed, the pioneers would step back into the road with their bags of rocks and continue to fill the holes.[8] Marion Andrews of the Thirteenth Field Artillery Regiment drove an ammunition supply wagon for his artillery battery. "Sometimes we would be alongside of the infantry," he remembered, "and again maybe we would be half a mile back. It all depended on the situation. We would go up to a bridge, and if the bridge was shot down, we put down pontoons and would go across. It took everybody, artillery, engineers, and everybody to do the job."[9]

Smith Cable, a private with the Fifth Field Artillery Regiment, was one of three soldiers responsible for an escort wagon in his battery. Cable explained: "I would say all together there were about four or five wagons to a battery. Then we had our caissons, all the ammunition to haul, and all our

Members of the 105th Engineer Regiment repair a road near Bellicourt, France, shortly after the Americans had broken through the Hindenburg Line on September 29, 1918. The engineers and pioneers had to work as quickly as possible rebuilding roads and bridges to maintain the supply line to the front. Their work often took them into combat areas where they were in as much danger from German artillery as the front-line infantry. Photograph from the files of the Division of Archives and History.

guns. I was assigned to this special wagon train that hauled ammunition. We used horses all the time. . . . I had a team of horses for hauling ammunition. . . . I rode one and the other was right there beside me. Each man had a team, and they had three teams to a wagon."[10] The American wagoners found that working with horses in France was at times challenging. French horses understood French, and captured German horses knew German, but neither responded to English commands. This resulted in miscommunication and confusion until a mutual understanding between man and horse could be worked out. Six horses were used to pull the heavy steel ammunition wagons, which carried several hundred rounds of ninety-pound 155mm shells. Typically, during battle the wagons would make two or three trips a night on existing roads or along paths cut through the forest.[11] Once the wagons reached the guns, another detail of soldiers unloaded the wagons and stacked the shells out of the enemy's view.

Taking supplies to the front could be confusing and dangerous. Otho Offman of the 321st Infantry Regiment was responsible for delivering ammunition each night to the front. He recalled that they had to be careful not to do anything that would attract enemy fire. "They said the Germans would drop a bomb on you if you lit a cigarette, so you had better not do that or somebody would get killed."[12] At night when no lights could be used, wagoners could easily get lost. Offman remembered that the only way they could keep on track was for an infantryman to come from the front and guide the ammunition wagons. This soldier, Offman recalled, "would walk in front of the team [of horses] with a piece of paper on his back so the driver could keep the team in the road."[13]

In addition to ammunition, food was carried to the front during the night. After a day of marching and fighting, the soldiers were hungry and usually received their daily rations after dark. Archie Ingram and Roby Yarborough were supply sergeants in the Thirtieth Division who delivered food to the front near Ypres, Belgium, at night. Ingram recalled that "one trip did them for the day," because in each nightly supply run they "had enough for two or three meals."[14] After the rations were cooked, they were loaded on two-wheel carts pulled by two mules or horses and guided by a soldier who rode one of the animals. Yarborough remembered one part of the trip to the Ypres front as being particularly hazardous: "The British had built this plank road over part of this distance from the base camp and the front line where the men were standing guard. That was low country, and a wagon would mire up almost anywhere. . . . From time to time the Germans would drop their artillery shells and blast part of [the road]. . . . I had the good fortune of never being caught in a barrage, but we did experience artillery shelling from time to time."[15]

Joe Thompson was a wagoner in the Thirtieth Division at Ypres. He recalled: "They gave us these instructions: 'Keep your head down all you can because the life you save might be your own. Pay attention to everything you see and hear and [don't] forget any of it, because it might help you get back!' "[16] Under the cover of darkness, Thompson would take his supplies to the front lines. He said: "You'd unload your equipment, and hear boom, boom, boom, boom, boom, boom, boom, and a big shell would come over and blow up over here, then over there, then over there. You were just lucky if you didn't get hit; it was all luck."[17] Thompson wasted no time on his return to the rear and had no difficulty driving his mules. "The mules I was working with, they had been wounded before," he said, "and I would unload my supplies and about half a mile I would run [them] about as fast as I could to get out of there, flying. They wanted to go, and I wanted them to go."[18]

The hungry soldiers at the front would never appreciate the perils faced by the ration supply teams each night because they lived every hour, day and night, under dangerous conditions. Nor would the frontline troops always be understanding when their rations arrived late. To be fair, however, the supply sergeants and the soldiers of the mess were not always to blame when the food was not delivered quickly enough. Sometimes they simply could not find the troops they were to feed, and at other times they had no food to prepare.

Sergeant Lawrence Crawford described the Services of Supply organization as it was supposed to work: "The army had a railhead somewhere in the area, and the division was supplied by that railhead. . . . Each company would bring in their request—how many men they had—and we would get that all together and consolidate it for the six companies. . . . We had a truck assigned to the headquarters, and we would take that truck and draw the rations and come back and divide it out."[19] This was the ideal situation, but many times what was divided out was inadequate. Even if it was sufficient, the mess sergeant's troubles were not over. Roby Yarborough remembered that "wood was so scarce we were sometimes hard put to find wood enough to keep the stoves going."[20] Despite these difficulties, the cooks made every effort, in most cases, to do their best for the soldiers, and the rations were delivered as soon as possible. Yarborough went so far as to switch the much-hated orange marmalade for strawberry jam when he could, because, as he put it, "I was partial to the men in my company, and I wanted to feed them the best I could," even at the risk of being caught by the English supply officers.[21]

The soldiers who hauled supplies and ammunition were not alone in traveling the roads of France and Belgium. As Smith Cable drove his team of horses pulling an ammunition wagon, he frequently encountered other

Truckers from the 306th Supply Train wait for trains delivering supplies at Rembervillars, France, on October 24, 1918. Trains would bring ammunition and food as close to the front as possible. Then the supplies were loaded on trucks or wagons to be taken to the battle lines. Photograph from the Military Collection, World War I, State Archives, Division of Archives and History, Raleigh.

114

doughboys returning from the front. "Oh Lord, have mercy," said Cable, "I've seen ambulance after ambulance loaded with wounded men."[22] Cable's duty was to carry forward the necessary supplies to keep the battle going, just as the Medical Corps was responsible for bringing back those who had suffered the consequences of war. During World War I, over 150,000 men and women served in the American Medical Corps, a military organization that worked with the American Red Cross in France.[23] Many of these "Red Cross Soldiers" were volunteers, including Charles Gibson, who enlisted in April 1918 at the age of twenty-three. "Colonel Fred Hanes and Colonel [J. Wesley] Long were organizing Base Hospital No. 65," Gibson recalled. "They were to have two hundred enlisted men. . . . I happened to become acquainted with some of the men who had enlisted, and that's why I enlisted."[24] After "joining up" he left Winston-Salem by train on April 5, 1918, with nineteen other volunteers and went into training at Fort McPherson, near Atlanta, Georgia.

In addition to the usual military drilling, every medical corpsman was taught basic battlefield first-aid techniques, which to Felix Brockman of the 321st Ambulance Company was "no medical training at all."[25] Corpsman Gibson did work for three weeks in the hospital at Fort McPherson, but he explained that he and the others were no more than stretcher-bearers, "to go out on the battlefield and bring in the wounded."[26] Any additional training was little more than the most elementary first aid, such as how to pin a blanket around an injured man and how to tie a tourniquet. William Grubb, a corpsman in the 321st Ambulance Company, also had a low opinion of the training that he had received before going to France. "We had some sessions on medical training," he said, "but I never did think they were too great. If you would find a man you would try to pick him up and get him where something could be done for him. That's the thing I worried about. I didn't care much about what they said."[27]

For the men of the Medical Corps, firsthand experience proved to be the best teacher, and even then what they learned often resulted from difficult and confusing situations. Most corpsmen served for a time in a camp hospital while still stateside. At other times they were on call for the almost predictable camp mishaps, and occasionally they had to respond to an unexpected disaster. While in training at Camp Jackson, South Carolina, the 321st Ambulance Company was confronted with one such tragic event. In May 1918, a troop train derailed while crossing a trestle, and several wooden boxcars toppled into a ravine. Nine soldiers were killed instantly in the crash, and many others were trapped in the wreckage. Felix Brockman saw the train as it fell from the trestle and knew that the results would be disastrous. He was a dispatcher in company headquarters at the time and rushed out to the sergeant. "They had just had an inspection," Brockman remembered, "and all of the ambulances were lined up. I told the sergeant in charge that there was an accident and a lot of men had been killed and to send the ambulances. He said, 'Where are your orders?' I told him to go to hell. You could hear the train whistle blowing. . . . The men disregarded the sergeant and went on to the wreck."[28] The corpsmen pulled about thirty-five injured soldiers from the broken debris and administered their newly learned first aid. Ambulances then carried the injured to the camp hospital for further treatment.[29] During their first medical emergency, these corpsmen disregarded regulations and acted on instinct, as they would continue to do once they were in France.

Four ambulance companies and four field-hospital organizations accompanied every infantry division to France.[30] In addition to these units, which served on the front lines with their divisions, the Red Cross and Army Medical Corps established numerous evacuation hospitals and 153 base hospitals behind the lines.[31] For the most part, the Red Cross initially secured personnel and equipment for these facilities. Ultimately, the hospitals were taken over by the Army Medical Corps, which supplied additional personnel and medical materials. Hospitals were usually located where the French had already established a medical facility or in a public building with sufficient space. They also needed to be near a railroad in order to transport the wounded from the front and to evacuation ports.[32] If a suitable location could not be found, the Army Corps of Engineers would build a hospital, and if necessary, construct a railroad.

During the fall of 1918, Corpsman Charles Gibson spent much of his time walking the wards of the newly constructed Base Hospital No. 65 in Kerhoun, France. The facility, located just four miles from the port of Brest, was established to alleviate the burden on three other American hospitals in the port city. In September, when the staff of approximately twenty doctors, one hundred nurses, and two hundred medical corpsmen arrived, the hospital buildings were unfinished. Long barracks, or wards, each containing beds for forty patients, two coal stoves, a kitchen, and a linen room, were soon thrown together. Though still lacking running water and electricity, the hospital was filled within two weeks with about two thousand influenza and pneumonia patients.[33] These sick soldiers came directly from the ships from the United States but little could be done for them. Gibson remembered that "they were just about dead before they got to us" and that "a lot of them didn't make it."[34] Gibson recalled that all they could do was to try to keep them warm, feed them if possible, and give them aspirin, the only form of medication administered. Of the some 3,300 influenza and pneumonia patients admitted to this one hospital, 569, or 17 percent, died.[35]

The influenza and pneumonia death rate for the American Expeditionary Force was as a whole much higher than that at Base Hospital No. 65. Nearly 70,000 cases of influenza were treated in the military hospitals in France during the fall and winter of 1918, and of this number, about 32 percent proved

Base Hospital No. 65 at Kerhoun, France, near Brest, was quickly constructed in the fall of 1918 to handle the growing number of sick and wounded American soldiers. Each building was a ward for forty patients. Within a week of the completion of construction, the hospital was overwhelmed with over three thousand influenza patients. Photograph from the files of the Division of Archives and History.

fatal.[36] In the training camps in the United States, there were 316,089 cases of influenza and 53,449 cases of pneumonia between September 14 and November 8, 1918. The fatality rate increased dramatically among soldiers training in the United States. Before mid-September, the cumulative fatality rate for all diseases for soldiers at home and abroad was five deaths for every one thousand soldiers per year. For the second week in October 1918 alone, the rate was four deaths per one thousand troops in the United States.[37]

The dreaded influenza epidemic appears to have been brought to the United States in the first shiploads of wounded from France in early 1918. In addition, infected recruits transported the disease to troops in Europe when they were shipped overseas. In this way the disease was continually spread back and forth between Europe and America, and from the army on the front to the soldiers in training in the United States. New recruits and medical personnel contracted the disease, including Julius Dillon of the Forty-sixth Engineer Regiment. Dillon saw many men die of the disease, including his friend Lewis J. Mumm of Mississippi, who lasted only a few days after the diagnosis. As for Dillon, he battled influenza for almost three weeks following the armistice before recovering.[38]

Influenza was not the only disease to plague the soldiers. Exposure to adverse weather conditions and other sick soldiers often caused problems. William Grubb and Horton Hall contracted pneumonia in the winter of 1917 while still in training in the United States. Grubb was at Fort Oglethorpe, Georgia, and was sent to the hospital. He was not attended by a doctor, and when a soldier in the next bed died of pneumonia, he became concerned and took his treatment into his own hands. He found a bottle of castor oil and drank about half of it. As soon as he could stand on his feet, he was assigned to hospital kitchen duty. This made the sick man so angry that he "just walked away from that damn place" and returned to camp.[39]

Horton Hall got sick at Camp Jackson and stayed in the hospital four weeks. He remembered: "I took the measles and was transferred to the base hospital, where I stayed for several weeks, taking pneumonia on top of the measles. . . . There were a lot of them with the measles and the flu—the old-timey flu that killed so many people during those years."[40] When he returned to camp, Hall had lost his coveted position as company clerk and was assigned as a machine gunner in an infantry squad.

During World War I, 83.6 percent of all disease fatalities in the U.S. Armed Forces were caused by the influenza-pneumonia pandemic. Of the remaining 16.4 percent, death was caused by a variety of diseases, including spinal meningitis, tuberculosis, typhoid fever, and measles.[41] At the time of the war, many diseases could be prevented because of recent medical break-throughs, and for the first time the military conducted mass inoculations of soldiers. After arriving in training camp and before being shipped overseas, every soldier received several types of inoculations. Many of the shots were potent, and some soldiers passed out. Isham Hudson remembered that many of his companions "would start to eat in the mess hall, and while standing in line to be served food, these men would just keel over and spill their beans, seven or eight [men] at a time."[42]

Not all of the diseases could be prevented, however. Influenza caused the greatest concern by far because of its high fatality rate. Measles was also dreaded because it usually preceded pneumonia. Spinal meningitis was highly contagious and could not be effectively prevented or treated. About two thousand American soldiers died from the disease during the war.[43] While in training at Camp Jackson, the Eighty-first Division had 244 cases, with 71 deaths.[44]

Two soldiers who served in the Eighty-first Division remembered the spinal meningitis outbreak. Felix Brockman of the 321st Ambulance Company recalled the panic that set in when the camp was confronted with the illness. "At Camp Jackson," he said, "we had a spinal meningitis epidemic. . . . I remember looking at one ambulance and there were a couple of guys in there rolling across [the floor]. The guy who was driving was afraid of catching the spinal meningitis from them, and he wouldn't slow down, and he was throwing them back and forth. They were quarantined, of course."[45] William Grubb was in training in the same company and remembered some unorthodox preventive measures that they were told to follow: "They told us to drink all the liquor, chew all the tobacco, and smoke all the cigarettes we wanted. We had a boy in our company who bought a suit of clothes and went to Florida and brought back a whole load of liquor. . . . They served it in the mess hall. The captain drank it, the colonel drank it, all of us drank it."[46] The use of these measures has been confirmed by other members of the division.

There was one disease General Pershing was determined to eradicate. Venereal disease was in this war, as in others, the enemy behind the front. In the first three years of World War I, the French army alone suffered some one million cases of venereal disease, and the rate of infection was also high among the British.[47] Secretary of War Newton Baker said, "I pledge my word to the mothers of America that their sons shall not be subject to undue temptation in America or in Europe."[48] While the secretary was given broad powers under the 1917 Army Bill to suppress prostitution in the United States, it was doubtful that effective measures could be taken once the soldiers were overseas. Nevertheless, Pershing was going to try. He pressed the medical department and combat officers to stress the need for moral behavior to the troops and stated that men who became unfit for duty because of "misconduct" would be punished.[49]

The results of Pershing's crusade against the disease were impressive, unmatched by any army up to that time. When he began his prevention campaign in November 1917, the rate of disability due to the disease was seventy-six ineffectives for every ten thousand soldiers in the American Expeditionary Force; by September 1918 the rate was down to nine per ten thousand.[50] This was a lower rate of infection than in the civilian population in the United States during the same period.[51] American military police were posted in the French "red light districts," much to the dismay of the French government. The presence of the MPs, Pershing's strict punitive measures, and the graphic medical education program caused many Americans to avoid these areas. The army's restrictions, however, did not end American liaisons with French women, nor during the postwar occupation, with German women. Isham Hudson expressed the thoughts of many of the soldiers interviewed when he said, "Some of the men didn't have better judgment, and they had to be guarded of the bad women, [but] they didn't have to guard me."[52] No soldier in Pershing's army could claim that he was not warned of the risks associated with unsafe sex.

Statistics for the AEF indicate that if stateside disease-related deaths of military personnel are excluded, the number of battle fatalities exceeded the number of deaths caused by disease for the first time in American military history. The number of combat-related deaths, 50,554 men, is more than double the 23,853 deaths caused by disease. Comparative percentages of American fatalities in Europe reveal that 64.9 percent died as a result of battle, 30.6 percent because of illness, and 4.5 percent due to various other causes. If the disease fatalities from stateside training camps are included, the combat percentage drops to 42.1 percent of total losses and the percentage of disease-related deaths rises to 52.2 percent, or 62,668 deaths.[53] Even with the inclusion of the training camp numbers, there is a reduction in the percentage of disease-related deaths compared to earlier American wars. In the Civil War twice as many soldiers died from disease as were lost in combat.[54] In the more recent Spanish-American War, more than five times as many men were lost to disease than to battle.[55]

The medical facilities behind the front lines were often well organized, but many times evacuating the wounded to those areas was difficult because of the intensity of combat, the broken terrain of the battlefield, and the shortage of medical personnel. If the wounded soldier could survive until he received medical attention, there was about a 95 percent chance of recovery and an 85 percent likelihood of returning to duty.[56] There was, however, a high risk that the wounded soldier would die on the battlefield before being found and evacuated.

Medical corpsmen, who struggled to locate and remove the wounded, knew that they too were at risk and that time was against them. Corpsman William Grubb recalled that when he found a fallen soldier, he "would get him on the litter anyway I could and get him in the ambulance as quick as I could."[57] Isham Hudson saw the corpsmen on the battlefield at St. Mihiel: "The stretcher-bearers would take off the pack of the wounded man, throw away his rifle, and would take him back to all the protection they could give him."[58] On a battlefield covered with the wounded of friend and foe alike, the medical corpsmen learned their priorities quickly. Smith Cable remembered that "they would pick up the wounded Americans quicker than the Germans. Until the battle was over they wouldn't mess with anybody else except the Americans. They would pick them up first thing, as soon as they could get to them."[59] To the wounded soldier, the corpsmen never arrived quickly enough, but despite the difficulties encountered, the doughboys of the Red Cross managed to save many from a battlefield death.

William Grubb of the 321st Ambulance Company was sent to the front several times to bring back the wounded. Grubb explained that once the men were placed in the ambulances and driven to the rear, they "would bring them to the first-aid dressing station first, [and] depending on how bad they were wounded, they were carried on to the field hospitals" located farther to the rear.[60] The medical team at the dressing station gave first consideration to the most severely wounded and tended the slightly wounded last. The corpsmen

William C. Grubb volunteered for military service in June 1917. In the fall of 1918, he was on the battlefields of the western front locating and transporting wounded men by ambulance to a field hospital behind the lines. Grubb said that he had received very little training as a medical corpsman and merely tried to find and take the wounded back to the doctors as quickly as possible. Photograph courtesy of Thomas A. Grubb.

"would patch up [the critically wounded soldiers] as little as they could and try to get them back to the field hospital as quick as they could," according to Grubb.[61] When the wounded soldiers arrived at the field hospitals, the men in danger of dying were immediately sent to the operating room, the men who had no hope of surviving were placed aside, and the others were sorted, and if severely wounded, sent on to the base hospitals.

Corpsman Julius Dillon of the Forty-sixth Engineer Regiment was assigned to a field hospital as soon as he arrived in France in July 1918. The hospital consisted of several tents and was staffed by four or five doctors and about twenty-five medical corpsmen. Here they handled every type of battle injury, including shrapnel and bullet wounds and injuries caused by poison gas. "If the wounded were too bad that they couldn't go back to the front," Dillon said, "then we would evacuate them back to the base hospital."[62] Those whose wounds were less serious were given time to recover and then sent back to the front to rejoin their units. After only a month this hospital was closed, and the staff was sent to other facilities.

The staff at Base Hospital No. 65 had not recovered from the overwhelming number of influenza cases when they received an allotment of battlefield wounded. At first, the wounded were either slightly injured or had no chance to live and were sent there to die. Shortly thereafter, however, they began to receive men whose wounds were not terminal but were serious. Most of these soldiers were wounded too severely to return to the front and were to be shipped to the United States when they were able to make the voyage. Corpsman Charles Gibson remembered these men and the difficult time the medical team had in treating their wounds. "Some of them didn't have but one leg," he said, "some of them one arm, some of them were crippled up with a shrapnel wound. . . . Shrapnel wounds were very hard to cure. Our medical supply was very limited. We didn't have much. We had aspirin, we had Vaseline gauze, and a baking solution to clean them."[63] Gibson, along with another enlisted man and two or three nurses, cared for the wounded in a ward of forty beds, assisted the doctors, and when necessary, carried out the dead.

Corpsman Gibson said that he received some satisfaction in knowing that he was relieving the pain of the wounded but that having to deal with the suffering and death "was quite an experience for me because I was right off the farm and [had] never seen anything like that."[64] Indeed, most never forgot the experience of caring for wounded soldiers. Carl Clodfelter was pulled from the infantry ranks during the battles of July 1918 and sent to several hospitals. He had never had any medical training but was soon working as an orderly in the operating room of one hospital and in a ward of another. He wrapped the damaged limbs of soldiers, once held a lantern over a patient during a brain operation, and like Gibson, carried the dead from the wards. Clodfelter described the feelings of many when he spoke of those who would not go

Charles H. Gibson joined the army in April 1918. He was trained as a corpsman at Fort McPherson, Georgia, before being sent to France in August. Gibson was assigned to Base Hospital No. 65 in Kerhoun, France, where first he cared for influenza patients off the ships from the United States and later tended the wounded from the front. This 1981 photograph was provided by the author.

home: "We buried them every day. We had a squad of Germans who dug the graves. They would take a ditch and dig it [twenty-five yards]. . . . Every morning we would carry the dead patients out. We would wrap a blanket around them and lay them down in there side by side. Yes, we lost a lot of men. Sometimes we would have a dozen or fifteen every morning who died in the hospital. . . . About the worst thing I've seen is maybe a dozen or fifteen men lying there wrapped in a blanket and those Germans throwing dirt in on them, with no protection, on those blankets."[65] When the Germans finished their task, Clodfelter and the other corpsmen tacked a dog tag to a board sticking up from the grave of each dead American.

Notes

1. Thompson, interview, December 19, 1985.
2. Thompson, interview, December 19, 1985.
3. American Battle Monuments Commission, *American Battle Fields*, 233.
4. Wise, interview, January 5, 1984.
5. Wise, interview, January 5, 1984.
6. Wise, interview, January 5, 1984.
7. Wade Latimer Marshall Jr., interview with author, Forsyth County, N.C., June 3, 1984.
8. Covington, interview, September 19, 1983.

9. Andrews, interview, October 30, 1981.
10. Cable, interview, September 16, 1983.
11. Cable, interview, September 16, 1983.
12. Offman, interview, January 12, 1984.
13. Offman, interview, January 12, 1984.
14. Ingram, interview, April 10, 1984.
15. Yarborough, interview, May 8, 1984.
16. Thompson, interview, December 19, 1985.
17. Thompson, interview, December 19, 1985.
18. Thompson, interview, December 19, 1985.
19. Crawford, interview, January 5, 1984.
20. Yarborough, interview, May 8, 1984.
21. Yarborough, interview, May 8, 1984.
22. Cable, interview, September 16, 1983.
23. Stallings, *Doughboys*, 381.
24. Gibson, interview, November 2, 1981.
25. Brockman, interview, January 5, 1984.
26. Gibson, interview, November 2, 1981.
27. Grubb, interview, January 5, 1984.
28. Brockman, interview, January 5, 1984.
29. Brockman, *Here, There, and Back*, 9-10.
30. *Division Insignia*, 28-29.
31. Stallings, *Doughboys*, 381.
32. Broun, *Our Army*, 159.
33. "Report of the Surgeon General," *War Department Annual Reports, 1919* , vol. 1, part 3 (Washington, D.C.: Government Printing Office, 1920), 3696.
34. Gibson, interview, November 2, 1981.
35. "Report of the Surgeon General," *1919*, 3697.
36. Pershing, *My Experiences*, 2:327.
37. Ayres, *War with Germany*, 125-126.
38. Dillon, interview, September 29, 1983.
39. Grubb, interview, January 5, 1984.
40. H. B. Hall, interview, November 3, 1981.
41. Ayres, *War with Germany*, 26.
42. Hudson, interview, October 27, 1981.
43. Ayres, *War with Germany*, 126.
44. Lemmon, *North Carolina's Role*, 60.
45. Brockman, interview, January 5, 1984.
46. Grubb, interview, January 5, 1984.
47. Stallings, *Doughboys*, 180.
48. Taft et al., *Service*, 1:116.
49. Pershing, *My Experiences*, 1:177.

50. Ayres, *War with Germany*, 128.
51. Taft et al., *Service*, 1:117.
52. Hudson, interview, October 27, 1981.
53. Vincent J. Esposito, "War Casualties," in *A Concise History of World War I*, ed. Vincent J. Esposito (New York: Frederick A. Praeger, 1964), 373.
54. E. B. Long, *The Civil War Day by Day: An Almanac, 1861-1865* (Garden City, N.Y.: Doubleday and Company, 1971), 710-711.
55. Ayres, *War with Germany*, 124.
56. "War Surgery," in *The European War*, vol. 17 (New York: New York Times Company, 1919), 119.
57. Grubb, interview, January 5, 1984.
58. Hudson, interview, October 27, 1981.
59. Cable, interview, September 16, 1983.
60. Grubb, interview, January 5, 1984.
61. Grubb, interview, January 5, 1984.
62. Dillon, interview, September 29, 1983.
63. Gibson, interview, November 2, 1981.
64. Gibson, interview, November 2, 1981.
65. Clodfelter, interview, September 19, 1983.

Chapter Seven
"Fighting to Beat the Band":
The Meuse-Argonne Campaign

On the afternoon of September 29, 1918, following the breakthrough of the Hindenburg Line, the Americans watched in wonder as captured German troops were marched down the roads to internment camps. One North Carolinian, William F. Crouse of the 105th Engineer Regiment, recalled: "That evening the Germans commenced coming back at us like flies, giving up. The road was full of them, some old men and some young boys. We knew they weren't going to last long. We had a lieutenant from Tennessee, one of the finest fellows ever I knew, and he said, 'Boys, this thing can't last much longer.' We had prisoners come back there, and they looked like they weren't sixteen or seventeen years old, just kids and old men."[1] For these Germans, and for thousands like them, the war was over. From the front, they came to be shuffled away to some distant prison camp behind the Allied lines.

After a brief rest following the breakthrough of the Hindenburg Line at Bellicourt, the American Thirtieth Division renewed its drive against the battle-weary Germans. In the weeks to follow, prisoners continued to filter through the American lines, many of whom "were just kids and glad to be captured," according to Archie Ingram.[2] Not all of the Germans were beaten so easily, however, as evidenced by American casualty figures. The Thirtieth Division suffered 4,113 casualties during the two-week period that ended October 20, 1918.[3] The British army to which the Thirtieth Division was attached sustained 121,000 casualties during October.[4]

Archie Ingram of the 119th Infantry knew firsthand the cost of the recent battles. At night he commanded a supply detail that took rations to the front and then returned with the dead loaded on two-wheel limbers. He recalled the struggle he had on the night of October 17, 1918, when he brought back a friend from High Point: "We took our rations up one night and brought back a load of dead, two or three. They were all wrapped up; you couldn't see them. Private [John D.] Grant was one of them. . . . He got a machine-gun bullet. We were coming out of there, and I met his brother [Charles E. Grant]. He told me about [John] getting killed and said, 'I'm going up there, and I'm going to shoot until they kill me.' I said, 'No, don't do that!' I talked him out of it."[5]

Archie Ingram was a resident of High Point and joined the local National Guard unit before the war. Companies were organized in most towns across the state. Men serving in these companies often had grown up together, and in many cases, brothers served in the same unit. Ingram encountered the tragic consequences of this arrangement when he had to calm a soldier whose brother had just been killed in combat. This photograph was taken in 1987 and provided courtesy of Norris Ingram, Ila Mae Canter, and Kenneth Ingram.

Despite Allied losses, the kaiser's forces were beaten on every front. Marshal Foch saw his opportunity and pushed French, British, Belgian, and American armies to the limit in order to win a decisive victory before winter weather stopped the advance. The Allies might suffer tremendous casualties, but the Germans would lose the war.

Far to the south of the British front, the American First Army under Pershing was engaged in a campaign of its own. As previously discussed, Pershing had to fight a personal battle with Foch on August 30, 1918, over Foch's plan to divide the American divisions among the Allied armies. This was unacceptable to Pershing, who was trying to build up his own army and keep it from being dispersed to foreign commanders. At this same conference Pershing proposed that a united American army assume the offensive in one of the two French combat sectors. In response to Pershing's insistence, Foch agreed to turn over the more difficult sector on the Meuse-Argonne front to the American First Army.[6]

This area was one of the most challenging on the western front in which to attempt an advance. The Germans had held the region since 1914, when they made their first drive on Verdun, and in 1917 and 1918 had constructed an elaborate defensive system. Unlike the defenses facing the British and central French fronts, where the German trenches were great distances apart, there were three strong German trench lines opposite Pershing that were close together and stretched back from no-man's-land for fifteen miles. The lay of the land also created problems for Pershing. The Argonne Forest, a great wooded area filled with deep ravines, wire entanglements, and countless machine-gun positions, stood on the American left flank. High ground along the Meuse River was on the far right flank. The forest and heights were held by the Germans. Between the forest and the river was the first German trench line, which included the fortified town of Montfaucon, situated on a hilltop commanding the entire region. Behind Montfaucon the land was relatively open, broken by small wooded areas, a few scattered villages, and two additional German trench lines.[7] Pershing was determined to break through the German positions within a few days. General Pétain, French veteran of many bloody campaigns, thought that the Americans would do no better than take the Montfaucon garrison by winter.[8]

The ultimate objective of the Meuse-Argonne campaign was to force the enemy back from their forward positions and cut the vital railroad at Sedan and Mézières. If this could be done the German armies would be divided, their lines of supply and communication disrupted, and the best route for a retreat to Germany blocked.[9] In the two weeks following the Battle of St. Mihiel, Pershing massed 600,000 American soldiers and moved them to the Meuse-Argonne front. Because the veteran American divisions had been exhausted in the previous months of battle, Pershing used mostly inexperienced troops in the initial assault on the morning of September 26, 1918. Five of the nine divisions in the attack had never been in combat, and four had not been equipped with their own artillery.[10] Nevertheless, the men began what was up until that time the largest battle in American military history.

The first phase of the forty-seven-day Meuse-Argonne campaign produced mixed results. Pershing was disappointed, though his army's accomplishments were impressive by most standards. Pershing had planned to drive the Germans back ten miles in the initial attack and break through the main enemy defensive line within two days. Instead, after two days the Americans had advanced only seven miles and had just breached the first of the three German trench lines, but could go no further. The delay was caused in part by the entanglements of the Argonne Forest, but this had been anticipated. The main reason for the delay was that the fortress at Montfaucon had stopped the Americans cold on the first day of battle. Rather than pushing ahead, the doughboys had to regroup and take an extra day to reduce the garrison. During this time, the Germans moved six reserve divisions into the Kriemhilde Line, the second and main defensive trench line between Pershing and the Sedan-Mézières Railway.[11] It was here that the American advance bogged down. The advancing force had outdistanced its artillery support, lost most of its armor (thirty tanks were destroyed in one two-mile advance), and its supplies were ensnared in the confusion far to the rear.[12] During the next four days the weary and now much-experienced American divisions straightened their lines, and then were finally replaced before the second attack.

Pershing was unjustly criticized by other Allied leaders for the breakdown in supply and support efforts during the first phase of the campaign. Several factors were responsible for the problems. Despite Pershing's good intentions and great effort, his army was not prepared for a major offensive. Troop ships from the United States could not provide men quickly enough to replace the American battlefield losses. Rather than being sent into combat training, many of the infantry divisions that arrived in the summer of 1918 were immediately dispersed to provide replacements to frontline divisions. Because these newly arrived soldiers were deficient in training and had no combat experience before being thrown into battle, they fell in greater numbers, thereby requiring yet another round of replacements. Because the shipment of men was paramount in 1918, the transporting of trucks, mules, and horses fell far behind schedule. In July, Pershing requested that 25,000 horses and mules be sent to France per month, but only 2,000 were received in the three months prior to the Meuse-Argonne battle. Too few trucks were received for the number of road construction projects, for hauling supplies, and for the transporting of soldiers to the front and the wounded to the rear.[13]

Closer to the actual battlefield, Pershing's troubles were almost insurmountable. There were few roads in the region, and those that did exist were severely damaged by shellfire. The rest of the terrain was also badly broken by shell holes and was far too muddy for wagons and trucks to cross. This was especially true after September 27 when rain fell for forty out of forty-seven days, so that every shell crater filled with water and each depression became a stream. In this morass the supply organization's attempts to struggle forward were constantly blocked or bogged down, leaving the infantry without sufficient food or ammunition. Ambulances returning from the front with the wounded were also mired in the mud and unable to reach the field hospitals. Each day the problems became more acute and more threatening to the success of Pershing's campaign.

The experiences of one Eighty-first Division soldier exemplify the difficulties a transport convoy could encounter. In September 1918, Robert Hamlin of the 306th Ammunition Train drove a Ford truck to the Meuse-Argonne front. His vehicle was part of a convoy of seventy-two trucks loaded with ammunition that left Dijon and arrived at the front just as the battle began. Hamlin, who was inexperienced in driving a horseless vehicle, carried machine-gun ammunition in his load. The trip was uneventful until the convoy neared the front, but then, Hamlin recalled, "just before dark we stopped at a little village to eat, and a German plane came over and bombed that town. They didn't see all of our seventy-two trucks sitting out there loaded. If they had just dropped a bomb on one of them the whole chain of them would have exploded."[14] Hamlin and the other drivers fled into the fields outside the village and watched the bombing with trepidation. After the enemy plane departed, the soldiers hurried to their trucks and continued their journey. After this near disaster, however, the driving was done only at night.

Hamlin and the other drivers encountered confusion at the front. They were not allowed to use their head lamps while driving and thus had to travel close to each other in order not to get separated. Hamlin made a mistake that almost had dire results for the drivers following him. "Our convoy had to pass an entire division that night to get in front of them," he said. "We had orders to, but one time we were blocked. I hadn't had any sleep in forty-eight hours and when we stopped I got out and walked around my truck to keep from going to sleep. But I went to sleep anyway on a pile of crushed stone. An artillery shell fell about twenty yards of me and killed some horses [but did not wake him]. Then somebody kicked me and woke me up and said, 'Get the hell out of here, you're holding up the entire convoy,' which I was because the others had gone. I didn't know which way they went except straight down the road. I came to the forks in the road, and I didn't know which way to go so I got out. The roads were dusty enough to make tracks so I followed those tracks and soon caught up with the rest of the convoy."[15]

After this experience Hamlin was determined not to lose sight of the other trucks again, but soon thereafter his truck blew a tire and he had to pull out of line. The tires "had those old fashioned rims that you had to prize [*sic*] apart to get the tire on and off," but Hamlin, who did not want to be left behind, got the tire repaired and back in place just as the last truck in the convoy passed.[16] Hamlin's tribulations are indicative of the problems faced throughout the supply organization and help to explain why Pershing's advance was slowly brought to a halt.

In this campaign all of the Americans did not fight on Pershing's immediate front. In addition to the divisions loaned to the British, about half a dozen other divisions were sent to other fronts, sometimes under Pershing's direction, occasionally under French supervision. The Eighty-first and Ninety-second Divisions began their active service in the Vosges Mountains, about eighty miles southeast of Verdun, and then were moved closer to the Meuse-Argonne front later in October 1918. The Vosges Mountain sector was considered a quiet area and was used to train new troops in the details of trench fighting. From September 1918 to the end of the war, however, the Americans increased their activity in the area to make the Germans believe that an attack in the Vosges Mountains was imminent.[17] When pressure was put on the enemy in this area, they responded in kind, and what was once a "quiet area" was quiet no longer.

Two soldiers, William Morris and Horton Hall, received their baptism of fire in the Vosges Mountains in the fall of 1918, and both had similar experiences. William Morris of Stokes County was a draftee in the Ninety-second Division. This division was offered initially to the British in May 1918 but was not accepted by the British government because it was composed of African American soldiers. Pershing was surprised at the British response and took these men back into his fold without reservation. He wrote Field Marshal Sir Douglas Haig that, unlike the British, he would not discriminate against these American citizens.[18] Accordingly, the soldiers of the Ninety-second Division were sent into the line previously held by the French. There they proved themselves to be equal in combat to any enemy or Allied soldier.

Morris had been in the trenches near St. Dié for a few weeks when he was first called to fire on the enemy. He was one of two gunners in his squad with a French Chauchat automatic rifle and was in a dugout when an officer came tumbling down and ordered him to the firing line. As he lifted his weapon into place, Morris saw several Germans in no-man's-land. "They were putting a mine under the hill we were on," he said. "We could hear them digging. We had an observation post, and a guy stayed on there, looking. He spied those guys over there digging. They called a French Chauchat squad up there, and it happened to fall on my luck to have to go. I opened up on them. . . . I never will forget it."[19] Morris was haunted by the results of his actions and did not want the details of this incident disclosed, but it can be said that the Germans did not return to their lines.

The following day Morris's regiment, the 365th Infantry, was called into the frontline trenches in anticipation of a German attack. The previous night had been much too quiet. They were usually shelled each evening, but that night nothing fell. The fears of a German assault were well-founded. The Americans were attacked, but as Morris remembered, that was not half the story: "The next morning they attacked. Their field artillery started shelling us, and we shot up a signal to our artillery [when the German infantry came in sight]. Our artillery got the wrong signal. The signal that they got was like the Germans had taken our front lines, and we had fallen back. So, when they threw it they threw it on our front lines, and we hadn't gotten out. . . . We were shelled by the German artillery and our own for a while . . . and we were still there holding the line."[20] Several Americans were killed or wounded by the shellfire. Morris firmly believed that many were hit by friendly fire, including a friend who was killed. The mistake was corrected when the same sergeant who had fired the wrong signal in the first place finally sent up the correct one, and the artillery adjusted its fire. Meanwhile, the German attack collapsed in all the confusion, and the German infantry returned to their lines. After this ordeal, the Ninety-second Division was pulled from their battered trenches and ultimately sent to the Meuse-Argonne front.

Horton Hall, along with the rest of the Eighty-first Division, was sent into the trench sector vacated by the Ninety-second Division. In the first week of October, Hall's regiment, the 323rd Infantry, occupied a segment of the trench line, and like their predecessors, they soon received their first shelling. On October 5, 1918, Hall wrote in his diary: "We are getting our first baptism of fire. All day and night the shells are screaming. Their warning shriek is a life saver. Standing watches of six hours or more and being under a continual hail of fire, while the mud of the trenches keeps our feet cold, and the least sound is magnified a thousand times, is not pleasant, but it is war."[21] It was war indeed, but luckily for Hall and his friends the vast majority of the enemy shells fell well behind their trenches. What Hall and the others did not know, however, was that the Germans were planning an assault on the American lines, an attack that came only a few days after his diary entry.

When the assault occurred Hall was in the front lines and saw about eight hundred Germans charging in four waves, firing as they came. The Americans were ordered to hold their fire until the enemy came to within one hundred yards and then to make every shot count. Hall recalled: "The first wave was shot down, didn't a single one of the Germans make it to our trenches. The second wave kept coming. It looked like they would have taken warning and not come on, but they kept coming until they walked over the dead men of the first wave, and they were shot down, the biggest part of them. . . . Then another wave came—the Germans were just suicidal."[22] By the time the third wave of Germans was decimated, the Americans were out of ammunition. When the last wave of Germans came close enough, most of the Americans were ordered to charge out of the trenches and "go at them with the bayonets."[23] The enemy was driven back, and many Germans were captured. Hall's squad had been told to remain in the trenches, however. He was not disappointed in being left behind, because as Hall put it, "I was more scared of a bayonet than anything else."[24] That night his company was relieved by other troops, and on October 19, the Eighty-first Division was pulled out of the St. Dié sector and sent into reserve near Verdun.

Another unit initially separated from Pershing's Meuse-Argonne campaign was the veteran Second Division. At the request of General Pétain, this division was sent to the French Fourth Army located on the front between the Argonne Forest and the city of Rheims. In conjunction with the American First Army, this French army attacked the German lines on September 26, 1918, but like Pershing's force, stalled after a few days of heavy fighting. The French were able to push the Germans back through the town of Sommepy at the base of the wooded Blanc Mont ridge but were unable to budge the Germans from the heights. On the night of October 1, the Second Division moved into the forward lines and replaced the exhausted French troops. It was hoped that the Americans would jolt the Germans out of the fortified heights and help the French regain their lost momentum.

The rolling countryside in this area was devastated by shellfire. Jack Marshall of the Fifteenth Field Artillery Regiment remembered that the "land there was really torn up, not any green anywhere. Everything was dead, and the ground was torn up with shell holes. All the trees were dead."[25] After his artillery battery established a position for the attack, Jack Marshall and his brother Matt hiked around the area and salvaged some scrap sheet metal to build a shelter. Before they could finish their work, Jack was called to the frontline trenches to be a forward observer. Matt continued to work on the shelter, but Jack was destined never to return there from the front.

On the evening of October 2, 1918, the infantry and marines of the Second Division made a preliminary attack to gain a suitable jumping-off point for the next morning's assault on Blanc Mont. The attack was made on a two-mile front west of Sommepy. While the infantry and marines advanced, the artillery shelled the German positions. Just prior to this barrage, Jack Marshall and a lieutenant moved forward to observe the fire of the guns and call in range adjustments. Marshall stood in a foxhole in front of the trenches with the phone set and relayed the coordinates shouted down by the officer, who stood with field glasses in the open ground. After the American bombardment began and the soldiers moved forward, the Germans returned fire.

One German shell exploded near the artillery lieutenant and Marshall. Somehow the officer was unharmed, but Jack Marshall, hidden in the foxhole, was hit by a shell fragment the size of a coffee cup. He thought he had lost his leg because of the intense pain he felt at that moment. "I didn't know where my leg was off," Marshall said. "I just kept feeling down until I found where it [the wound] was. . . . I just heard it hit down in the hole, and my whole leg went numb. The officer asked where I was hit, then pushed me back into the hole and told me to stay there until he got help. I stayed there until the stretcher-bearers came and pulled me out."[26]

As it so happened, Marshall's brother Matt was one of the stretcher-bearers who carried him to an ambulance. Jack was placed in a Ford truck with four other wounded soldiers and rushed to a field hospital, then ultimately to a base hospital where he remained until January 7, 1919.[27]

As Marshall lay in the hospital with a wound in his right ankle, the men of the Second Division continued to fight for Blanc Mont. After a fierce struggle, the Germans yielded the position, one they had held since 1914, and retreated behind the Aisne River. For the Second Division, this battle ended on October 9, when it was relieved by the American Thirty-sixth Division. The veteran Second Division had driven the Germans back about four miles, had taken 1,963 prisoners, and had captured a large quantity of supplies. The

CLASS OF SERVICE	SYMBOL
Telegram	
Day Letter	Blue
Night Message	Nite
Night Letter	N L

If none of these three symbols appears after the check (number of words) this is a telegram. Otherwise its character is indicated by the symbol appearing after the check.

WESTERN UNION

TELEGRAM

NEWCOMB CARLTON, PRESIDENT   GEORGE W. E. ATKINS, FIRST VICE-PRESIDENT

CLASS OF SERVICE	SYMBOL
Telegram	
Day Letter	Blue
Night Message	Nite
Night Letter	N L

If none of these three symbols appears after the check (number of words) this is a telegram. Otherwise its character is indicated by the symbol appearing after the check.

RECEIVED AT   258PM

5 Rd Ms-23 Gov

WA Washington,D.C. 12/9/18.

Mr.William M.Marshall,RFD 4,
        Walnut Cove,N.C.

Deeply regret to inform you that it is officially reported that
private Roy J.Marshall field artillery was slightly wounded in
action about October third further information when received.
                        Harris the Adjutant General.

The telegrams that every family with a serviceman overseas dreaded came with increasing frequency to North Carolina homes during the latter stages of the war. This telegram was sent to the parents of Jack Marshall to notify them of the wounding of their son during the Meuse-Argonne offensive. Fortunately for this family, the news was not as bad as it might have been. Their son recovered and came home in 1919. Telegram courtesy of the R. Jack Marshall family.

division lost 209 officers and 4,764 enlisted men, killed, wounded, or missing, during the eight-day battle.[28] At the end of October, the Second Division moved into the front line in the Meuse-Argonne sector and again assisted in breaking the German lines.

Progress on the Meuse-Argonne front was slow during the first week in October. Pershing, who was receiving harsh criticism from the Allies because of his lack of success, reopened the offensive on October 4 after moving several veteran divisions into line. Even then the Germans could not be driven from the Argonne Forest or the Kriemhilde Line, though some advances were made. The attack on the Kriemhilde Line was still held up by enfilading artillery fire from the heights above the Meuse River. To prevent additional losses from the bombardment, Pershing changed his plans and on October 8 sent two divisions across the river to assist the French in clearing the enemy from the area. At the same time, he redoubled his efforts to clear the Argonne Forest, which was finally captured on October 10. Several days later, when the Meuse River heights were cleared, Pershing resumed the attack on the Kriemhilde Line.[29] American losses dating from the opening of the battle already totaled about seventy-five thousand men, of whom over eight thousand were killed in action.[30]

For those who fought in the Meuse-Argonne campaign, the endless pounding of German shellfire was unforgettable. Jack Marshall was under enemy artillery fire several times before he was finally wounded. He saw the effects of the shelling and soon learned to listen for each incoming projectile. "The trees were all shot up," he said. "Most of the time you couldn't even walk. Some of the German shells had fuses on them that a twig would set off if it hit it. Some of their shells had impact fuses. I've seen many shells hit the ground and keep going until hitting hard dirt before going off. When they went off it would throw dirt everywhere."[31]

Generally, the Germans fired their shells behind the American lines to disrupt the support and supply lines and isolate the frontline troops. For this reason, the men who served behind the lines considered themselves to be in as much danger as the infantrymen on the front. According to Marion Andrews of the Thirteenth Field Artillery Regiment: "Some say that the infantry had the worst part of it, but that's not true. If you were in the infantry you could get behind a tree, and a man could shoot at you all day and not hit you. But if he throws a big shell at you, one of those big 4.7s [155mm] at you, then you and the tree are both gone."[32]

Andrews went on to observe: "I didn't mind the ones that woozed-bammed, but the ones that bammed-woozed, they were dangerous. The [shells] coming over, you could detect where they were going to be. But if it bangs and then wizzed, then it has done what it is going to do and then it's too late to duck your head. Most of those shells you could hear coming, and you could halfway protect yourself."[33] Only a few days after the Thirteenth Field Artillery Regiment reached the front, a shell found Andrews and a group of his friends. "Five of us were in an escort wagon sleeping," Andrews recalled. "Another man was under the wagon. Two studhorses [were] tied to the front wheels, and two studhorses [were] tied to the back wheels. [The shell] killed one of the four horses and one of the men and wounded four. . . . I was one of the four wounded."[34] A small piece of shell fragment passed through the calf of Andrews's left leg. Thinking the wound to be rather minor, Andrews refused to report to the field hospital. After a week, however, he had blood poisoning and had to undergo weeks of treatment.

Marshall and Andrews, who were both wounded by shellfire, understandably believed shellfire to be the greater threat during war. Many others almost lost their lives or were killed by the shells. Isham Hudson and other soldiers of the Forty-second Division were sent to the front about October 14 and were immediately subjected to the endless German shelling. Hudson described the terrible experience: "We were under constant artillery fire during that time. . . . It was awfully hard and hazardous to get food into where the men were on those front lines. . . . Two soldiers brought it [the food] in a big wooden container. . . . They didn't attempt to parcel it out; they said, 'Here it is, if you want it come and get it.' We had this one fellow in our outfit who was shell-shocked, and he was so afraid he wouldn't get his food, but I brought him some food. I recall that one man had eaten in a deep hole he had dug, but a shell fell right on top of him, right in the hole he had dug, and just split him open. Of course, he was killed."[35]

Perhaps the only thing worse than sitting in a foxhole waiting for that one shell to make a direct hit was being detailed to unload ammunition while under fire. Robert Hamlin of the 306th Ammunition Train arrived at the front with a convoy, and while he and others were removing ammunition from the trucks, the Germans opened fire. Hamlin remembered that he and his fellow soldiers did not remain at their post very long. "Machine-gun bullets were kicking up the dirt all around us," he said. "There was a dugout out there about a hundred yards from us, and we all went to the dugout, and if we missed the hole we made one. A good run is always better than a bad stand."[36]

Sometimes, however, taking cover was impossible. Smith Cable of the Fifth Field Artillery Regiment was in that situation one day when he was on the Meuse-Argonne front. He was riding one of six horses pulling an ammunition wagon when the Germans began to shell the area. He recalled: "They shelled us pretty heavy. . . . That's where I had a horse killed right beside me. A shell hit right under it, but I was on the other horse, and this other one was beside me. . . . A shell [fragment] hit him in the throat and cut his jugular vein, and he had to be shot."[37]

Marion A. Andrews (right) poses with an unidentified friend, ca. 1919. Andrews volunteered in 1917 and became a wagoner in the Thirteenth Field Artillery Regiment, Fourth Division. The division arrived in France in May 1918 and went into action almost immediately. Andrews was subjected to heavy artillery fire in three battles and was wounded in the left leg by a shell fragment on the Meuse-Argonne front in October 1918. Photograph courtesy of the Marion A. Andrews family.

In the artillery duel during the Meuse-Argonne campaign, the Americans gave as well as they got. Over two thousand artillery pieces were used by the Americans during the Meuse-Argonne campaign. The pounding of these guns and the relentless infantry assaults finally resulted in the defeat of the German divisions in the region, but not the total collapse of the enemy. After the Americans broke out of the Argonne Forest, they attacked the German Kriemhilde Line, which was breached October 14. On November 1, the last German trench line was broken by American troops. The Germans retreated toward Sedan, with the American First Army and the newly created Second Army still pressing forward. The Americans had suffered tremendous casualties—by November 1, over 24,000 men had been killed since the beginning of the battle.[38]

Pershing's advance was too slow for some Allied leaders, however, and they talked of having him relieved of command. Marshal Foch would not permit it. Foch realized that Pershing was doing more than merely winning back a limited area of French territory. Pershing's campaign was causing the Germans to transfer twenty-seven reserve divisions to face the Americans, thus making advances by the other Allied armies easier.[39]

General Erich Ludendorff resigned his command under pressure on October 27, 1918, and therefore was not in control of the crumbling German army when Pershing initiated his last offensive in the Meuse-Argonne campaign. On November 1, after moving additional reserve divisions to the front, the American commander sent his troops finally to cut the Sedan-Mézières Railway. In just over a week the Americans advanced twenty-four miles, over twice the distance covered in the month of October. On November 7, the vital railroad fell into American hands, thus cutting off communication and supplies to the German armies in northern France from the city of Metz and insuring the ultimate defeat of the kaiser's forces.[40]

The last of Germany's allies, Austria-Hungary, fell on November 3, and the German kaiser abdicated on November 9. The German government had asked the American president for terms to end the war as early as mid-October, while the fighting was raging in the Argonne Forest. Although the men in the field were unaware of these events, rumors about a possible German surrender were circulating among the American soldiers during the first week of November. But while the talk was of peace, the fighting continued.

Corporal John Adams, a newcomer to the war, marched to the front with the 321st Infantry Regiment, past men who had fallen a few days before. "The first thing I saw going up to the front," Adams remembered, "was five men lying on the ground dead. Some of them had their guts hanging out where they had been killed by shrapnel, and it was pretty bad to see."[41] The sight of the slain American soldiers left a lasting impression on Adams. He recalled that after marching from the spot where he had seen the dead soldiers and on to the front, he thought about the possibility of being hit. He said, "If I was hit by shrapnel or a bullet I was hoping it would kill me so I wouldn't have to suffer or be left behind."[42] Adams did not experience combat until the week before the armistice, unaware that the politicians had already decided to end the war and merely had to work out the details of a cease-fire. Meanwhile, Adams and his friends would continue to fight, and some would die.

"You had to be a little bit particular when you were on the front lines," recalled Gladney Clarke of the 322nd Infantry Regiment.[43] Adams and Clarke, with the other infantrymen of the Eighty-first Division, were sent into the front lines on November 7. They had come from the Vosges Mountains and, after being in reserve for a few weeks, were called into action on the far right flank of the American First Army. The division, which included many North Carolina draftees, was sent "over the top" across the Woëvre Plain on the east side of the Meuse River, northeast of Verdun, on November 9. These

John F. Adams was drafted in December 1917 and assigned to the 321st Infantry Regiment, Eighty-first Division. He arrived in France in July 1918, soon after being promoted to corporal. After training in a quiet sector, his division went into action northeast of Verdun on November 9. Adams recalled seeing the dead on his way to the front and remembered his fear of being wounded and left behind. The photograph on the left was taken ca. 1918; the one on the right, November 7, 1981. Photographs courtesy of the John Flem Adams family and the author.

mostly inexperienced doughboys captured abandoned trenches and several villages with minimal losses. The German resistance soon stiffened, however, and these new recruits had to fight harder. Clarke remembered that the Germans were "fighting to beat the band" and in the last few days had killed two members of his company who shared his last name, only "they didn't have the 'e' on the end of it."[44] He was concerned that his poor mother might mistakenly be informed that he had been killed, but fortunately the military kept the paper work in order.

The German positions, hastily constructed across the rolling countryside in front of the Eighty-first Division, slowed but did not stop the American advance. Horton Hall, an automatic rifleman in the 323rd Infantry Regiment, recalled that "we advanced that day [November 10] approximately a mile or two miles from our trenches, from where we had taken the German trenches away from them and driven them out, and they left machine guns with one or two men to man the machine guns to try to hold us back. The sector we came under the heaviest fire on that day was on a hillside where the grass was about knee high, and when we started up that hill every man had to crawl like a snake, [and] we crawled all day long up that hill."[45] Not once during the long maneuver did Hall or the others have a chance to return fire. He spent the entire time pushing his new American-made Browning automatic rifle ahead of him as he crawled under the weight of 150 rounds of ammunition packed in .30 caliber twenty-shot clips. Two other men in his squad followed with an

Horton B. Hall was a schoolteacher in Wilkes County when he was drafted in December 1917. He was assigned to the 323rd Infantry Regiment, Eighty-first Division, as an automatic rifleman. As he recalled, he spent most of November 10, 1918, crawling under fire toward German positions. At the end of the day, he and his squad were put out of action by poison gas. This 1981 photgraph was provided by the author.

additional 150 rounds of ammunition for Hall, along with their own rifles and ammunition.

As the infantrymen neared the top of the hill, they were told "not to hide behind the bushes because that was the most dangerous place to be." Hall remembered that "there was a bunch of bushes not far from my squad, just on one side of it. Our squad had moved over one way, and the squad adjoining us had moved over the other way. We were going to bypass the bushes about ten or fifteen feet because it was a very dense bush grown up into shrubbery. . . . Just about the time we were bypassing it, the Germans cut loose from a machine gun from another hill and shot that bunch of shrubbery all to pieces. They shot thousands of shells through that bunch of shrubbery."[46]

The 323rd Infantry continued to push forward, and by the end of the day, the Germans started firing poison-gas shells to try to stop the American advance. This time Hall and his squad were caught unprepared. "We had been on the go driving them back all day long," he said, "and my whole squad got gassed. We were ordered by our lieutenant to march back down the hill to the first-aid station. . . . When we got to the first-aid station the medics examined us for gas. . . . Everyone who showed the effects of it was put into the ambulance . . . and sent further back to a field hospital for treatment."[47] Hall's squad leader, Corporal Rolin K. Pope, a South Carolinian, received the worst dose of phosgene gas of the group, but most of them, including Hall, returned to the front on November 12, the day after the armistice.[48]

Corporal Pope's squad was not alone in suffering from poison gas during the last days of the war. Matt Marshall of the Fifteenth Field Artillery Regiment and Robert Hamlin of the 306th Ammunition Train were also victims. After jumping into a shell hole to avoid enemy fire, Marshall was choked with mustard gas before he could put on his mask.[49] Hamlin was on a supply train with two other guards when he was affected by poison gas. The three men were asleep in one of the railroad cars, and Hamlin was awakened when he started to cough. He revived the other two soldiers, who were quickly sent to a field hospital, but Hamlin, like Marshall, refused treatment.[50] Both men suffered respiratory problems for the rest of their lives. They were two of over seventy thousand reported gas-injury cases the Americans suffered during the war.[51]

William Morris of the Ninety-second Division also knew what it was like to be gassed and shot at near the end of the war. His regiment, the 365th Infantry, was sent into action east of the Meuse River on November 10 as part of the American Second Army. They attacked the Bois Frehaut and were subjected to a terrific storm of German machine-gun and artillery fire. Morris recalled that "if you stuck your head up, they would hit it. It would rain bullets."[52] The Germans, however, could not hold their position, and a

Henry Clyde Holt of Randolph County is shown in these photographs wearing the standard uniform of an American soldier on the western front in 1918. On the left, his gas mask is in a canvas carrier across the front of his chest. On the right, Holt is wearing the mask, which covers his face entirely. Clips inside the mask were used to pinch the nose shut, while the wearer breathed through a mouthpiece attached to a rubberized hose. The hose was attached to a canister inside the carrier that filtered the air. Soldiers on the front never went anywhere without their gas masks. Photographs courtesy of the Henry Clyde Holt family.

number of them were taken prisoner. "Some of [the Germans] would give up, and some of them wouldn't," Morris remembered, and "as long as he kept that helmet on we would fight him, but if he pulled off that helmet and just had his cap on, we wouldn't kill him."[53]

James Covington of the Fifty-sixth Pioneer Regiment saw many of the German prisoners captured in the Meuse-Argonne battles sent to the rear. To him, "they looked dirty and nasty, they looked like fighters."[54] William Morris added, "Don't let anybody tell you the Germans are not good fighters."[55] The Germans would fight until their capture was inevitable. They would cut down the advancing Americans with their machine guns until all hope was lost, and then, and only then, would they throw up their hands and bellow, "Kamerad!" Because of this practice, which was common knowledge among the doughboys, Noah Whicker, a newly promoted platoon sergeant in the 321st Infantry Regiment, believed that a group of prisoners his unit sent back under guard never survived beyond the nearest hill or broken patch of trees. "I don't imagine they lived very long," Whicker recollected. "The one in charge took them back . . . and probably killed them all."[56]

Felix Brockman and a friend stumbled into a group of prisoners one night but did not realize it. Brockman was trying to deliver a message to a battalion headquarters in the frontline trenches and had already had difficulty in just getting to the front. Not only did he have to travel while under fire, but a colonel's car knocked Brockman, who was riding in a motorcycle sidecar, into a ditch after hitting the cyclist head on. Stunned but unharmed, Brockman and his partner continued to the front where they were told by a sentry to proceed on foot. Then, in the rambling trenches, they got lost. "It was dark as the dickens," Brockman remembered. "We started walking and got in with this group marching, blump-blump-blump, keeping step like that. There was a green light up there [in a doorway], and they were keeping single file. We found out we were mixed in with German prisoners going under the intelligence department green light. When we got there these two fellows were checking them, and they said, 'What the hell are you guys doing in here?' "[57] Luckily, Brockman and his friend did not break rank when they neared the intelligence dugout; if they had, they probably would have been shot.

After delivering his message, Brockman returned to the headquarters of the 321st Ambulance Company. Weary from his evening of hard work, Brockman lay down to rest on some boxes and equipment. He was off to the side, supposedly asleep, when some officers gathered for a discussion. "There were a lot of officers," he recalled, "and [Captain W. E.] Brackett said, 'Tomorrow at 11 A.M. there could be an armistice.' "[58] From that moment on, though he could not tell anyone, Brockman knew what most of the soldiers had been wondering about for several weeks—the war was going to end.

Many soldiers spent the cold night of November 10 speculating about the war's end. Noah Whicker did not sleep and "walked all night to keep from freezing."[59] He knew that the next morning he was scheduled to "go over the top." William Morris and his friends also pondered the possible conclusion of the war. That afternoon Morris was surprised by the remarks of a German prisoner. "We captured a couple of Germans in a dugout up there," Morris explained, "and one of them said, 'Tomorrow at eleven o'clock, Deutschmann free.' He knew more about it than I did."[60] Hour after hour passed, however, and the men at the front heard no word of a cease-fire. The scheduled assaults would take place as planned. The armistice was signed at 5 A.M. on November 11 but did not take effect until eleven that morning.[61] In the hours between the signing and the actual cease-fire, thousands of American soldiers left their lines and assaulted the German lines. Hundreds died.[62] The Eighty-first Division, composed primarily of North Carolinians, participated in one of these attacks. The assault began at 6 A.M., the same hour that Pershing received word that the war was to end. The 321st Infantry Regiment was part of the front line of the assault. The attack had scarcely begun when the Americans were met by heavy machine-gun fire and then shelling from artillery. Noah Whicker was in Company D, which had only just managed to fill a gap in the line when the enemy fire became intense. "We were lucky that morning, it was foggy and you couldn't see a thing," Whicker recalled. "They would have killed us all if it had not been foggy."[63]

Under such fire the entire American line fell to the ground. Some men were killed or wounded, while others hugged the earth for protection. Corporal John Adams was one of the men caught in the open ground. "We were taking machine gun fire and we were crawling on the ground," Adams explained. "The shells were bursting overhead and the machine gun bullets were hitting all around."[64] Sergeant Whicker, who was also caught in the fire, occasionally would attempt a short run forward to try to gain additional ground. He recalled: "I had them cut weeds down around me. We crossed over a big mine [placed under a bridge], but it didn't go off. It was set for tanks, but we didn't have any tanks. There was one building there, and a bridge to get to it, and it looked like there had been a hog killed there [because] there was so much blood on the ground."[65] Whicker added: "You just can't imagine. You would think you would be scared to death, but I was only scared enough to take care of myself while I was running through it."[66]

The doughboys of the Eighty-first Division were subjected to the German fire for five hours, then suddenly there was silence.[67] John Adams did not know what to think at that moment. He remained on the ground,

Noah Whicker was a platoon sergeant in the 321st Infantry Regiment, Eighty-first Division, when he went "over the top" against the German lines on November 11, 1918. He and his men were unaware that an armistice would go into effect that day. Whicker remembered being pinned down by machine-gun and artillery fire when the war abruptly ended at 11:00 A.M. The photograph on the left was taken at Camp Jackson, South Carolina, ca. 1917. In the photograph on the right, Whicker is wearing his World War I uniform at a Bicentennial celebration in 1976. Photographs courtesy of Katherine Whicker Linville.

still fearful of death, and wondered what to do. "I didn't know what was happening," he said. "We had strict orders to keep our heads down, but after a few moments it was still quiet, so I raised up to look around and I saw a lieutenant stand up."[68]

Sergeant Noah Whicker was also on the ground when it all came to an end. Like Adams, he did not know what to think when it got quiet. He remembered: "I was scared a little bit. I was afraid it wasn't over. . . . I was out there in no-man's-land about two or three hundred yards from the German lines. . . . There wasn't any word, it just cut off all at once. The whole line stopped, [there] wasn't any firing."[69] The sergeant stood and with a lieutenant walked around the battlefield and gathered papers from the dead. All across the line soldiers began to stand up and walk around, amazed it had ended so suddenly.

John Adams said that when the fighting ended "it was like you were starting out on a new life."[70] The officer he first saw stand up was crossing back and forth in front of the troops. Adams remembered that "the lieutenant hollered, 'It's all over. The war is over. It's all over, and you can go home now!' We started getting up pretty fast after it got quiet, and some of the boys were hugging each other because it was over."[71] Everyone did have a new lease on life, except for the men who lay dead and wounded on the battlefield.

Felix Brockman stepped away from the door of the first-aid dressing station that morning at 11:00 and heard the roar of the gunfire abruptly end, exactly on the hour, just as the officer said it would the previous night. He remembered the impact it had on him: "I was helping the wounded, shipping them out to the field hospital. So at 11:00 I went outside, and it sounded like hell with these shells going over, and it stopped so quick I thought I was going to pieces. It was just like being in a thunderstorm with lightning striking, and then all of a sudden the sun comes out."[72] The front fell quiet, but behind the medical corpsman there remained a seemingly endless sound of war. Hundreds of men had been wounded in those last hours of combat, and many of them had been brought into the triage where Brockman worked. "To tell you the truth, I was about sick, and I had only seen one day's wounded brought in."[73] Sick or not, Brockman had to work quickly. Each ambulance delivered more wounded soldiers, and they would continue bringing in the wounded until the afternoon of November 12.

Brockman and the other corpsmen assigned to triage prepared the wounded men for surgery by removing any equipment and cutting away the blood-stained clothing from the wounds. These soldiers were wounded in every imaginable way. Brockman recalled that "some of the patients were very talkative and tried to tell us all about the fighting that they had just come out of," while others were in far worse shape and said very little.[74]

Felix Brockman (right) of the 321st Ambulance is shown with his brother Harry Lyndon Brockman, who served in the U.S. Navy. The night before the armistice, Felix Brockman overheard his captain tell other officers that the war was going to end. On the morning of November 11, 1918, Brockman was working in a first-aid dressing station, which was overwhelmed with casualties, when the roar of artillery and machine-gun fire suddenly stopped. Brockman and many other soldiers did not understand why men were sent into battle when the commanders knew that the war was to end that morning. Photograph courtesy of L. Becky Brockman.

Brockman never forgot one soldier in particular whose right arm was badly wounded. "Now and then he would groan," Brockman recalled, "and say, 'Oh God, will they never get ready to help me.' "[75] To try to ease the soldier's pain, they put his stretcher on two wooden sawbucks and placed an oil lantern beneath him. Finally, the medical team tended his injuries, while Brockman stood by and watched. "He had a bad shrapnel wound in his right shoulder," Brockman said. "When they took his blanket off, his arm dropped down, over the side, hanging by just a little muscle. And he said, 'Oh God, why did they send us over the top when they knew it was going to end?' "[76] To this, Brockman had no answer.

Notes

1. Crouse, interview, September 22, 1983.
2. Ingram, interview, April 10, 1984.
3. American Battle Monuments Commission, *30th Division*, 35.
4. Terraine, *Great War*, 366.
5. Ingram, interview, April 10, 1984.
6. Pershing, *My Experiences*, 2:254.
7. American Battle Monuments Commission, *American Battle Fields*, 117; Stallings, *Doughboys*, 225; Harbord, *American Army*, 432-433.
8. Pershing, *My Experiences*, 2:293.
9. American Battle Monuments Commission, *American Battle Fields*, 116; Stallings, *Doughboys*, 224; Harbord, *American Army*, 428-429.
10. Esposito, "Western Front," 126.
11. Simonds, *World War*, 5:298.
12. Pershing, *My Experiences*, 2:302.
13. Harbord, *American Army*, 442; Pershing, *My Experiences*, 2:308-309; Timothy K. Nenninger, "Tactical Dysfunction in the AEF, 1917-1918," *Military Affairs*, 51 (October 1987): 178-179.
14. Hamlin, interview, January 13, 1984.
15. Hamlin, interview, January 13, 1984.
16. Hamlin, interview, January 13, 1984.
17. [Spaulding and Wright], *Second Division*, 164-165.
18. Pershing, *My Experiences*, 2:45.
19. Morris, interview, February 2, 1984.
20. Morris, interview, February 2, 1984.
21. Horton Bower Hall, "Memoirs of H. B. Hall," unpublished manuscript in private possession.
22. H. B. Hall, interview, November 3, 1981.
23. H. B. Hall, interview, November 3, 1981.

24. H. B. Hall, interview, November 3, 1981.

25. R. J. Marshall, interview, September 21, 1976.

26. R. J. Marshall, interview, September 21, 1976.

27. R. J. Marshall, interview, September 21, 1976.

28. [Spaulding and Wright], *Second Division*, 191.

29. Allen et al., *Triumph*, 339; Harbord, *American Army*, 444-446; American Battle Monuments Commission, *American Battle Fields*, 122-124.

30. Ayres, *War with Germany*, 120; Pershing, *My Experiences*, 2:328.

31. R. J. Marshall, interview, September 21, 1976.

32. Andrews, interview, October 30, 1981.

33. Andrews, interview, October 30, 1981.

34. Andrews, interview, October 30, 1981.

35. Hudson, interview, October 27, 1981.

36. Hamlin, interview, January 13, 1984.

37. Cable, interview, September 16, 1983.

38. Ayres, *War with Germany*, 120; Allen et al., *Triumph*, 340, 459-460; Harbord, *American Army*, 452.

39. Esposito, "Western Front," 127-128.

40. Pershing, *My Experiences*, 381-382; Simonds, *World War*, 5:311; Harbord, *American Army*, 460.

41. Adams, interview, November 7, 1981.

42. Adams, interview, November 7, 1981.

43. Clarke, interview, January 4, 1984.

44. Clarke, interview, January 4, 1984.

45. H. B. Hall, interview, November 3, 1981.

46. H. B. Hall, interview, November 3, 1981.

47. H. B. Hall, interview, November 3, 1981.

48. H. B. Hall, interview, November 3, 1981.

49. R. J. Marshall, interview, July 7, 1978.

50. Hamlin, interview, January 13, 1984.

51. "Report of the Surgeon General," *War Department Annual Reports, 1920*, vol. 1 (Washington, D.C.: Government Printing Office, 1920), 491.

52. Morris, interview, February 2, 1984.

53. Morris, interview, February 2, 1984.

54. Covington, interview, September 19, 1983.

55. Morris, interview, February 2, 1984.

56. Whicker, interview, September 21, 1983.

57. Brockman, interview, January 5, 1984.

58. Brockman, interview, January 5, 1984.

59. Whicker, interview, September 21, 1983.

60. Morris, interview, February 2, 1984.

61. Allen et al., *Triumph*, 369.

62. Ayres, *War with Germany*, 120.
63. Whicker, interview, September 21, 1983.
64. "Doughboys Still Remember," *Winston-Salem Journal*, November 12, 1978.
65. Whicker, interview, September 21, 1983.
66. Whicker, interview, September 21, 1983.
67. "Doughboys Still Remember," *Winston-Salem Journal*, November 12, 1978.
68. "Doughboys Still Remember," *Winston-Salem Journal*, November 12, 1978.
69. Whicker, interview, September 21, 1983.
70. Adams, interview, November 7, 1981.
71. Adams, interview, November 7, 1981.
72. Brockman, interview, January 5, 1984.
73. Brockman, *Here, There, and Back*, 24.
74. Brockman, *Here, There, and Back*, 24.
75. Brockman, *Here, There, and Back*, 24.
76. Brockman, interview, January 5, 1984.

Chapter Eight
"Peace without Victory":
Occupation and the Return Home

"We heard this a.m. Germany has surrendered. I do hope this is so, but don't want to build on false hopes."[1] These lines, written on November 8, 1918, were sent by the mother of marine corporal Wade Marshall to her son. The rumor of Germany's surrender, however, was not only premature but indeed built on false hopes. On November 11, Germany did not surrender unconditionally, as General Pershing continually insisted they be forced to do, but instead was granted a cease-fire. The armistice brought an end to the fighting, and in accordance with President Wilson's "Peace without Victory" policies, the German army was allowed to quit the field still intact, beaten but not defeated.

Pershing's Meuse-Argonne campaign, forty-seven days of continuous fighting, ended just as the Americans broke through the last German defenses and cut a critical enemy supply line.[2] The Americans had advanced some thirty miles, inflicted over 100,000 German casualties—including taking 26,000 prisoners—and captured 847 field guns and 3,000 machine guns. To pay for these spoils, the American First Army of over one million men (including 135,000 French soldiers) sustained 117,000 casualties, including 29,446 Americans killed in action.[3] This was a high price for a victory cut short by policy makers.

Though somewhat expected, the armistice occurred rather abruptly and caught most of the soldiers in the field by surprise. More than one doughboy stood on the battlefield those first few moments after the cease-fire in nothing less than a stupor. After those awkward minutes, however, the celebration began, and as Otho Offman of the Eighty-first Division recalled, "You could hear the American soldiers hollering for ten miles."[4] Smith Cable of the First Division remembered that when they learned of the armistice the fellows in his outfit "went crazy" and started firing their rifles and pistols until there "was a solid roar of guns shooting."[5] Cable gathered up his blankets and sought a safe place to try to get some rest, but got little sleep because he "was more worried than when the war was going on with those jokers shooting."[6]

The Americans were not the only ones to react with joy. Other Allied soldiers and German troops had suffered far more in the war and therefore celebrated the end of the conflict with even greater enthusiasm. Lawrence Crawford of the 321st Ambulance Company saw the reaction of a few of the Allies: "There were some French soldiers who were moving back from the front, and they spent the night up the road in the field. They were yelling and shooting their rifles. There was a bunch of Chinese working on the railroad, and they were whooping and hollering."[7] A few days later Crawford wrote home to his sister: "At exactly eleven o'clock all the noise stopped and for a minute everything was quiet. All of a sudden train whistles, church bells, automobile horns, army rifles, and automatics turned loose almost drowning out the full lung shouts of the American and French soldiers. Believe me, Tritz, these Frenchmen are a happy bunch. Of course, we are happy the war is over too, but it is nothing in comparison with them. Four years of war and destruction to their country is enough to make a man go wild when he finally realizes it is all over and Kaiser Bill has been knocked out."[8] In a rock quarry

Lawrence Crawford of Greensboro was a sergeant in the 321st Ambulance Company. Like most soldiers, he was surprised that the war ended so abruptly on November 11, 1918. To Crawford, no troops seemed more relieved than the French, who had seen their country nearly destroyed and had suffered six million casualties. The photographs of Crawford were taken in May 1918 and in the 1970s. Photographs courtesy of Larry A. Crawford Jr.

behind the lines, Guy E. Wise saw his work crew of German prisoners clap their hands and have "a hullabaloo" when they heard of the armistice.[9] Next to the men on the battlefield, the prisoners of both armies probably took the news of the cease-fire with the greatest expectation of a change for the better.

Starting on the day of the armistice and continuing through the rest of November, the German army withdrew from war-torn France and Belgium and returned to their homeland. On November 17, the Allied soldiers began their advance, following close behind the retiring German troops, into the areas vacated by the enemy. Private Ernest James of the Forty-second Division kept a diary during the march to Germany, recording much of what he saw as he passed through Belgium and Luxembourg. The Belgians often met the Americans with flags, banners, and music, as the doughboys marched along, covering an average of twelve miles a day. In the village of Eischen, Luxembourg, however, the Americans received a more wary reception. James wrote: "When we first marched into this village the people seemed to be kindly shy of us, but are awfully willing to do anything for you. They say the Germans went through here only a week ahead of us and they just took possession of everything, taking anything they wanted without paying for it. I guess they thought we were going to do the same thing."[10]

The Forty-second Division stopped briefly on the Luxembourg-Belgian border before entering Germany, the destination of all of the American divisions that were to be part of the Army of Occupation. Another division, the Second Regulars, crossed the Rhine River and held a position in force on German soil. The infantrymen and marines were glad, at first, to be part of the occupation force. Matt Marshall made the historic crossing of the Rhine on December 13, 1918. A few days later he wrote home: "We are now on the eastern side of the Rhine, the side next to Berlin, and have reached our destination, for the time being at least. It sure has been a long, long, hike to get here, but as in everything else the old Second Division came in on time. Our Marines and Doughboys simply can't be beat."[11] The pride shown in Marshall's letter was typical of that exhibited by soldiers who marched into Germany. Unfortunately, their enthusiasm would wane during the long months of occupation, as the peacemakers continued their prolonged negotiations.

"The Germans were good to us when they were given a chance," admitted Clarence Moore of the Thirtieth Division.[12] Many of the American soldiers found the German people pleasant to deal with once the hostilities had ended. Because of a lack of facilities, many doughboys were billeted with German families. Private Ernest James stayed with a German family in the town of Waldorf. In a letter to his mother, James explained: "The people where I stay are just as good to me as you could be, although I would prefer you. This woman had five sons in the war. She said two of them were 'capoot,' this is the

The Second Division entered Germany on December 1, 1918, and crossed the Rhine River at Remagen on December 13. As part of the Allied Army of Occupation, the division served in the area around Koblenz until July 1919. In this photograph, Battery A of the Fifteenth Field Artillery is shown crossing the Rhine. Photograph courtesy of the author.

German word for no good. She meant they were killed; one is a prisoner of war, and the other two are at home. One of them was in the submarine service. I love to talk to him. He is only a kid, looks to be about 18."[13] After serving almost the entire war with the British, Luther Hall said of the Germans: "They were good soldiers, and in general, they were wonderful people. To tell you the truth, I think more of them than I do the English."[14]

Actually, fewer than half of the thirty active American combat divisions were sent into Germany. The others remained in France and Belgium, waiting to return home. Neither the Thirtieth nor the Eighty-first Division, which were made up primarily of North Carolinians, was part of the occupation force in Germany. They stayed in France during the winter of 1918-1919.

Regardless of whether a division was sent across the Rhine or stayed behind, long hard marches were made to reach the areas set aside for temporary billeting. Immediately following the armistice the Thirtieth and Eighty-first Divisions marched from the front to villages far behind the lines. The Eighty-first Division trekked 175 miles with full equipment. For Noah Whicker this meant carrying a ninety-pound pack each day, "rain or shine."

He recalled that "come nighttime we would have wet clothes on. We would find an old French shelter and sleep in wet clothes, and get up the next morning and go again."[15] The march was over demanding terrain, much of which was similar to the Blue Ridge Mountains, according to Horton Hall. The hills were so steep that the men had difficulty carrying their packs. This prompted Hall's captain to tell the soldiers, "If any of you have anything that you can lighten your load while climbing these hills, I won't be looking at you."[16] One item no one wished to carry any farther was extra shoes; hundreds were thrown down the mountainside. Another Eighty-first Division soldier, Lawrence Crawford, described the mood of his friends in a letter home: "The general opinion of all American soldiers regarding this country is that the more we see of it the more we love the good old U.S.A., or as one of the boys expressed it: 'France is one of the prettiest and best countries in the world—to go home from.' "[17]

The greatest hardship endured on the marches, either to Germany or across France, was hunger. The infantry had scarcely begun their march when the supply groups fell far behind the soldiers. The troops went each day with little or nothing to eat, while being pushed to keep some prescribed schedule. At first, the men had their emergency rations to eat, but after these were gone there was almost nothing to serve the hungry men. Horton Hall described the dilemma faced by his company on their march through France: "On that hike we ran out of food, and we didn't have anything left but sugar and coffee. Our captain, he rode horseback all the time. He would circle around that company while we were hiking. Everywhere he could find a French farm he would see what he could buy for food. He found somebody who had a couple hundred pounds of rice; he bought that. We had rice, sugar, and coffee for a couple of days. That's all we had, didn't have anything else."[18]

In addition to the captain's efforts to find food for his troops, the men would at times take care of themselves. Hall and his squad were in line directly behind the water and ration carts, and every time the column slowed or stopped Private Andrew Boyce Love of Mecklenburg County "would take anything he could get his hands on." Hall recalled that Love was not too particular. "It didn't matter what it was, if it could be eaten he would take it."[19] More than once he obtained onions and hard bread for the squad to devour as they moved forward.

Soldiers who remained in France after the armistice found that getting to know the French people was easier during peacetime but that the results were not always agreeable. Noah Whicker recalled one bad experience: "The chinches ate me up, that was about the worst thing I ran into. It's a little bug that gets in your bed. I was quartering with a French family . . . and they told me, 'You come up here and sleep in our bed.' So, I went up to that fancy bed with the curtains hanging down from the ceiling all around the bed. It was a feather bed. I fell into that thing and thought, 'Boy, I have it now.' I slept that night pretty good, but these scoundrels about ate me up."[20] John Collins, a soldier of the Thirtieth Division, also had a memorable encounter with the French. "I was in a little town one night by myself," he recalled. "A blame old girl came around a corner, and she threw a gun on me. I didn't know what she meant. I didn't know. I never did ask her. I knocked her down and ran like a turkey."[21]

Other American soldiers had more typical experiences. Lawrence Crawford described his stay in France after the armistice in a letter home: "You can't imagine what a total wreck the northern part of France is. Towns where before the war two or three thousand people lived is today a pile of ruins with not a single house left that hasn't been shot to pieces. I don't see how in the world they will ever rebuild unless they haul the old town out and dump it in a hole and start over again. . . . We are pretty lucky as we are now located in one of the few towns in this part of the country that has not been totally destroyed [Les Monthairons, south of Verdun]. Our billets and sleeping quarters is located in the home of a French captain who is away in the army and the rest of the family has moved away. There are four of us in a twelve by twelve room. When we all four get in with our equipment at the same time there is hardly enough room left to breathe good. It is warm though and that is what counts."[22]

After the armistice the common soldiers waited for any news about the peace conference and an agreement that would finally end the war. Until such an agreement was reached, however, the soldiers had to continue to drill, practice for battles they hoped would never come, and perform other duties. Ernest James described the difficulties that he faced in a letter he wrote to his mother in March 1919: "I don't like the army when it is real cold. The only real cold weather I have seen over here was in February and believe me it was cold. Think of standing guard at midnight hours and it below zero, and a lot of responsibility on you. I can't say for sure that I love it."[23]

Guard duty was at times miserable work and at other times disconcerting. Henry Holt was on guard duty late one night in Germany and had to make an embarrassing arrest. "I had to arrest two Catholic sisters," Holt said. "They were out too late and came down my beat. I said, 'I'm sorry, but I have to take you to my sergeant.' "[24]

Although the fighting had stopped, the soldiers still faced danger, and casualties still occurred. Robert Hamlin narrowly avoided death one night while serving as a guard on a supply train. During a stop Hamlin got out in the open air to stretch his legs. He was told not to wander off because the train might leave at any moment. Hamlin remembered: "On one of those trips the train stopped, and I got out and walked around in the night, waiting for the train to go. Those French locomotives didn't have a big headlight, just an oil

Ernest James was a draftee from Forsyth County. He arrived in France and was on his way to the front as a replacement in the Forty-second Division when the war ended. James was assigned to Company D, 168th Infantry Regiment, and served in the Army of Occupation. Photograph courtesy of June Hastings Michael.

lamp. The train was on a double track, and I was across on the other side. One of those durn French trains came over the grade and almost got me. I couldn't see anything. There was no light, and I came near to getting killed as anywhere else."[25]

Robert Gaither was nearly killed performing a task that was part of his daily routine. "After the war was over we got the horses from the Seventy-seventh Division," Gaither said. "We were up on the front, and they were going home, so we had to tend their horses and mules. They had four or five studhorses, and some of them were mean, hard to handle. We took them down to the river to water them, and this fellow let his studhorse get loose. We didn't have anything on them but halters. I had two mules, and this studhorse got loose and carried away my mules. He ran up behind my mules, and those mules just ran over me. They knocked the life out of me. When I came to there was a soldier on each side of me carrying me to the doctor."[26] Gaither never returned to his outfit after being trampled on February 6, 1919. He was admitted to the hospital at Valahoun, France, and remained there until transferred to Walter Reed Hospital in Washington, D.C., in June 1919. He was so badly injured that he stayed there until October.[27]

Robert Gaither was lucky to have survived his disaster, but many soldiers were not as fortunate. Robert Hamlin and other members of the 306th Ammunition Train were awakened one morning when an explosion collapsed their sleeping quarters. Later the soldiers learned that a guard posted outside near an ammunition dump had lit a cigarette, causing a terrific blast. A huge hole was left where the ammunition had been, and nearby pine trees were knocked down and stripped of their bark "as slick as wheat straw."[28] Needless to say, the sentry did not survive.

Jack Marshall of the Fifteenth Field Artillery Regiment recalled another incident in which a soldier died while in Germany. "The Rhine River was fast and strong," Marshall explained. "You couldn't even go near that river. Our garbage and horse manure from the stables were picked up and hauled by wagon to be dumped into that river. The driver would back the wagon just a little way back into the river and shovel the manure out. One time he backed up too far, and the river pulled him, the wagon, and horses all into the river. We never saw him or anything else of him again. We got word to a town downriver to watch for him, but they never did see him. I don't know what they wrote home, missing in action or what."[29] This fatality was probably added to the list of almost three thousand accidental deaths suffered by the AEF, of which about three hundred were from drowning.[30]

When not on duty the doughboys engaged in a variety of activities. Baseball teams and boxing matches were organized, and as David Edwards of the Eighty-first Division recalled, "Each division would put on a show over there, and then people would go around from the different divisions to see

THE INDIAN

PUBLISHED WEEKLY BY THE SECOND DIVISION ASSOCIATION

E.L.Palmer   2.A.T.

While diplomats spent months negotiating terms for a permanent peace, army commanders had to find ways to alleviate the boredom of the troops in the Army of Occupation. Boxing and baseball became popular pastimes, and most of the divisions began publishing newspapers or magazines, like *The Indian*, a Second Division weekly. Baseball photograph from a scrapbook in the Robert R. Bridgers Papers, Private Collections, State Archives, Division of Archives and History, Raleigh; *The Indian* cover courtesy of the author.

those shows, which furnished a good deal of entertainment."[31] Mail call provided another favorite pastime. Soldiers opened letters and packages from home and shared their news with others.

Cigarettes and chewing tobacco were valued by the soldiers when off duty, but quality tobacco was hard to find. Otho Offman, like most of the soldiers, chewed tobacco but did not smoke because the cigarettes that were available "didn't have any more flavor to them than if they were made of oak leaves."[32] While tobacco was limited, French beer and wine were abundant. The prohibition against the sale of hard liquor to American soldiers did not prevent drinkers from getting drunk. Sergeant Guy Wise recollected that "if you were a drinker you could find all the beer you could drink in France," and a soldier could consume all he desired as long as he was back in the barracks by nine o'clock.[33]

Gambling was another popular diversion. As David Edwards remembered: "There were certain fellows who were good gamblers, dice shooters. When the troops did get any money, why those gamblers usually had it, most of it anyway."[34] Gladney Clarke's 322nd Regiment of the Eighty-first Division was stationed in Bouy, France, after the armistice. Because of one crap game there, Clarke thought he had lost his newly acquired corporal's stripe. Clarke was supposed to be on duty; instead he was gambling. He recounted the story of that particular Sunday morning: "I was a good crap shooter. I could win money to beat the band. This fellow told me, 'There's a good crap game, so when you get through go down there and you'll have a good time.' So, I took the morning report and stuck it in my pocket. I went on down there and got in the crap game, and of course I won because I knew how to handle them and how to beat them. Anyhow, the colonel came over and wanted to see the morning report. Well, they said, 'Clarke has it.' He said, 'Where is Clarke?' 'He's up at the crap game.' So, somebody came to me and said, 'You had better get back to the company; the colonel's looking for you.' So, I got up and was walking and the colonel stopped me. I stopped and saluted and clapped my heels together. He said, 'Corporal Clarke, where's my morning report?' I said, 'It's in my pocket.' So, he came up there and I handed it to him, and he wanted to know—'Where have you been?' I said, 'I've been in a crap game.' [He asked], 'How did you come out?' I said, 'I won, I always win.' "[35] The colonel let Clarke remain a corporal, but according to Clarke, the scare was punishment enough. "What could he do to make it any worse than I was having already?" the corporal confessed.[36]

Often the one thing that could cause the most excitement, and sometimes the most misery, was a visit from General Pershing. Pershing spent much of his time traveling to the various camps across France and Germany to review the troops. When he did show up, as Noah Whicker recalled, "it didn't matter if there was snow on the ground or not, or how far away you were, you had to walk there and pass in review in front of him to let him see what you looked like."[37] Carl Clodfelter remembered his day with the general as being one of terrible discomfort: "One day we hiked and passed review before General Pershing. It rained that day where we passed review and there was a big swamp and there was water there about knee deep. We had to line up with about fifty or more men in a line, and you had to march right through that water. It took us all day to hike over there and pass review before him and get back to camp."[38]

Every soldier wished that when Pershing came to see a parade that he would bring the news that the men in that particular division would soon return home. Rumors to that effect often floated in the billets, but such hopes were usually dashed, as was the case when Pershing visited the camp of the Eighty-first Division. John Adams remembered: "We all lined up, and he made about a thirty-minute speech, and he said, 'The Eighty-first Division is one division to soon be sailing to America.' Well, that sounded good. But one of the officers said, 'That doesn't mean a thing. That's the way they talk all the

After the armistice, General John J. Pershing conducted reviews of the troops still in Europe. The American commander was highly respected by his men, but the doughboys sometimes resented having to stand in review for the general, particularly when the weather was bad. They all hoped, however, that on such occasions Pershing would bring the news that they were going home. Photograph from a scrapbook in the Robert R. Bridgers Papers, Private Collections, State Archives, Division of Archives and History, Raleigh.

time.' When we got back to the barracks Sergeant [William B.] Baker [of Wingate, North Carolina] went to packing up, getting his things ready to sail. He thought he was going to sail the next week. Somebody said, 'What are you doing?' And he said, 'I'm getting ready to go home. You heard General Pershing say we are soon to go back.' That was four or five months before we left."[39]

With each passing month after the armistice, boredom, and finally depression, slowly spread throughout the American army. Thanksgiving and then Christmas came and went, and the soldiers were still not home. The peace conference accomplished nothing as the politicians could not settle on the details of Germany's surrender. Meanwhile, the common soldier waited for orders to return home. Veterans in some divisions were in France and Germany almost as long after the armistice as they were before the cease-fire.

Matt Marshall's increasing depression was evident in the letters he wrote home to Forsyth County. Just before Christmas 1918, he wrote: "We have had all the war we want and more than enough to last a life time [sic]. Nothing matters now but getting home, as the fighting is over."[40] Much later, in May 1919, Marshall sent another letter expressing the melancholy he felt after a memorial ceremony in his regiment. "Today has been decoration day," he wrote. "We had a short service this a.m. but are not near enough to any graves to decorate. We all thought of the difference between this 30th of May and last year. We had learned what war was then, but not tasted of the bitter dregs as we now know them. We thought of our comrades who were absent, and will ever remain so, not only to us, but to those who love them best back in the U.S.A."[41] Within the next two months a lieutenant and a sergeant-major in Marshall's regiment committed suicide.[42]

On June 17, 1919, the American divisions in the occupation force in Germany were called to prepare immediately for combat. The German delegation, rejecting the harsh terms for surrender, had bolted the peace conference. For a few days it seemed that the war would reopen, this time on German soil. Then, to the relief of all, except perhaps the Germans, the terms were signed on June 28 as written. The war with Germany was over as far as the Germans were concerned, and the majority of Americans were free to go home. President Wilson took the treaty back to the United States, where, much to his dismay, the Senate rejected it. The Americans would sign a separate treaty with Germany on August 25, 1921.

Fortunately, the War Department did not wait for an American treaty before withdrawing the doughboys from Europe. By the end of February 1919, over 400,000 soldiers had been returned to the United States, and by the first of June an additional 800,000 men had been sent home.[43] Generally speaking, the national divisions of drafted men were sent back first, then the men of the National Guard, and finally the soldiers of the regular army. By following this schedule the soldiers who had arrived in France first and had fought the most were the last to go home, while those who had been drafted and had arrived in France just before the armistice went home before all others. The veterans of all the hard-fought battles were not impressed with this arrangement, nor were they appeased by speeches in which they were told how much more they were needed because of their experience. These veterans, many of whom were volunteers and most of whom had served in the Army of Occupation, thought even less of the draftees after the months of dull life in Europe, knowing full well that the conscripts were at home with their families.

All of the American soldiers, no matter when they were shipped home, had to go through the same preparations before making the voyage. They marched across France one last time to one of the many embarkation camps located near port cities. There they were given a vaccination for a multitude of illnesses, if they had not received it prior to arriving at the camp, and all the men were deloused a final time. Ernest James received his vaccination while still in Germany before starting his return home, and he wrote to his mother of its effects: "I was vaccinated day before yesterday morning for the fever and it made me sick. I was in bed all day yesterday, but am feeling pretty good today. Kindly have the headache. I hardly think you will wonder at it making me sick when I tell you that they put three doses in our arm at one time. I think it was enough to kill a mule."[44] Noah Whicker, like hundreds of other soldiers, had one last encounter with the delouser before he boarded his ship for home. "I had a wool overcoat and had a pair of kid gloves in the pocket," he remembered. "I went through delousing, came back, and those kid gloves, why a child couldn't have gotten them on they were so drawn up, and my overcoat, it was all drawn up."[45] Whicker was not pleased about having to return to the United States with overcoat sleeves halfway up to his elbows, and after some arguing he persuaded the supply sergeant to give him one that was a better fit.

The voyage back to the United States was a far better trip than the crossing to Europe. First of all, the soldiers came home on American ships with American crews, which meant better food than that served by the English on the first voyage. On the way home Ernest James wrote in his diary: "For breakfast we had eggs, oatmeal, butter bread, coffee, and apples. For dinner we had turkey, cream potatoes, butter bread, coffee, fruit cake, and apple pie."[46] Felix Brockman also ate well on his ship. He wrote: "We had grapefruit, oatmeal, and eggs for breakfast; beans, stewed beef, pickles, greens, and sweet potatoes for dinner, and sauerkraut, with pickles and wieners for supper. Irish potatoes and good bread at all meals."[47] The good food must have made a difference; far fewer soldiers got seasick on the voyage home to America.

Though better than the voyage to Europe, the trip home was not without difficulty. Some of the ships were caught in storms with frightening results. Horton Hall was aboard the *Walter A. Luckenback* when it hit stormy weather. "We had a terrible storm one time that we had to head into," he remembered. "It looked like it was going to sink the ship. I was getting scared about it. I think everybody was, even the captain of the ship. . . . The waves were so high they came plumb over the bow of the ship. When the waves passed over, that part of the ship would go down, down like it was going down into a ditch, and the back end of the ship would come plumb out of the water."[48] Clarence Moore of the Thirtieth Division came home on a captured German mail ship, and it too was caught in several storms. Moore thought on one occasion that the ship would certainly sink. During the storm he watched "some of the boys praying, some of them cussing, some of them shooting craps."[49] Clarence Moore seemed to be more the praying type.

Moore's 117th Infantry Regiment arrived at Charleston, South Carolina, during the first week of April, then traveled by train to Memphis, Tennessee. Because most of the men in the regiment were Tennesseans, the people of Memphis expected a parade of their troops. The parade was a grueling experience for the soldiers. Moore remembered: "We had those woolen uniforms on, collars up high. We sweated those things out; that's hell. And we didn't have to, we were home."[50] After satisfying the people and politicians, the regiment was sent to Fort Oglethorpe, Georgia, where the men were discharged.

By far the majority of the soldiers did not march in parades, and the only celebrations held in their honor were given by their families. The Eighty-first Division came home in June 1919 by way of Newport News, Virginia, then to Camp Lee, Virginia, where most of the soldiers were given sixty dollars and discharged. Other divisions arrived in various ports up and down the East Coast and were then fragmented, with men being sent to the camps nearest their home state. Guy E. Wise, a sergeant in the 534th Engineer Battalion, arrived at Boston Harbor on July 4, 1919. To his recollection, few Bostonians came out to welcome the soldiers home. Wise, a white noncommissioned officer in a company of African American troops, boarded a train with some of his men and went to Camp Lee where he was discharged. Wise took his sixty dollars travel pay and caught a train to Salisbury, North Carolina. The former sergeant described his trip home, which was typical of that experienced by many North Carolinians: "There was a little old place called Richfield that was close to my home, about sixteen or eighteen miles. . . . I got on the train in Salisbury and went to Richfield. My father was there to meet me. . . . They had a big dinner fixed up when I got home, and it was a sight to the world."[51]

For other North Carolinians the final train ride home was not as easy and the arrival at the homeplace almost overwhelming. Young men went to war; weary soldiers with memories of battle and death returned. The Second

Troops returning from Europe landed at various ports along the eastern seaboard. In the top photograph, members of the 113th Field Artillery Regiment march down a street in Newport News, Virginia, where they landed on March 18, 1919. Once home, the doughboys were often feted by their communities. In the bottom photograph, Rowan County veterans are the guests of honor at a barbecue dinner. The top photograph is from A. L. Fletcher, *History of the 113th Field Artillery, 30th Division* (Raleigh: History Committee of the 113th F.A., 1920), 137; the photograph below is from the files of the Division of Archives and History.

In Raleigh, returning soldiers march down North Wilmington Street (above), and on Fayetteville Street, a crowd, including Gov. T. W. Bickett and other dignitaries, waits for a parade of the 113th Field Artillery Regiment. The original of the top photograph was provided by Eleanor H. Mason, copy from the files of the Division of Archives and History; the bottom photograph is from A. L. Fletcher, *History of the 113th Field Artillery, 30th Division* (Raleigh: History Committee of the 113th F.A., 1920), 138.

Regular Army Division arrived in New York City on August 4, 1919, and paraded on Fifth Avenue four days later. The men were then sent to various camps to be discharged. Three friends from this division, Jack Marshall, his older brother Matt Marshall, and Hugh Edwards from Winston-Salem, were discharged on August 14 at Camp Lee, and on that day they traveled as far as Roanoke, Virginia, which was halfway home. Each man was a 1917 volunteer, had survived five battles in about as many months, and had served over eight months in the Army of Occupation. The past two years had been hard, and now that they were finally approaching home, the two Marshall brothers found that they had one more obstacle to overcome. The conductor said that the train would not stop at Dennis Station, which was almost in sight of their home. Instead they would have to ride an additional fifteen miles to Winston-Salem. The confrontation that ensued overshadowed the good feelings of the Fifth Avenue celebration and left Jack Marshall with a bad memory. He described the incident: "The next morning we caught the first train out. After a while we told the conductor where we wanted to get off, but he told us that they would not stop at the Dennis Station. We had to get off in

Jack Marshall (left) and Wade Marshall, brothers from Forsyth County, are shown with their nieces Emily and Lucy Gray Smither in Winston-Salem after the war. Photograph courtesy of the R. Jack Marshall family.

Winston-Salem. Well, Matt told the conductor he didn't care if it wasn't on the schedule to stop at Dennis, that Winston-Salem was out of the question, and he was going to have to change his plans. . . . We still had our uniforms on, [but] he just turned around and left. After a while he came back and said that the engineer agreed to stop at Dennis. . . . Only [our little brothers] Karl and Vance were at the station waiting when we got there. . . . Everything had changed so much while we were gone. I didn't really know how to feel."[52]

Notes

1. Alice Haizlip Marshall to Wade Latimer Marshall, November 8, 1918, manuscript in private possession.
2. Pershing, *My Experiences*, 2:388-389; Simonds, *World War*, 5:313; American Battle Monuments Commission, *American Battle Fields*, 129.
3. Ayres, *War with Germany*, 120; Harbord, *American Army*, 461; Pershing, *My Experiences*, 2:389.
4. Offman, interview, January 12, 1984.
5. Cable, interview, September 16, 1983.
6. Cable, interview, September 16, 1983.
7. Crawford, interview, January 5, 1984.
8. Lawrence Alyette Crawford to his sister, November 17, 1918, manuscript in private possession.
9. Wise, interview, January 5, 1984.
10. Diary of Ernest Luther James, November 26, 1918, manuscript in private possession.
11. James Madison Marshall to his sister, December 19, 1918, manuscript in private possession.
12. Moore, interview, November 5, 1981.
13. Ernest Luther James to his mother, March 24, 1919, manuscript in private possession.
14. L. P. Hall, interview, April 10, 1984.
15. Whicker, interview, September 21, 1983.
16. H. B. Hall, interview, November 3, 1981.
17. Lawrence Alyette Crawford to his sister, November 17, 1918, manuscript in private possession.
18. H. B. Hall, interview, November 3, 1981.
19. H. B. Hall, interview, November 3, 1981.
20. Whicker, interview, September 21, 1983.
21. Collins, interview, April 12, 1984.
22. Lawrence Alyette Crawford to his sister, November 17, 1918, manuscript in private possession.

23. Ernest Luther James to his mother, March 11, 1919, manuscript in private possession.
24. Holt, interview, January 6, 1984.
25. Hamlin, interview, January 13, 1984.
26. Gaither, interview, October 3, 1983.
27. Gaither, interview, October 3, 1983.
28. Hamlin, interview, January 13, 1984.
29. R. J. Marshall, interview, September 21, 1976.
30. Esposito, "War Casualties," 373.
31. Edwards, interview, October 5, 1983.
32. Offman, interview, January 12, 1984.
33. Wise, interview, January 5, 1984.
34. Edwards, interview, October 5, 1983.
35. Clarke, interview, January 4, 1984.
36. Clarke, interview, January 4, 1984.
37. Whicker, interview, September 21, 1983.
38. Clodfelter, interview, September 19, 1983.
39. Adams, interview, November 7, 1981.
40. James Madison Marshall to his sister, December 19, 1918, manuscript in private possession.
41. James Madison Marshall to his sister, May 30, 1919, manuscript in private possession.
42. R. J. Marshall, interview, September 21, 1976.
43. Ayres, *War with Germany*, 37.
44. Ernest Luther James to his mother, May 23, 1919, manuscript in private possession.
45. Whicker, interview, September 21, 1983.
46. Diary of Ernest Luther James, April 20, 1919, manuscript in private possession.
47. Brockman, *Here, There, and Back*, 35.
48. H. B. Hall, interview, November 3, 1981.
49. Moore, interview, November 5, 1981.
50. Moore, interview, November 5, 1981.
51. Wise, interview, January 5, 1984.
52. R. J. Marshall, interview, September 21, 1976.

Epilogue
The War to End All Wars

"We always said that the ones to die early were the lucky ones because they didn't have to go through what we did."[1] This statement, made by a North Carolina veteran of World War I, is representative of the sentiments of those men who survived the hardships of 1918. Many American soldiers did not come home, and though the number of American casualties was small compared to that of the European armies, the few months of battle in World War I were one of the deadliest periods in American military history. Some 275,948 American soldiers were casualties after only a year of fighting; of these, 50,554 were killed in action or died of wounds, and an additional 69,590 men died of disease or other causes in France and the United States.[2] North Carolina shared in these losses. The Old North State sent 86,457 of its young men to fight in the war. Of these, 629 were killed in combat; 3,859 were wounded, resulting in the subsequent deaths of an additional 204 men; and 1,542 died of disease.[3]

Most of the North Carolina veterans who were interviewed firmly believed that the accomplishments of the United States in the war were not only worth the loss, but were justified and essential in the struggle to defeat the kaiser. "Germany had France and England just about whipped when we went in," said Smith Cable. "If we had not gone into it the Germans would have jumped on us."[4] Instead, America "jumped" on Germany, and by Armistice Day Pershing's soldiers actually held more miles on the front with more men than even the British Expeditionary Force.[5] Certainly, the United States did not win the war alone, but without the American doughboy, Belgium, France, and England could not have brought about a successful conclusion to the conflict on the western front. "We had to whip the kaiser, there was no question about that," said Charles Gibson.[6] "The old kaiser said he was going to conquer the whole world," as Carl Clodfelter recalled, "but he didn't get it done."[7] To a large degree, the kaiser had the American soldier to blame for his failure.

When the doughboys returned from their "crusader's task," as Isham Hudson put it, they wanted to believe with all their hearts that they had truly secured a lasting peace for the world. Harvey Maness said, "I felt I had an opportunity to make history. I can't imagine anything more justifiable than to say, 'I'll help kill war. There will never be another war.' "[8] But was it really going to be the end of all wars, and was the world really as safe for democracy as President Wilson desired? Many American soldiers felt the need to look back over their shoulder and wonder. The question was answered, and their idealism, or what was left of it after the Great Depression, was finally shattered when war broke out again in Europe only twenty years later.

The Second World War made "Pershing's Crusaders" question the purpose of the 1918 sacrifice. Many were terribly disillusioned. Their efforts, the death, and the destruction in the First World War were made worthless in 1939. To make matters worse, many World War I veterans had to watch their sons leave home to fight in World War II. One veteran of the First World War, James Covington, summed up his thoughts by saying: "We made a mess and came home, and then the Second World War started, and we went over there and made another mess, and came home. . . . We fought two world wars and never got anything."[9] Luther Hall, who was wounded in 1918, believed that "you can't make peace by fighting" and did not think America accomplished anything in World War I.[10] "All wars are useless, nobody wins," concluded World War I veteran Robert Hamlin.[11]

World War I, "that was the war to end all wars," recalled Archie Ingram. "No," he said, "it wasn't worth fighting."[12] When he volunteered in 1917, he thought it would be. The veterans perceived World War I as America's forgotten war, a historical footnote to World War II, but for them—the men who fought the war and survived—it remained a horrific memory that they wished to forget. Some, like Jack Marshall, suffered from depression and nightmares after returning home. This was so troubling to his family that they put away his uniform and photographs during what they called "the bad years."[13] Smith Cable, in the years following the war, refused to talk about it. He said: "It was the front, I never talk about it. I have never talked about it. . . . I've seen boys going around bragging, but I never liked that. I never thought about it. I didn't even want to hear anything about it. I would just walk away from it."[14] Many of the veterans quoted in this volume had never talked about their war experiences, even with their own families, until being interviewed for this study over a half century after the war's end. For some, like Clarence Moore, who quietly wept when recalling the wounding of his captain, the memories were painful, but something they wanted to share. Felix Brockman was philosophical about his experience when shortly after the war he wrote: "Every generation has its interesting episodes and no matter during which generation your destiny places you on earth, you will see practically the same things that people have seen in all other times."[15] History repeats itself; war repeats itself—only the location of the battlefield changes. On November 11,

1918, a cease-fire silenced the battlefields of World War I, but as these old veterans realized, their "war to end all wars" never really came to an end.

Notes

1. R. J. Marshall, interview, September 21, 1976.
2. Esposito, "War Casualties," 373.
3. Connor, *North Carolina*, 2:544-545.
4. Cable, interview, September 16, 1983.
5. William L. McPherson, *A Short History of the Great War* (New York: G. P. Putnam's Sons, 1920), 384; Ayres, *War with Germany*, 103.
6. Gibson, interview, November 2, 1981.
7. Clodfelter, interview, September 19, 1983.
8. Maness, interview, December 19, 1985.
9. Covington, interview, September 19, 1983.
10. L. P. Hall, interview, April 10, 1984.
11. Hamlin, interview, January 13, 1984.
12. Ingram, interview, April 10, 1984.
13. Lucy Gray Drake, interview with author, Winston-Salem, N.C., January 28, 1981.
14. Cable, interview, September 16, 1983.
15. Brockman, *Here, There, and Back*, 1.

Biographical Sketches of the Veterans

John Flem Adams (November 6, 1895–June 3, 1992) was born in Stuart, Virginia. In 1909, he moved to Leaksville, North Carolina (Rockingham County), where he was employed as a grocery clerk at the time of the war. He was drafted on December 28, 1917, in Reidsville and sent to Camp Jackson, South Carolina. Adams was assigned to Company C, 321st Infantry Regiment, Eighty-first Division. On June 20, 1918, just before the division was sent to France, he was promoted to corporal. He fought in the St. Dié sector and in the Meuse-Argonne offensive. The Eighty-first Division was sent back to the United States in June 1919, and Adams was discharged on June 27, 1919, at Camp Lee, Virginia. After the war he returned to the grocery business in Leaksville. In 1934, he moved to Winston-Salem and was self-employed as a café supplier and later as an insurance agent until his retirement.

Marion Alvin Andrews (May 15, 1899–March 12, 1991) was born in Sandy Ridge (Stokes County). At the time of the war, he resided in Winston-Salem and was a factory worker for the R. J. Reynolds Tobacco Company. Andrews volunteered at an army recruiting station in Winston-Salem and was sent to Fort Thomas, Kentucky, where he was inducted on December 8, 1917. He was assigned to the Supply Company, Thirteenth Field Artillery Regiment,

Marion Alvin Andrews, 1981

Fourth Division, as a wagoner. He arrived in France on May 22, 1918, and served in the attack at the Vesle River in the Aisne-Marne offensive, in the Battle of St. Mihiel, and in the Meuse-Argonne offensive. During this last campaign he was wounded in the left leg by a shell fragment (date unknown). He was then treated in a field hospital and released. Still troubled by his wound, he returned to the United States on July 31, 1919, and was sent to Camp Lee, Virginia. There he was given the choice of being transferred to Walter Reid Hospital in Washington, D.C., for further treatment, to remain at Camp Lee for treatment, or to be discharged immediately without reference to his wound. Desiring to return home, he selected a discharge, which was granted on August 5, 1919. Because of this decision he was denied future governmental assistance in the treatment of his wound and never received a Purple Heart. He reenlisted in the Marine Corps in early 1920 and served in Cuba and Haiti before being discharged in 1921. After the service he lived in Winston-Salem, where he owned and operated a small business until he retired. *Photograph courtesy of the author.*

Felix Elbridge Brockman (December 17, 1895–October 2, 1997) was a construction worker in Mecklenburg County when the United States went to war. He volunteered for service on June 25, 1917, in Greensboro and joined Ambulance Company Thirty-one. This unit was sent initially to Fort Oglethorpe, Georgia, and later to Camp Jackson, South Carolina. On September 22, his unit was redesignated as the 321st Ambulance Company, 306th Sanitary Train, Eighty-first Division. Brockman was promoted to private first class on August 20, 1917, and on May 1, 1918, was transferred to the headquarters detachment of the 306th Sanitary Train. He arrived in France on August 8, 1918, with the Eighty-first Division and was sent to the front. He served on the St. Dié sector and in the Meuse-Argonne offensive. He was discharged on June 26, 1919, at Camp Lee, Virginia. After the war he lived in Charleston, South Carolina, briefly, then returned to Greensboro, where he worked for the

Felix Elbridge Brockman, 1996

Mitchell-Dixon Office Supply Company until his retirement. He moved to Florida in 1989 to live near his daughter. He died at the age of 101 in the Veterans Administration Hospital in Miami. *Photograph courtesy of L. Becky Brockman.*

Smith Coy Cable (January 22, 1897–September 19, 1986) was born in Watauga County, North Carolina. In 1912-1913, he moved to Akron, Ohio, where he was employed by a street construction company. Cable volunteered for service on May 29, 1917, in Columbus, Ohio. He was sent to Fort Bliss, Texas, where he was assigned to Battery C, Fifth Field Artillery Regiment, First Division, as a wagoner. His unit arrived in France in August 1917. In the following year he served in the battles at Cantigny, Soissons, and St. Mihiel, and

Smith Coy Cable as a Winston-Salem police officer, 1928-1930.

in the Meuse-Argonne offensive. Cable was discharged from service in Koblenz, Germany, on August 4, 1919, just before the First Division was sent home. He reenlisted the following day and served another year in France with the Quartermaster Department. He returned to the United States in 1920 and went back to his old job in Ohio. In 1921 he moved to Winston-Salem to work as a wagon driver and guard with the Forsyth County Prison Department. In 1928, he became a police officer and in 1930 a detective in the Winston-Salem Police Department. He retired in 1969 after forty-two years on the force. *Photograph courtesy of Mrs. Kay Chunn, niece of Smith C. Cable.*

Lamar Gladney Clarke (September 13, 1895–December 24, 1985) was born in Albemarle County, Virginia, and moved to Greensboro in 1908. At the time of the war, he worked at Cone Mills in Greensboro. He volunteered for service and reported to the Thirtieth Division at Camp Sevier, South Carolina, only to be sent home to be drafted. He was inducted on October 9, 1917, in Greensboro and sent back to South Carolina, to Camp Jackson. Clarke was assigned to Company M, 322nd Infantry Regiment, Eighty-first Division. On October 12, only days after his arrival, he was promoted to corporal, then reduced in rank to private on November 24. On January 2, 1918, he was again promoted to corporal. He arrived in France on July 31, 1918, and served in the St. Dié sector and in the Meuse-Argonne offensive. He was discharged on June 25, 1919, at Newport News, Virginia. After the war he returned to Greensboro and worked as an accountant for Cone Mills until he retired.

Carl William Clodfelter (September 2, 1893–July 2, 1987) was living and working on his father's farm in his native Davidson County when the United States entered the war. He was drafted in Lexington on March 5, 1918. He was sent to Camp Sevier, South Carolina, and assigned to the 120th Ambulance Company, 105th Sanitary Train, Thirtieth Division, as a private. After arriving in France on June 4, 1918, he was transferred to several hospitals to help with the overwhelming number of wounded. He was discharged on April 7, 1919, at Camp Jackson, South Carolina. After the war he returned to farming in Davidson County.

John Henry Collins (November 19, 1895–December 27, 1987) was born in Pilot Mountain (Surry County). At the time of the war, he was farming in Westfield (Surry County). He was drafted in Danbury on October 5, 1917, and sent to Camp Jackson, South Carolina. There he was assigned to Company B, 322nd Infantry Regiment, Eighty-first Division, as a private. On October 16, 1917, he was transferred to Company C, 120th Infantry Regiment, Thirtieth Division, at Camp Sevier, South Carolina. Collins arrived in France on May 12, 1918, and fought in the Ypres-Lys offensive in Belgium and in the Hindenburg Line attack. He was wounded by shellfire on October 10, 1918, at Vaux-Andigny near the Selle River during the battle of Montbrehain. On November 4, 1918, he was promoted to corporal. He returned to his company after recovering from his wound. He was discharged on April 17, 1919, at Camp Jackson, South Carolina. After the war he moved to Stokes County where he farmed until 1947, then to Guilford County where he farmed until he retired.

James Vance Covington (December 31, 1896–October 1, 1988) was born in Danbury (Stokes County) and resided in Old Town (Forsyth County), where he was a farmer at the time of the war. He was drafted on August 19, 1918, at Winston-Salem and sent to Camp Wadsworth, South Carolina. Covington was assigned to Company G, Fifty-seventh Pioneer Infantry Regiment (no division affiliation), as a private. On August 29, 1918, just prior to being sent to France, he was transferred to Company E, Fifty-sixth Pioneer Infantry Regiment. He served in France from September 4, 1918, to June 25, 1919, primarily constructing roads behind the battle lines during the Meuse-

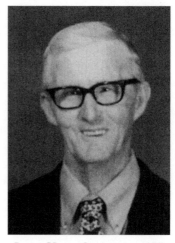

James Vance Covington, 1977

176

Argonne offensive. He was discharged on July 5, 1919, at Camp Lee, Virginia. After the war he went back to Winston-Salem and worked for the Frank L. Blum Construction Company. During World War II, he worked in the ship-yards in Norfolk, Virginia. After the Second World War, he returned to Winston-Salem and worked for the Blum Construction Company until his re-tirement. He then returned to farming. *Photograph courtesy of the James Vance Covington family.*

Lawrence Aylette Crawford (June 17, 1895–March 31, 1984) was born in Paint Lick, Kentucky, and moved to North Carolina to attend Davidson Col-lege, where he graduated in 1916. His family moved to Greensboro in 1914, where he joined them to work at the Southern Life and Trust Insurance Com-pany. He volunteered in Greensboro on June 25, 1917, and joined Ambulance Company Thirty-one. The unit was sent initially to Fort Oglethorpe, Geor-gia, and then to Camp Jackson, South Carolina. On September 22, his unit was redesignated the 321st Ambulance Company, 306th Sanitary Train, Eighty-first Division. Crawford was promoted to private first class on August 20, 1917. On May 1, 1918, he was transferred to the headquarters detachment of the 306th Sanitary Train. On July 1, 1918, he was promoted to sergeant. He arrived in France on August 8, 1918, with the Eighty-first Division and was sent to the front. He served in the St. Dié sector and in the Meuse-Argonne offensive. Crawford was discharged on June 29, 1919, at Camp Lee, Virginia. After the war he resided in Greensboro and worked for the Pilot Life Insurance Company. He was employed by that company for forty-three years before retiring in 1960.

William Foster Crouse, 1982

William Foster Crouse (May 16, 1897–December 7, 1986) was living in his native Winston-Salem at the time of the war. On June 16, 1916, he left his job with the R. J. Reynolds Tobacco Company and volun-teered for military service. He enlisted in Company C, First North Carolina Infantry Regiment, and served in the Mexican border campaign. He returned home in February 1917, only to be called back to active duty in July. On arrival at Camp Sevier, South Carolina, the First North Carolina was reor-ganized as the 105th Engineer Regiment, Thirtieth Division. Crouse was assigned to Company E as a private. He arrived in France on May 26, 1918, and served in the

177

Ypres-Lys offensive in Belgium, in the Hindenburg Line attack, and in the battles of Montbrehain and the Selle River. On August 1, 1918, he was promoted to private first class and on January 11, 1919, to corporal. He was discharged on April 24, 1919, at Camp Jackson, South Carolina. After the war he returned to work at R. J. Reynolds Tobacco Company for a year, rejoined the army for a short term, and then operated a grocery store near Winston-Salem until he retired. *Photograph courtesy of Carl R. Crouse.*

Frank Lewis Devane (December 20, 1898–March 13, 1987) was born in Florence, South Carolina, and was living in Wilmington, North Carolina, when the United States entered the war. He left high school on April 3, 1917, and volunteered in Troop C, First Squadron, North Carolina Cavalry. His cavalry troop reported to Camp Sevier, South Carolina, on September 1, and later that month was reorganized as Company C, 115th Machine-Gun Battalion, Thirtieth Division. Devane was promoted to private first class (date unknown), then to corporal on May 1, 1918. He arrived in France on May 11, 1918, and served in the Ypres-Lys offensive in Belgium, in the Hindenburg Line attack, and in the battles of Montbrehain and the Selle River. Devane was reduced in rank to private first class on August 1, 1918, and promoted once more to corporal on December 3, 1918. He was discharged on April 2, 1919, at Camp Jackson, South Carolina. After the war he returned to Wilmington and worked as a bank clerk. He was later an officer and assistant accountant with the North Carolina National Bank in Greensboro, where he worked until he retired.

Julius Franklin Dillon (March 25, 1895– November 27, 1992) was born in Oak Ridge (Guilford County), and in 1900 he and his family moved to Forsyth County. He was working as a farmer near Kernersville at the time of the war. He was drafted into service at Winston-Salem on March 21, 1918. Dillon was sent to Camp Jackson, South Carolina, and assigned to the 156th Depot Brigade as a private. On April 22, he was transferred to the medical detachment at Fort Oglethorpe, Georgia. Dillon was transferred again on May 31 to the medical detachment, Forty-sixth Engineer Regiment (no division affiliation). The regiment arrived in France on July 10, 1918. In December he was assigned to Camp Hospital No. 43. Dillon returned to

Julius Franklin Dillon, 1987

178

the United States and was discharged on March 24, 1919, at Camp Jackson, South Carolina. After the war, he was primarily a farmer near Walkertown (Forsyth County) until his retirement, though he periodically worked for the R. J. Reynolds Tobacco Company in Winston-Salem. *Photograph courtesy of the Julius Dillon family.*

David Nesbit Edwards, 1977

David Nesbit Edwards (February 15, 1892– December 29, 1985) was born in Ronda (Wilkes County). He graduated from the University of North Carolina in 1917, then moved to Winston-Salem to work in the sales department of the R. J. Reynolds Tobacco Company. He was drafted into service at Wilkesboro on April 28, 1918. Edwards was sent to Camp Jackson, South Carolina, and assigned to the 156th Depot Brigade as a private. On May 25, he was assigned to Company A, 306th Ammunition Train, Eighty-first Division, and on June 26 was promoted to corporal. His unit arrived in France on August 7, 1918. He served in the St. Dié sector and in the Meuse-Argonne offensive. Edwards was reduced to the rank of private on October 1. On June 15, 1919, just before Edwards returned to the United States, he was promoted to private first class. He was discharged on June 26, 1919, at Camp Jackson, South Carolina. After the war he lived in Winston-Salem, where he worked in the advertising department of the R. J. Reynolds Tobacco Company. He worked for this company for a total of forty-four years before retiring in 1962. *Photograph courtesy of David N. Edwards Jr.*

Robert Franklin Gaither (May 6, 1892–April 10, 1988) was born in Davie County and was a farmer in Mocksville at the time of the war. He was drafted at Mocksville on May 28, 1918. He was sent to Camp Jackson, South Carolina, and assigned to Battery C, 317th Field Artillery Regiment, Eighty-first Division, as a private. The regiment arrived in France on August 7, 1918, was detached from the division, and served in the Battle of St. Mihiel and in the Meuse-Argonne offensive. On February 6, 1919, Gaither was trampled by runaway mules and severely injured. He received medical treatment in France, then departed for the United States on May 28, 1919. On his return he was admitted to Walter Reid Hospital in Washington, D.C., where he remained until discharged from service on October 6, 1919. After the war he farmed near Walkertown (Forsyth County).

Charles Herbert Gibson (November 27, 1895–December 21, 1990) was born in Madison (Rockingham County). In January 1918, he moved to Winston-Salem to work as a drugstore cashier. He volunteered for service on April 5, 1918, in Reidsville and joined Dr. John Wesley Long's medical unit in training at Hospital No. 6 at Fort McPherson, Georgia. On August 30, the unit arrived in France and was assigned to Base Hospital No. 65, where it remained during the war. Gibson was promoted to private first class on December 1, 1918, and to corporal on April 26, 1919. He was discharged at Camp Mitchell Field, New York, on July 18, 1919. After the war he lived in Winston-Salem. He reenlisted in the Marine Corps during World War II and was stationed in Washington, D.C. Following the war he worked for the W. R. Weir Auction Company in Winston-Salem, where he was employed for forty-five years until his retirement.

William Carloe Grubb (December 26, 1899–December 23, 1986) was born in Jamestown (Guilford County). When the United States entered the war, he was living in Greensboro and working for the National Biscuit Company. He volunteered for service on June 26, 1917, in Greensboro and joined Ambulance Company Thirty-one. The unit was sent initially to Fort Oglethorpe, Georgia, and then to Camp Jackson, South Carolina. On September 22, the unit was redesignated as the 321st Ambulance Company, 306th Sanitary Train, Eighty-first Division. Grubb was promoted to private first class on November 1, 1917, and to musician (company bugler) on December 28. He arrived in France on August 8, 1918, with the Eighty-first Division and was sent to the front. He served on the St. Dié sector and in the Meuse-Argonne offensive. He was discharged on June 26, 1919, at Camp Lee, Virginia. After the war Grubb returned to the National Biscuit Company in Greensboro, then worked for the Southern Railway Company, and finally was a salesman for the Red Band Flour Company, part of General Mills, until his retirement.

Horton Bower Hall (July 21, 1895–May 2, 1990) was born in Wilkes County. At the time of the war, he was a schoolteacher in McGrady (Wilkes County). He was drafted at Wilkesboro on December 27, 1917, and sent to Camp Jackson, South Carolina. He was assigned to Company L, 323rd Infantry Regiment, Eighty-first Division, as a private. His regiment arrived in France on July 31, 1918, and on August 20, Hall was promoted to private first class. He served in the St. Dié sector and in the Meuse-Argonne offensive, during which he was exposed to poison gas on November 10, the day before the armistice. He was discharged on June 26, 1919, at Camp Lee, Virginia. After the war he returned to Wilkes County to teach. In 1926, he moved to Winston-Salem and began working for Duke Power Company. He retired from the company in 1961.

Luther Pinkney Hall (April 3, 1896–June 11, 1990) was a farmer in his native Surry County at the time of the war. On September 20, 1917, he was drafted into service at Mt. Airy. He was sent to Camp Jackson, South Carolina, and assigned to Battery B, 317th Field Artillery, Eighty-first Division. Hall was transferred to Camp Sevier, South Carolina, and reassigned to Company A, 119th Infantry Regiment, Thirtieth Division, as a private

on October 16. His regiment arrived in France on May 11, 1918, and served in the Ypres-Lys offensive in Belgium, in the Hindenburg Line attack, and in the battles of Montbrehain and the Selle River. Hall was wounded in the right arm by machine-gun fire while on night patrol in no-man's-land at Ypres on September 1. He was able to return to his company, however, to participate in the Hindenburg Line attack and other battles through the end of the war. He was discharged on April 7, 1919, at Camp Jackson, South Carolina. After the war he returned to tobacco farming for a year, then worked at the Dan River Cotton Mill in

Luther Pinkney Hall, holding his Purple Heart Certificate, 1984.

Danville, Virginia. During the Great Depression he was employed at a textile mill in New Jersey. He then moved to High Point where he worked for the Triangle Hosiery Mill until his retirement. He did not receive his Purple Heart until September 1984. He received it then through the assistance of the author. *Photograph courtesy of the author.*

Robert Colon Hamlin (July 28, 1895–June 9, 1984) was born in Asheboro (Randolph County) and was living on his father's farm in Randleman (Randolph County) at the time of the war. He had recently left home to attend school in Kansas City, Missouri, when he was drafted. He returned home, entered the service at Asheboro on May 3, 1918, and was sent to Camp Jackson, South Carolina. Hamlin was assigned to Company B, 306th Ammunition Train, Eighty-first Division, as a private and was promoted to private first class on July 5. His unit reached France on August 8, 1918. He served in the St. Dié sector and in the Meuse-Argonne offensive. During the latter campaign, Hamlin was was exposed to poison gas (date unknown) but refused to go to the field hospital. As a result, there is no official record of his injury. He was discharged on June 26, 1919, at Camp Jackson, South Carolina. After the war he resided in Greensboro, where he farmed, worked in a knitting mill, and was employed by a motor company. Ultimately, he owned and operated his own business, manufacturing belts and buckles. He operated this company until his retirement. Before his death he was plagued with severe respiratory problems, which he believed were caused by injuries suffered from poison gas during the war.

Henry Clyde Holt (May 11, 1893–December 4, 1991) was born in Ramseur (Randolph County), where at the time of the war he was working at the local textile mill. He was drafted on May 3, 1918, at Asheboro and sent to Camp Jackson, South Carolina. There he was assigned to Company D, 306th Ammunition Train, Eighty-first Division, then transferred to the Fourth Field Artillery Regiment (no division affiliation) on June 21, as a private. He was finally reassigned to Battery F, 341st Field Artillery Regiment, Eighty-ninth Division, on August 9. Holt's new division had been in France a month before he arrived on August 22, 1918. He fought in the St. Mihiel sector (following the battle) and in the Meuse-Argonne offensive. Later he served in the

Henry Clyde Holt, 1986.

Army of Occupation. He was discharged on June 4, 1919, at Camp Lee, Virginia. After the war he moved to Greensboro, where he worked for the Vicks Chemical Company briefly, then at the Cone Mills Revolution Plant until his retirement. *Photograph courtesy of the Henry Clyde Holt family.*

Isham Barney Hudson, 1981

Isham Barney Hudson (June 11, 1895– October 7, 1986) was born near Spiveys Corner (Sampson County). At the time of the war, he lived in Dunn (Harnett County). In 1917, he graduated from Buies Creek Academy. He was drafted on May 26, 1918, at Clinton and was sent to Camp Jackson, South Carolina, and assigned to the 156th Depot Brigade as a private. On June 28, he was transferred to Company F, 323rd Infantry Regiment, Eighty-first Division. His regiment arrived in France on July 31, and while in training, Hudson was reassigned to Company M, 168th Infantry Regiment, Forty-second Division, to replace battlefield casualties. He fought at St. Mihiel and in the Meuse-Argonne offensive. While serving in the Army of Occupation, Hudson taught basic skills in reading and writing to other soldiers in his unit. He then secured a scholarship to attend school in Edinburgh, Scotland, where he remained until his return to the United States. He was discharged on August 1, 1919, at Camp Mills, New York. After the war Hudson attended Wake Forest College and received his undergraduate degree in 1925. He worked as a teacher, principal, and school superintendent for forty-four years in several North Carolina county school systems before retiring in 1969. *Photograph courtesy of the author.*

Archie Clifford Ingram (June 6, 1899–November 10, 1989) was born in Buncombe County. He moved to High Point in 1912 and was working there as a printer at the time of the war. He volunteered for service on June 22, 1916, and joined Company M, First North Carolina Infantry Regiment, and served in the Mexican border campaign. He returned home in February 1917, only to be called back to active duty in July. On September 1, his company reported to Camp Sevier, South Carolina, where Ingram was placed in the Fifty-fifth Depot Brigade until October 23, 1917. He was then assigned to Company I, 119th Infantry Regiment, Thirtieth Division. He was promoted to corporal on July 15, 1917, and to sergeant on January 17, 1918. His regiment arrived in France on May 12, 1918, and served in the Ypres-Lys offensive in Belgium, in the Hindenburg Line attack, and in the battles of Montbrehain and the Selle River. He was discharged on April 7, 1919, at Camp Jackson, South Carolina. After the war he returned to High Point and worked as a typesetter for the *High Point Enterprise* and Hall Printing Company. He was state adjutant quartermaster of the Veterans of Foreign Wars from 1942 to 1965. During World War II, Ingram became known for his weekly address on "Voice for Democracy," a WMFR radio program. *Photograph courtesy of Norris Ingram, Ila Mae Canter, and Kenneth Ingram.*

Archie Clifford Ingram giving a radio address during World War II.

Ernest Luther James (March 30, 1894–May 25, 1986) was a farmer in his native Forsyth County when the United States entered World War I. He was drafted on August 12, 1918, in Winston-Salem and sent to Camp Wadsworth, South Carolina, where he was assigned to Company A, Fifty-seventh Pioneer Infantry Regiment (no division affiliation), as a private. On August 28, he was reassigned to Company D, 168th Infantry Regiment, Forty-second Division, which was already fighting in France. James arrived in France on September 15, 1918, received his equipment and additional training, and was on the march to the front to join his new company to fight in the Meuse-Argonne offensive when the war ended. He served in the Army of Occupation in the winter and spring of 1919. He was promoted to private first class on February 1, 1919. James was discharged on May 9, 1919, at Camp Lee, Virginia. After the war he returned to farming in Forsyth County.

Harvey Clinton Maness, 1985

Harvey Clinton Maness (April 20, 1896–May 22, 1987) was born in Hemp (now Robbins, Moore County). At the time of the war, he was living in Raleigh and working as a store clerk. He volunteered on June 2, 1917, in Raleigh and joined Company B, Third North Carolina Infantry Regiment, as a private. On August 31, 1917, his company reported to Camp Sevier, South Carolina, and in September was redesignated as Company B, 120th Infantry Regiment, Thirtieth Division. Maness was reassigned to the sanitary detachment, Sanitary Squad No. 28, in the regiment on January 18, 1918. His unit arrived in France on May 27 and served in the Ypres-Lys offensive in Belgium, in the Hindenburg Line attack, and in the battles of Montbrehain and the Selle River. Maness was discharged on April 22, 1919, at Camp Jackson, South Carolina. After the war he worked as an agent for an insurance company in Raleigh and for fifteen years worked for an independent agent in Florida. He returned to Raleigh to live following his retirement. *Photograph courtesy of the author.*

James Madison "Matt" Marshall (August 8, 1885–February 9, 1934) was born in Forsyth County near Walnut Cove (Stokes County). He left home in 1909 to attend Elon College for a short period. He then served abroad in the merchant marine for a few years and was engaged as a merchant broker in the food business at the time of the war. On October 11, 1917, he went to Pine Camp, New York, to visit his younger brother Jack, who was already in the army and preparing to be shipped to France. During the visit Jack persuaded Matt to enlist. Matt volunteered as a private in Battery A, Fifteenth Field Artillery Regiment, Second Division. The regiment arrived in France on December 12, 1917, and on March 8, 1918, Matt was promoted to private first class. He served at the front in the battles at Belleau Wood, Soissons, St. Mihiel, Blanc Mont, and in the Meuse-Argonne offensive. During the latter campaign, in October (specific date unknown) Matt Marshall was injured by poison gas. He served in the Army of Occupation until August 1919, when his regiment returned to the United States. He was discharged on August 14, 1919, at Camp Lee, Virginia, and came home with his brother Jack. After the war Matt Marshall returned to the wholesale food business and ultimately owned his own company in Washington, D.C., until the business failed during the Great Depression. He was killed in an automobile accident near Walkertown, North Carolina, on a return trip to Washington to try to collect debts that were owed to him. *Photograph (p. 187) courtesy of the author.*

Roy Jackson "Jack" Marshall (October 28, 1895–January 12, 1980) was born in Forsyth County near Walnut Cove (Stokes County), where he was living and working on his father's farm when the United States entered World War I. On August 16, 1917, he volunteered for service at an army recruiting station in Winston-Salem. He was sent to Fort Thomas, Kentucky, and assigned to Battery A, Fifteenth Field Artillery Regiment, Second Division, as a private. He was promoted to private first class on October 16. The regiment was sent to Pine Camp, New York, and then to France, arriving on December 12, 1917. Jack Marshall served at the front in the battles at Belleau Wood, Soissons, St. Mihiel, and Blanc Mont. On October 2, during fighting at Blanc Mont, he was wounded in the right leg by a shell fragment. After treatment in a hospital, he returned to his regiment in January 1919 and served in the Army of Occupation. On June 16, he was promoted to corporal. He was discharged on August 14, 1919, at Camp Lee, Virginia, and returned home with his brother Matt. After the war he worked on the family farm and as a carpenter. During World War II, he was employed in the shipyards in Norfolk, Virginia. He then worked for the Post Office in Winston-Salem. After retirement he returned to farming in Forsyth County. *Photograph courtesy of R. Jackson Marshall Jr.*

Roy Jackson "Jack" Marshall, 1973

Wade Latimer Marshall (March 3, 1898–November 22, 1971) was born in Forsyth County near Walnut Cove (Stokes County). At the time of the war, he was living and working on his father's farm close to Walnut Cove. He wanted to volunteer in 1917 after two of his older brothers, Matt and Jack, had enlisted, but his parents would not permit it. The struggle at home continued until the spring of 1918 when they reluctantly yielded to his persistence. He volunteered at a marine recruiting station in Winston-Salem on May 6, 1918. He was sent to Parris Island, South Carolina, and was assigned to the Fourth Squadron, First Marine Aviation Force, as a private. On June 17, Marshall was transferred to the Marine Flying Field in Miami, Florida, for training, and on September 12, he was promoted to corporal. His squadron arrived in France on October 5 and served only briefly, primarily on bombing raids in northern France and Belgium. As soon as the war ended, the unit was sent back to the United States, arriving in Norfolk, Virginia, on December 15 and then continuing on to Miami. On March 13, 1919, it was redesignated as the Second Division, Squadron D, First Marine Aviation Force. Marshall was discharged on March 31, 1919, and returned home. After the war he resided in his home community. He later moved to Madison and worked as a distributor for Gulf Oil Company in Forsyth, Stokes, and Rockingham Counties until his retirement. *Photograph courtesy of the author.*

Wade Latimer Marshall (left) and James Madison "Matt" Marshall, 1920s.

Clarence Cicero Moore (July 8, 1890–April 20, 1987) was born in Iredell County. At the time of the war, he was residing in Winston-Salem and working as a barber. He was drafted on April 1, 1918, in Winston-Salem and sent to Camp Jackson, South Carolina, where he was assigned to the Nineteenth Company, 156th Depot Brigade, as a private. On April 24, he was transferred to Camp Sevier, South Carolina, and assigned to Company K, 117th Infantry Regiment, Thirtieth Division. His regiment arrived in France on May 11, 1918, and served in the Ypres-Lys offensive in Belgium, in the Hindenburg Line attack, and in the battle of Montbrehain in France. On October 8, during the battle of Montbrehain, Moore was severely wounded in the shoulder and hip by machine-gun fire. He was sent to a hospital for medical treatment and returned to his regiment before it was sent back to the United States. He was discharged on April 16, 1919, at Fort Oglethorpe, Georgia. After the war he returned to Winston-Salem and worked as a barber until his retirement in 1970.

William Morris (July 19, 1895–March 6, 1988) was born in Walnut Cove (Stokes County). In 1913, he moved to Williamstown, West Virginia, where he was working as a mechanic for the Norfolk and Western Railroad when the United States entered the war. He was drafted on April 27, 1918, in Danbury. He was sent to Camp Grant, Illinois, and assigned to Company F, 365th Infantry Regiment, Ninety-second Division, as a private. This division was composed of African American enlisted men and noncommissioned officers and white commissioned officers. His regiment arrived in France on June 10 and served in combat at St. Dié and in the Meuse-Argonne offensive. Morris was promoted to corporal on January 3, 1919. He was discharged at Camp Lee, Virginia, on

William Morris, 1962

March 12. Following the war, Morris returned to Williamstown, West Virginia, and resumed his job with the Norfolk and Western, which he held for fifty years. When he retired he returned to live in his hometown of Walnut Cove. *Photograph courtesy of Lenora Crews Morris.*

Otho Fredrick Offman (March 25, 1894–February 7, 1984) was born in Randolph County. At the time of the war, he lived in Julian and worked as a printer. He was drafted on September 17, 1917, in Asheboro and sent to Camp Jackson, South Carolina. He was first assigned to the Supply Company, 321st Infantry Regiment, Eighty-first Division, but on October 15, he was transferred to the division's Ordnance Depot Company. He was promoted to corporal on November 1. His unit arrived in France on July 31, 1918, and he served in the St. Dié sector and in the Meuse-Argonne offensive. On October 1, 1918, Offman was transferred back to the Supply Company, 321st Infantry Regiment. He was promoted to sergeant on May 1, 1919, and then to supply sergeant the same day. He was discharged on June 27 at Camp Lee, Virginia. After the war he lived in Greensboro and was employed as a printer with the Fisher-Harrison Corporation until his retirement.

Matt Marshall Strader (August 12, 1893–February 24, 1936) was born in Forsyth County near Walnut Cove (Stokes County). He was living in Winston-Salem and working for the Norfolk and Western Railroad at the time of the war. Strader was drafted on May 25, 1918, in Winston-Salem. He was sent to Camp Jackson, South Carolina, and assigned to the 156th Depot Brigade. On June 24, he was transferred to the Headquarters Company, 321st Infantry Regiment, Eighty-first Division, as a private. His regiment arrived in France on July 30 and served in the St. Dié sector and in the Meuse-Argonne offensive. Strader was discharged on June 28, 1919, at Camp Lee, Virginia. After the war he lived in Winston-Salem and operated a grocery store. He died after a prolonged illness at age forty-three.

Joe Willoughby Thompson (May 31, 1900–November 23, 1992) was born in Wayne County. When the United States entered the war, he was living in Smithfield and working as a lumber-wagon driver. He volunteered at age sixteen on April 16, 1917, in Goldsboro. He joined the Supply Company, Second North Carolina Infantry Regiment, as a wagoner. His company reported to Camp Sevier, South Carolina, on August 1, and in September, it was redesignated as the Supply Company, 119th Infantry Regiment, Thirtieth Division. Before the company was sent to France, the captain tried to persuade Thompson to resign because of his youth, but Thompson refused. He told the captain that as an orphan he had no other home than the army. His company arrived in France on May 11, 1918. On September 3, during the Ypres-Lys offensive, Thompson was severely wounded in the left leg by an exploding shell near Ypres. He was sent to a hospital in England for medical treatment and never returned to his regiment. He was sent back to the United States and discharged on January 27, 1919, at Camp Greene, North Carolina. After the war he resided in Rockingham and worked for the Seaboard Railroad. When Thompson retired from the railroad, he moved to Raleigh. He did not receive his Purple Heart until November 11, 1991, a year before his death.

Noah Lester Whicker (May 5, 1896–October 28, 1993) was a farmer in his native Forsyth County when the United States entered World War I. He was drafted on September 18, 1917, in Winston-Salem. Whicker was sent to Camp Jackson, South Carolina, and assigned to Company D, 321st Infantry Regiment, Eighty-first Division, as a private. He was promoted to corporal on June 13, 1918, and arrived in France on July 31. He served in the St. Dié sector, was promoted to sergeant on September 1, and then fought in the Meuse-Argonne offensive. He was discharged on June 28, 1919, at Camp Lee, Virginia. After the war he lived in Forsyth County, near Walkertown, where he was a farmer and a carpenter until he retired.

Isaac Enos Winfrey (January 10, 1895–July 7, 1990) was born in Mocksville (Davie County). At the time of the war, he was living in Winston-Salem and working at the Chatham Blanket Mill. He was drafted on September 18, 1917, in Winston-Salem. Winfrey was sent to Camp Jackson, South Carolina, and assigned to Company D, 321st Infantry Regiment, Eighty-first Division, as a private. On October 12, he was transferred to Camp Sevier, South Carolina, and assigned to Company C, 119th Infantry Regiment, Thirtieth Division. His company arrived in France on May 11, 1918. On August 31, during the Ypres-Lys offensive, Winfrey was severely wounded by shellfire in the trenches near Ypres. His wounds resulted in the loss of his left arm and injury to his right arm and chest. He was sent to a hospital in England for medical treatment and never returned to his regiment. He was sent back to the United States on December 16 and admitted to Walter Reid Hospital in Washington, D.C. He remained there until discharged on March 11, 1919. After the war Winfrey lived in Winston-Salem, where he owned and operated a grocery store and woodyard, managed rental property, and farmed until his retirement.

Guy Earl Wise (September 7, 1895–June 20, 1985) was born in Cabarrus County and was residing in Richfield (Stanly County) at the time of the war. He was employed as a carpenter and was away from home building barracks at an army camp when he was drafted. He returned home, was inducted at Salisbury on May 29, 1918, and then sent to Camp Jackson, South Carolina. He was assigned to the 156th Depot Brigade and promoted to private first class on June 1. He was then transferred to Company D, 534th Engineer Battalion, an African American unit (no division affiliation), on June 13. Three days later Wise, who was white, was promoted to corporal as one of the white noncommissioned officers. On August 1, he was promoted to sergeant and sent with his unit to France, arriving on August 30. His unit constructed roads in France. In addition, he supervised the work of German prisoners

Guy Earl Wise, 1980

of war. Wise was discharged on July 17, 1919, at Camp Lee, Virginia. After the war he moved to Salisbury and worked on the Bladen Lake Dam construction project. He moved to High Point in 1925, where he worked for the R. K. Stewart and Son Construction Company for twenty-five years. Later, he was employed by the J. A. Jones Construction Company and the Coltrane and Graham Construction Company. Over the years he worked on projects in North Carolina, Tennessee, Florida, and Virginia until his retirement. *Photograph courtesy of Raymond M. Wise.*

Roby Gray Yarborough, 1982

Roby Gray Yarborough (October 25, 1895–January 25, 1997) was living and working as a store clerk at the J. F. Ward Company in his native Lexington (Davidson County) at the time of the war. He was persuaded to join Company A, Third North Carolina Infantry Regiment, by his brother Grady, who had just returned with the company from service on the Mexican border. Roby volunteered on May 31, 1917, and with the company reported to Camp Sevier, South Carolina, on September 2. During September his company was redesignated as Company A, 120th Infantry Regiment, Thirtieth Division, and Yarborough was promoted to private first class. In November he was promoted to corporal, and in February 1918, to sergeant, in part to replace his brother who had left for officers' training school. His regiment arrived in France on May 12 and served in the Ypres-Lys offensive in Belgium, in the Hindenburg Line attack, and in the battles of Montbrehain and the Selle River. He was discharged on April 17, 1919, at Camp Jackson, South Carolina. After the war Yarborough lived in Lexington and worked as an accountant until he retired at the age of ninety-two. *Photograph courtesy of the Roby G. Yarborough family.*

Bibliography

Interviews with Veterans

All of the interviews were conducted by the author.

Adams, John Flem. Winston-Salem, N.C., November 7, 1981.

Andrews, Marion Alvin. Winston-Salem, N.C., October 30, 1981.

Brockman, Felix Elbridge. Greensboro, N.C., January 5, 1984.

Cable, Smith Coy. Winston-Salem, N.C., September 16, 1983.

Clarke, Lamar Gladney. Greensboro, N.C., January 4, 1984.

Clodfelter, Carl William. Forsyth County, N.C., September 19, 1983.

Collins, John Henry. Guilford County, N.C., April 12, 1984.

Covington, James Vance. Forsyth County, N.C., September 19, 1983.

Crawford, Lawrence Aylette. Greensboro, N.C., January 5, 1984.

Crouse, William Foster. Forsyth County, N.C., September 22, 1983.

Devane, Frank Lewis. Greensboro, N.C., January 4, 1984.

Dillon, Julius Franklin. Forsyth County, N.C., September 29, 1983.

Edwards, David Nesbit. Winston-Salem, N.C., October 5, 1983.

Gaither, Robert Franklin. Forsyth County, N.C., October 3, 1983.

Gibson, Charles Herbert. Winston-Salem, N.C., November 2, 1981.

Grubb, William Carloe. Greensboro, N.C., January 5, 1984.

Hall, Horton Bower. Winston-Salem, N.C., November 3, 1981.

Hall, Luther Pinkney. High Point, N.C., April 10, 1984.

Hamlin, Robert Colon. Greensboro, N.C., January 13, 1984.

Holt, Henry Clyde. Greensboro, N.C., January 6, 1984.

Hudson, Isham Barney. Winston-Salem, N.C., October 27, 1981.

Ingram, Archie Clifford. High Point, N.C., April 10, 1984.

James, Ernest Luther. Forsyth County, N.C., January 19, 1984.

Maness, Harvey Clinton. Raleigh, N.C., December 19, 1985.

Marshall, Roy Jackson. Forsyth County, N.C., September 21, 1976; July 7, 1978; December 18, 1979.

Moore, Clarence Cicero. Winston-Salem, N.C., November 5, 1981.

Morris, William. Walnut Cove, N.C., February 2, 1984.

Offman, Otho Fredrick. Greensboro, N.C., January 12, 1984.

Thompson, Joe Willoughby. Raleigh, N.C., December 19, 1985.

Whicker, Noah Lester. Forsyth County, N.C., September 21, 1983.

Winfrey, Isaac Enos. Walnut Cove, N.C., September 15, 1983; January 27, 1984.

Wise, Guy Earl. Greensboro, N.C., January 5, 1984.

Yarborough, Roby Gray. High Point, N.C., April 19, May 8, 1984.

Unpublished Manuscripts

Crawford, Lawrence Aylette. Correspondence. In private possession.

Hall, Horton Bower. "Memoirs of H. B. Hall." In private possession.

Hudson, Isham Barney. Diary. Military Collection, World War I Papers, Private Collections, I. B. Hudson, State Archives, Division of Archives and History, Raleigh.

James, Ernest Luther. Diary and correspondence. In private possession.

Ledger for the 120th Infantry. In private possession.

Marshall, James Madison. Diary and correspondence. In private possession.

Marshall, Roy Jackson. Diary and correspondence. In private possession.

Marshall, Wade Latimer. Correspondence. In private possession.

Memorandum to the Division Surgeon, August 31, 1918, Military Collection, World War I Papers, Private Collections, John Van B. Metts, State Archives, Division of Archives and History, Raleigh.

Strader, Matt Marshall. Correspondence. In private possession.

Books, Articles, and Newspapers

Allen, George H., et al., eds. *The Wavering Balance of Forces*. Vol. 4 of *The Great War*. Philadelphia: George Barrie's Sons, 1919.

————. *The Triumph of Democracy*. Vol. 5 of *The Great War*. Philadelphia: George Barrie's Sons, 1921.

American Battle Monuments Commission. *A Guide to the American Battle Fields in Europe*. Washington, D.C.: U.S. Government Printing Office, 1927.

————. *30th Division: Summary of Operations in the World War*. Washington, D.C.: U.S. Government Printing Office, 1944.

Arnett, Alex Mathews. *Claude Kitchin and the Wilson War Policies*. Boston: Little, Brown and Company, 1937.

————. "Claude Kitchin Versus the Patrioteers." *North Carolina Historical Review* 14 (January 1937): 20-30.

Aston, George. *The Biography of the Late Marshal Foch*. New York: Macmillan Company, 1929.

Ayres, Leonard P. *The War with Germany: A Statistical Summary*. Washington: Government Printing Office, 1919.

Brief History of the 4th Division. Germany: Fourth Division Headquarters, 1919.

Brockman, Felix E. *Here, There, and Back*. Greensboro: Felix E. Brockman, 1925.

Broun, Heywood. *Our Army at the Front*. New York: Charles Scribner's Sons, 1919.

Catlin, A. W. *"With the Help of God and a Few Marines."* Garden City, N.Y.: Doubleday, Page and Company, 1919.

Churchill, Winston S. *The World Crisis: 1916-1918*. Vol. 2. New York: Charles Scribner's Sons, 1927.

Connor, R. D. W. *North Carolina: Rebuilding an Ancient Commonwealth, 1584-1925*. Vol. 2. New York: American Historical Commission, 1929.

Conway, C. B., and George A. Shuford, comps. *History, 119th Infantry, 60th Brigade, 30th Division, U.S.A.: Operations in Belgium and France, 1917-1919*. Wilmington, N.C.: Wilmington Chamber of Commerce, n.d.

Division Insignia: The Insignia of Pershing's Crusaders with a Brief History of Each Unit. Camp Dix, N.J.: I. L. Cochrane, n.d.

"Doughboys Still Remember." *Winston-Salem Journal*, November 12, 1978.

Drinker, Frederick E., ed. "America's Part in the War." In *The World War for Liberty*, edited by Francis Rolt-Wheeler and Frederick E. Drinker. N.p.: National Publishing Company, 1919.

Esposito, Vincent J. "War Casualties." In *A Concise History of World War I*, edited by Vincent J. Esposito. New York: Frederick A. Praeger, 1964.

———. "Western Front, 1918: The Year of Decision." In *A Concise History of World War I*, edited by Vincent J. Esposito. New York: Frederick A. Praeger, 1964.

Falls, Cyril. "Western Front, 1915-17: Stalemate." In *A Concise History of World War I*, edited by Vincent J. Esposito. New York: Frederick A. Praeger, 1964.

Fletcher, A. L. *History of the 113th Field Artillery, 30th Division*. Raleigh: History Committee of 113th F.A., 1920.

———. *Ashe County: A History*. Jefferson, N.C.: Ashe County Research Association, 1963.

Frothingham, Thomas G. *The American Reinforcement in the World War*. New York: Doubleday, Page and Company, 1927.

Gibbons, Floyd. *"And They Thought We Wouldn't Fight."* New York: George H. Doran Company, 1918.

Harbord, James G. *The American Army in France, 1917-1918*. Boston: Little, Brown and Company, 1936.

Hill, Daniel Harvey. *Young People's History of North Carolina*. Rev. ed. Raleigh: Alfred Williams and Company, 1923.

Hudson, Isham B. "Going Over at St. Mihiel." *Wake Forest Student* 40 (March 1921): 303-309.

James, D. Clayton. *The Years of MacArthur*. Vol. 1, *1880-1941*. Boston: Houghton Mifflin Company, 1970.

Johnson, Clarence Walton. *The History of the 321st Infantry: With a Brief Historical Sketch of the 81st Division*. Columbia, S.C.: R. L. Bryan Company, 1919.

Lemmon, Sarah McCulloh. *North Carolina's Role in the First World War*. Raleigh: State Department of Archives and History, 1966.

Lloyd, Nelson. *How We Went to War*. New York: Charles Scribner's Sons, 1919.

Long, E. B. *The Civil War Day by Day: An Almanac, 1861-1865*. New York: Doubleday and Company, 1971.

McPherson, William L. *A Short History of the Great War*. New York: G. P. Putnam's Sons, 1920.

March, Francis A. *History of the World War*. Vol. 5. New York: Leslie-Judge Company, 1918.

Martin, Santford, comp., and R. B. House, ed. *Public Letters and Papers of Thomas Walter Bickett, Governor of North Carolina, 1917-1921*. Raleigh: Edwards and Broughton Printing Company, 1923.

Murphy, Elmer A., and Robert S. Thomas. *The Thirtieth Division in the World War*. Lepanto, Ark.: Old Hickory Publishing Company, 1936.

Nenninger, Timothy K. "Tactical Dysfunction in the AEF, 1917-1918." *Military Affairs* 51 (October 1987): 177-181.

"Operations of the Second American Corps Against the Hindenburg Line, September 27-October 1, 1918." In *Source Records of the Great War*, vol. 6, edited by Charles F. Horne. Indianapolis: American Legion, 1930.

Operations of the 2d American Corps in the Somme Offensive. Washington, D.C.: Government Printing Office, 1920.

Pershing, John J. *My Experiences in the World War*. 2 vols. New York: Fredrick A. Stokes Company, 1931.

Pratt, Joseph H. "Diary of Colonel Joseph Hyde Pratt, Commanding 105th Engineers, A.E.F." Parts 4 and 5. *North Carolina Historical Review* 1 (October 1924): 475-540; 2 (January 1925): 117-144.

"Report of the Surgeon General." *War Department Annual Reports, 1919*. Vol. 1, part 3. Washington, D.C.: Government Printing Office, 1920.

"Report of the Surgeon General." *War Department Annual Reports, 1920*. Vol. 1. Washington, D.C.: Government Printing Office, 1920.

Reynolds, Francis J., Allen L. Churchill, and Francis Trevelyan Miller, eds. *The Story of the Great War*. 8 vols. New York: P. F Collier and Son, 1916-1920.

Shermer, David. *World War I*. London: Octopus Books, 1975.

Simonds, Frank H. *History of the World War*. 5 vols. Garden City, N.Y.: Doubleday, Page and Company for the Review of Reviews Company, 1917-1920.

[Spaulding, Oliver Lyman, and John Womack Wright]. *The Second Division, American Expeditionary Force, in France, 1917-1919*. New York: Hillman Press and Historical Committee, Second Division Association, 1937.

Stallings, Laurence. *The Doughboys: The Story of the AEF, 1917-1919*. New York: Harper and Row, 1963.

Sullivan, Willard P., and Harry Tucker, comps. *The History of the 105th Regiment of Engineers*. New York: George H. Doran Company, 1919.

Taber, John H. *The Story of the 168th Infantry*. Vol. 2. Iowa City, Iowa: State Historical Society of Iowa, 1925.

Taft, William H., et al., eds. *Service with the Fighting Men*. 2 vols. New York: Association Press, 1922.

Terraine, John. *The Great War, 1914-1918: A Pictorial History*. Garden City, N.Y.: Doubleday and Company, 1965.

Tyson, L. D. "The Breaking of the Hindenburg Line at the St. Quentin Canal." In *Proceedings of the State Literary and Historical Association of North Carolina*, compiled by R. D. W. Connor. Raleigh: Edwards and Broughton Printing Company, 1920.

Walker, John O., William A. Graham, and Thomas Fauntleroy. *Official History of the 120th Infantry*. Lynchburg, Va.: J. P. Bell Company, n.d.

"War Surgery." In *The European War*. Vol. 17. New York: New York Times Company, 1919.

Index

A

B